REFORMING HUMAN SERVICES

Volume 142, Sage Library of Social Research

RECENT VOLUMES IN
SAGE LIBRARY OF SOCIAL RESEARCH

95 Roberts **Afro-Arab Fraternity**
96 Rutman **Planning Useful Evaluations**
97 Shimanoff **Communication Rules**
98 Laguerre **Voodoo Heritage**
99 Macarov **Work and Welfare**
100 Bolton **The Pregnant Adolescent**
101 Rothman **Using Research in Organizations**
102 Sellin **The Penalty of Death**
103 Studer/Chubin **The Cancer Mission**
104 Beardsley **Redefining Rigor**
105 Small **Was War Necessary?**
106 Sanders **Rape & Woman's Identity**
107 Watkins **The Practice of Urban Economics**
108 Clubb/Flanigan/Zingale **Partisan Realignment**
109 Gittell **Limits to Citizen Participation**
110 Finsterbusch **Understanding Social Impacts**
111 Scanzoni/Szinovacz **Family Decision-Making**
112 Lidz/Walker **Heroin, Deviance and Morality**
113 Shupe/Bromley **The New Vigilantes**
114 Monahan **Predicting Violent Behavior**
115 Britan **Bureaucracy and Innovation**
116 Massarik/Kaback **Genetic Disease Control**
117 Levi **The Coming End of War**
118 Beardsley **Conflicting Ideologies in Political Economy**
119 LaRossa/LaRossa **Transition to Parenthood**
120 Alexandroff **The Logic of Diplomacy**
121 Tittle **Careers and Family**
122 Reardon **Persuasion**
123 Hindelang/Hirschi/Weis **Measuring Delinquency**
124 Skogan/Maxfield **Coping With Crime**
125 Weiner **Cultural Marxism and Political Sociology**
126 McPhail **Electronic Colonialism**
127 Holmes **The Policy Process in Communist States**
128 Froland/Pancoast/Chapman/Kimboko **Helping Networks and Human Services**
129 Pagelow **Woman-Battering**
130 Levine/Rubin/Wolohojian **The Politics of Retrenchment**
131 Saxe/Fine **Social Experiments**
132 Phillips/Votey **The Economics of Crime Control**
133 Zelnik/Kantner/Ford **Sex and Pregnancy in Adolescence**
134 Rist **Earning and Learning**
135 House **The Art of Public Policy Analysis**
136 Turk **Political Criminality**
137 Macarov **Worker Productivity**
138 Mizruchi **The American Corporate Network**
139 Druckman/Rozelle/Baxter **Nonverbal Communication**
140 Sommerville **The Rise and Fall of Childhood**
141 Quinney **Social Existence**
142 Toch/Grant **Reforming Human Services**

REFORMING HUMAN SERVICES
Change Through Participation

Hans Toch
J. Douglas Grant

Foreword by Ross Stagner

Volume 142
SAGE LIBRARY OF
SOCIAL RESEARCH

SAGE PUBLICATIONS
Beverly Hills / London / New Delhi

To the Memory of
JEANNE BLOCK,
good friend and
respected colleague

For information address:

SAGE Publications, Inc.
275 South Beverly Drive
Beverly Hills, California 90212

SAGE Publications India Pvt. Ltd.
C-236 Defence Colony
New Delhi 110 024, India

SAGE Publications Ltd
28 Banner Street
London EC1Y 8QE, England

Printed in the United States of America

Library of Congress Cataloging in Publication Data

Toch, Hans.
    Reforming human services.

    (Sage library of social research ; v. 142)
    Bibliography: p.
    1. Social work administration.   I. Grant, James
Douglas, 1917-   . II. Title. III. Series.
HV41.T58 1982   361'.0068   82-10527
ISBN 0-8039-1886-0
ISBN 0-8039-1887-9 (pbk.)

FIRST PRINTING

CONTENTS

Foreword
>ROSS STAGNER   7

Acknowledgments   13

Preface   14

I. THE PROBLEM

  1. Definition of the Problem   18

  2. Alienation and Burnout   35

  3. Shape of the Work Problem   51

  4. Cynicism: The Human Equation   63

II. THE PROSPECT

  5. The Notion of "Job Enrichment":
    From Chores to Challenges   74

  6. Job Enrichment in the Human Services   85

  7. The Notion of "Quality of Work Life":
    Humanizing the Assembly Line   98

  8. Humanizing Client Assembly Lines   110

III. THE PRESCRIPTION

  9. The Notion of Participation   124

  10. Participation and Change   135

  11. Receptivity to Change   147

  12. Research, Action, and Action Research   159

IV. THE DEMONSTRATION

  13. Grass-Roots Management   174

  14. The New York Prison Survey   192

  15. The Correction Officer Teams   207

16. Team Proposals   218
17. From Cup to Lip: Implementation of Proposals   238
18. Epilogue: Where Do We Go From Here?   252

References   266
About the Authors   272

FOREWORD

Ever since William Blake wrote of the "dark Satanic mills" two hundred years ago, periodic concern has been expressed over the dehumanizing effect of modern industry. These complaints intensified with the adoption of assembly-line production, the microscopic fragmentation of tasks, and rigid constraints on work behavior.

In strictly dialectical fashion, these dehumanizing processes have given rise to various efforts at modifying this industrial reality to take account of human realities. Historically, of course, these attempts go back to the utopian communes of the nineteenth century, but they have taken clearer shape in the middle of the twentieth, with more pragmatic, less romantic proposals. Various writers, including Douglas McGregor (*The Human Side of Enterprise*), A. H. Maslow, Rensis Likert, and Chris Argyris, have proposed ways of restructuring industry to take account of man's noneconomic needs. Books such as that by Meltzer and Wickert (*Humanizing Organizational Behavior*) discuss and criticize many such recommendations.

An industrial psychologist looking at these humanistic commentaries may be impressed with their failure to recognize the enormous contribution to human welfare made by the "dark Satanic mills." Poor people, who had dressed only in patched rags, gained access to cheap cloth when the power loom revolutionized weaving. Millions of Americans attained freedom of movement when Henry Ford, Sr., arranged for mass production of automobiles. The "dehumanized" industries were indeed serving human needs of human beings; but these were the consumers, those who used the commodities, not the workers inside the factories. What was required was another Industrial

Revolution that would humanize working conditions to an extent comparable with that already in effect for consumers.

The problem arises from the fact that human beings are not merely biological units demanding food, freedom from pain, sexual gratification, and protection from the weather. While there be still a few psychologists holding to this diminished view of human nature, it is generally recognized that an individual also needs dignity, a feeling of self-respect, a sense of achievement, freedom to make decisions affecting his or her fate, and self-actualization. The essentially new contribution of the "humanizing" movement currently expanding in American industry is the view of the person in his or her totality, including not only the raw physiological needs—which have, on the whole, been met by the tremendous expansion of commodity production—but also the subtler, higher-level needs for self-worth and achievement. This restructured perception of human nature has been a guide to improved patterns of interaction of supervisors and subordinates in industry.

The great spurt in commodity production was achieved, at least in part, by applying the dehumanizing tactics we now deplore. Frederick W. Taylor (*Principles of Scientific Management*) laid down the basic rules of maximum production and minimum personal freedom for the worker: The manager must dictate to the workers "not only what is to be done, but how it is to be done and the exact time allowed for doing it" (1947: 39). Taylor realized that this meant rigid control over workplace behavior: "It is only through *enforced* standardization of methods, *enforced* adoption of the best implements and working conditions, and *enforced* cooperation that this faster work can be assured" (1947: 83). Thus the pattern was established for working conditions in which the employee lost all individuality and freedom to choose ways of doing the job.

This same pattern of tight organizational control and supervision has been taken over by service agencies. Bureaucratic regulations seek to ensure that every staff person handles cases in the same way, without regard to individual differences in external circumstances or the nature of the client's problems.

This rigidity in the bureaucratic system did not occur by chance. It is easy to forget—though Max Weber pointed it out a century ago—that the rule of law came into existence as people rebelled against capricious, arbitrary decisions based on the whims of rulers and their delegates. The rigid administration of rules characterizing modern service agencies seems intolerable—until one considers the alternative.

If we think back to the days of Charles Dickens, when the poor had the option of going to jail or to a workhouse, we can surely agree that modern welfare programs are more humane. And if we compare Aid to Families with Dependent Children to the Christmas basket brought by a Lady Bountiful who sorrowed for the poor regularly, once a year, or to the soup kitchens set up by religious orders, we must concede that bureaucratized public services provide more dignity and self-respect to the recipient while doing a better job of meeting physiological needs.

It is not necessary to enumerate all of the factors operating to require bureaucratic controls over these human service programs. The change from a rural to an urban population was an influence; home care of the aged was much easier in a farm home than for a two-child family in a one-bedroom flat. The population explosion is important. Advances in medicine, with greater numbers living to the age of weakness and of limited physical vigor, have compounded the problems. Crime rates may not have changed as drastically as statistics suggest; but the village constable who knew all of the restless boys in town has been replaced by hundreds of uniformed police officers who know only a tiny sample of the thousands of disturbed adolescents they must try to monitor. Thus, individual attention and flexible policies have been replaced by rules, laws, and due process requirements that deny individual differences.

Along with the shift to public financing of welfare, medical care, old age pensions, and the like has gone a taxpayer cry for an end to fraud and misuse of public funds. If agency personnel are given flexible authorization to spend money, some will be tempted to pocket a portion of the available cash. One consequence has been a proliferation of laws and administrative rules that make possible a tight check on the possible generosity of clerks and caseworkers. Arbitrary control by employer and foreman in private industry has its parallel in arbitrary control by laws and by supervisors in the service agencies.

The parallels go farther. Workers rebelling against perceived dictatorial control in industry formed unions and won some influence over the working conditions they hated. In the process they have negotiated contract clauses that impose tight constraints on the freedom of the foreman or manager. Likewise we now observe in service agencies a decided trend toward unionism, with contract provisions that protect low-level employees from capricious supervisors. But these same contract clauses result in a further proliferation of rules that deny freedom of decision making to the staff personnel who were to be protected by the contract, as well as to the supervisory personnel appointed by the agency.

"Humanizing" programs in industry have so far produced more promises than examples of conflict-free operation. While some unpleasant factories have been turned into satisfactory workplaces, the amount of overt conflict and covert hostility is still substantial. It should not be surprising that in service organizations conflict is very widespread. Unemployment clerks snarl at applicants for insurance payments; mothers seeking help explode at case workers. Teachers who once stayed late to help students now rush to escape the school building at the ringing of the final bell. Students heckle, harass, and assault teachers. Jail guards beat prisoners and are attacked by prisoners.

To understand these phenomena we must inquire into how the participants perceive the situation. With virtually no exceptions, the offender (staff or client) considers the hostile behavior to be completely justified. An unemployed worker with a sick child, behind on his mortgage payments, his car repossessed, demands immediate action on his claim; when he is told to come back in ten days, he blows up, denouncing the clerk as cold, cruel, and heartless. She, in turn, calls him a spoiled brat, an egomaniac who expects all the rules to be broken for his emergency to be met. Neither perceives the other correctly; neither can empathize with the other. But perception is what guides action, and misperceptions lead only to conflict and confrontation.

The bureaucrat develops an attitude of indifference to protect against real suffering over clients' problems that are insoluble. But the studied distancing of self from client, to avoid pain, is bolstered by a misperception of the client as childish, impulsive, and too stupid to understand regulations. Behavior based on this perception will result primarily in hostile attacks on the clerk and the agency.

Bureaucrats are also human, and "humanizing" these services must involve humanizing the work situation of the agency staff. This will involve primarily changes in the supervisor/subordinate relationship, but to some extent also changes in the staff/ client relationship.

Reforming Human Services represents an attempt to sift some of the most dependable generalizations from the industrial literature on humanizing programs, and then to apply these guiding principles to the humanizing of service organizations. This is a very large but very important undertaking. On the whole, it is my judgment that Toch and Grant have been judicious in their selections from and interpretation of the industrial material. Further, it appears that their translations of these guiding principles into rules for the modification of staff/agency relationships have been well conceived.

Toch and Grant recognize that supervisors and staff personnel are human beings first, role takers second. At the same time they make it clear that they do not consider agency conflicts to be due to "bad" people. Rather, these result from ill-conceived institutional arrangements. This is not a book about sadistic agency heads who delight in torturing their subordinates; it is about people at various levels in the organization who find themselves trapped in a bureaucratic maze. The recommendations, consequently, focus on changes in modes of agency management, not on selection of or therapy for individual employees.

"Humanized" programs in industry have taken many forms. They include decreasing the number of layers of supervision, pushing decision making as low as possible in the hierarchy, "quality control circles" where workers can offer suggestions without being slapped down by foremen, shifts from assembly lines to team production in which the work group takes some responsibility for deciding who does what, when, and for how long. Observers of the industrial scene believe that there is a real rainbow here, and that instead of a pot of gold at the end, we shall find a great increase in employee satisfaction, with a concomitant decrease in friction, conflict, and hostility. Typically, one observes a reduction in buck passing, better information at the top about conditions at the bottom, and more cooperation among employees at varying levels in the organization.

Toch and Grant propose that these benefits can be achieved in agency/client relations as well as in industry. The details of these expectations, and of the manipulations they propose in an effort to bring about humanization, are explored in the pages to follow.

—*Ross Stagner*
Wayne State University

ACKNOWLEDGMENTS

This book could not have been written without the background of sponsored research done over the past two decades. We are much indebted to the Center for Studies in Crime and Delinquency of the National Institute of Mental Health for underwriting Projects MH 08970, MH 12068, and MH 20757, which covered our violence-related work, particularly in the Oakland Police Department (we review this activity in Chapter 13). Some of this book draws on the unpublished final report of a project ("Corrections Officer Research/Training/Development") that was funded by the National Institute of Corrections of the Federal Prison System. We are grateful to NIMH and NIC for their faith and support. We are also grateful to our hosts, Chief Charles Gain and Commissioner Thomas A. Coughlin III. Our heaviest indebtedness, of course, is to our grass-roots colleagues, and we treasure the commitment and friendship of the men with whom we have worked.

Ross Stagner, Peter Manning, Joan Grant, and John Klofas have contributed significantly to this book. We also have partners who we do not know whose influence is reflected in these pages.

Needless to say, all opinions expressed herein are ours, and where we fall short, we jointly share the blame.

PREFACE

Several years ago, we were privileged to watch police patrolmen—some with checkered careers—work to improve a police department. We later observed other such experiments, including one in which correction officers wrote proposals for prison reform.

As psychologists, we are hard put to separate "organization change" and "person change." We know that people—including people in organizations—learn and grow and fulfill themselves as they become involved. Often, the *product* of focused involvement is *change*. To put the matter differently, when persons become concerned with efforts to improve their environments—particularly, their work environments—the inhabitants and their environments are liable to benefit. The reasons for this fact, the documentation for it, and the implications of it will be key concerns of this book.

Throughout our individual careers we have often worried—at times aloud—about the ability of "human service" organizations (schools, hospitals, mental hospitals, social work agencies, prisons, police departments) to deliver meaningful services—to become or to remain compassionate, humane, and responsive to people's needs. One problem that *appeared* to us to get in the way of "helping" was bureaucracy—traditional management adopted (or maladopted) from assembly lines.

Assembly-line management seemed counterproductive when it was applied to organizations that are designed to serve, deal with, and respond to people. The difference in goals between organizations that seemed to *legitimately* engage in mass-manufacture (such as car assembly lines) and those that become Kafkaesque nightmares when they were converted to assembly lines, implied that there must be differences in how workers in different types of organizations should be properly supervised, and in the way their work should be planned and coordinated.

What makes such an assumption about "appropriate management" outdated is the worker alienation of the sixties and the decade of "work reform" that followed. These developments demonstrated that organizations of every description can be (and in fact must be) differently run than they have been run in the past.

In this book we try hard not to downgrade the continuum of work-related problems. We stress this continuum by surveying the highlights of recent organizational reform, including (as reviews must) the "classics" that have inspired reformers. We assume that our survey of work reform efforts may strike students of industrial management as somewhat familiar, though (we hope) not as redundant. We feel simultaneously confident that our peers—students, critics, workers, and managers in the human services—will find the recent history we review both suggestive and helpful. What is most apt to surprise our readers (as it did us) is that today the winds of organizational change seem to blow from factories to clinics, offices, schools, and prisons.

This book is *in part* a primer or a summary recapitulation of today's trends in organizational change theory and experimenta-tion. It is also a blueprint, and as such, contains a prescription or "model" of planned change. The prescription is eclectic. It combines elements of what are now the "mainline" work reform strategies (job enrichment, quality of work life, and action research) into a package that we hope is coherent and deployable.

We can document our prescription by drawing on a few past reform efforts in human service settings, which include experiments in schools and in hospitals. Our "first-hand" illustration—the experience with prison guards that we have referred to—derives from a criminal justice agency. If a criminal justice agency seems remotely, if at all, "human service," our choice may be doubly relevant: Pejorative stereotyping *as well* as inappropriate management are compounded grounds for workers feeling, and acting, alienated.

In this book we contend that workers work best and most contentedly, that they are most apt to exercise ingenuity and decency and helpfulness, when they have a voice in shaping organizational goals and defining their own jobs. This ideal condition—which we call "grass-roots management"—is neither utopian, nor revolutionary, nor hard to create. We shall outline how organizational democracy can be achieved, and how it has— to varying degrees—been attained. We shall suggest why the strategy works—why, in fact, it *must* work. In this connection, we assume that strategies vested in "classic management" have been tried and found wanting. Reasons for the shortfall are many: some have to do with changing needs or expectations, some with needs we have known but ignored. The reason (whichever it may be) is academic, because manifest needs of workers, whether they are new or "discovered," are intense and irreversible. If we ignore workers' needs, we violate human nature. And nature (as the commercial points out) has a way of avenging itself when it is violated.

—*H. T.*
—*J. D. G.*

PART I

THE PROBLEM

CHAPTER 1

DEFINITION OF THE PROBLEM

> The officer stands in the sundrenched
> yard, bursting with its shifting humanity,
> whispering, tenuously controlled. The
> guard feels lonely.
>
> The teacher faces the board, sensing
> trouble. The apathy behind her contains
> festering pockets of chaos. The teacher
> writes faster.
>
> A figure leaves and a form drops in the
> box. Another figure fills the chair,
> another variation on the theme. Again,
> the incantation about new limits to
> benefits . . .
>
> The mother is insistent, and the beefy,
> bleeding man hovers. "I'll call your
> name," the nurse repeats. "We call
> names when we're ready."

Incumbents of human service jobs increasingly feel afraid, impotent, vulnerable, and bored. They increasingly face clients who feel neglected, put upon, sullen, and angry.

A vicious cycle links expanding human needs to shrinking human services. Some costs are direct and traceable. Others are subtle and inestimable. What price do we pay for crowded classrooms, wards, and tiers, for community nonprograms for the extruded, for eroding remediation options? How many such costs are increments in deficits (educational, mental health, and so forth) that expand the gap between needs and resources? How is this chasm experienced? "Insiders" intuit a crisis, often in vague inarticulate ways. They know—or at least, sense—that mass processing of children, patients, criminal suspects, inmates, applicants, and supplicants creates climates that are multifariously destructive.

Such climates are almost equally destructive for clients, staff, and managers of human service settings. The jobless, whose esteem problems are compounded through wait-and-rush routines that are inflicted by an overburdened bureaucracy, are no more victims than are the impotent workers who must delay and then rush them (and who must live with the resentment they engender) and their scapegoated supervisors. The child who is ignored in a congested classroom is no more a victim than the teacher who cannot attend to that child, or than the principal who must deal with the restlessness, tension, and out-of-control mob scenes under his or her auspices. Joint fates link prison guards and underoccupied and irritable inmates, link the staff and patients of overtaxed emergency wards, and join resourceless clients to welfare workers who have no welfare to disburse.

In this book we center primarily on one component (the staff component) of human service transactions. The choice is strategic in the sense that it has to do with the interventions we shall describe and prescribe. It is also one way of facilitating diagnosis, of teasing out current problems that exemplify longer-term trends—problems that have preexisted the current crisis and are likely to reemerge if/when the emergency is over.

One feature of crises is that they impede our capacity to diagnose, project, and predict trends (Toch, 1957). This problem is not new to human history. It is one that hounded the pharaoh in Exodus, who panicked during the great plague and expelled the captive aliens who received credit for it (12:31). The pharoah's misdiagnosis is obvious from the fact that he had shrugged off a cattle epidemic (9:6), a rash of boils and other symptoms (9:11), dietary deficits occasioned by bad weather and by infestations of locusts (9:3; 10:14), serious pollution problems (7:18), the urgent need for pest control (8:6, 8:24) and horrendous sanitation problems (8:7). Acute maladies that are superimposed on (or that partially result from) chronic conditions can mislead us, especially if they are dramatic or mobilize emergency responses.

Some of the concerns we shall review have emerged gradually; others have made headlines. The public has been often regaled with portraits of asphalt jungles and snakepits, of bins for the retarded and riot-prone prisons. It has read of issues that are related to turnover (the nursing crisis), maladministration (adult home scandal), alienation (teacher strike), and morale (police stress). The icebergs that lie beneath such tips make up the world of human service clients and staff.

A modern pharaoh who reacts to crises would miss key trends. One such trend relates to the enhanced meaning of work, and this trend compounds the crises that specific groups of workers (such as teachers, prison guards, and nurses) must face and adjust to. More of our lives today are invested in our work. Other institutions—such as churches, community groups, families, and extended families—play a relatively less important role in our lives. It is not that we spend more time at work (many of us do; most of us do not), but we expect more satisfactions and rewards from work. We can also be more hurt and disillusioned by work. This is a long-term trend shared by *all* work, including blue-collar, white-collar, and human service work. Daniel Bell has written,

> A business corporation, like a university, or a government agency, or a large hospital—each with its hierarchy and status system—is now a lifetime experience for many of its members. Necessarily, therefore, it can no longer be an instrument satisfying a single end—in the case of the business corporation, only turning out its goods and services—*but it has to be a satisfactory way of life for its members. It not only has to satisfy its customers it has to be agreeable to its "self."*

> To the extent that the traditional sources of social support (the small town, church, and family) have crumbled in society, new kinds of organizations, particularly the corporation, have taken their place; and these inevitably become the arenas in which the demands for security, justice, and esteem are made. To think of the business corporation, then, simply as an economic instrument, is to fail totally to understand the meaning of the social changes of the last half century [1976: 288-289].

The Work Problem, Generally

Work-related problems in the human services are neither unique nor are they more dramatic than counterpart problems elsewhere in the work spectrum. As this spectrum shifts—and it is shifting—work increasingly denotes delivery of services. Diagnoses of the "postindustrial" syndrome thus apply (with suitable variations) to white-collar and human service organizations.

The Diagnosis

In 1973, a university press released a widely quoted report that summarized the thinking of a federal government task force. The book, *Work in America*, became an instant classic, and its diagnoses and prescriptions have been widely quoted. There are many reasons for the book's influence, but one such reason is the urgency the text reflects, and the quiet passion it conveys. The book's concluding section opens with the words of Albert Camus, "Without work all life goes rotten. But when work is soulless, life stifles and dies." The report continues:

> Our analysis of work in America leads to much the same conclusion: Because work is central to the lives of so many Americans, either the absence of work or employment in meaningless work is creating an increasingly intolerable situation. The human costs of this state of affairs are manifested in worker alienation, alcoholism, drug addiction, and other symptoms of poor mental health. Moreover, much of our tax money is expended in an effort to compensate for problems with at least a part of their genesis in the world of work. A great part of the staggering national bill in the areas of crime and delinquency, mental and physical health, manpower and welfare are generated in our national policies and attitudes toward work. Likewise, industry is paying for its continued attachment to Tayloristic practices through low worker productivity and high rates of sabotage, absenteeism, and turnover. Unions are paying through the faltering loyalty of a young membership that is increasingly concerned about the apparent disinterest of its leadership in problems of job satisfaction. Most important, there are the high costs of lost opportunities to encourage citizen participation: the discontent of women, minorities, blue-collar workers, youth, and older adults would be considerably less were these Americans to have an active voice in the decisions in the workplace that most directly affect their lives.
>
> Our analysis . . . indicates that to do nothing about these problems in the short run is to increase costs to society in the long run

[Special Task Force to the Secretary of Health, Education and Welfare, 1973: 186].

The eloquent paragraph makes it clear that the distinguished group had developed misgivings about the meaningfulness of work experiences available to the average American. According to the task force, many of the problems our society faces result from the despair, frustration, and resentment of people who cannot find work or who are turned off at work. The task force's remedy for work alienation was what we shall call grass-roots management—the opportunity for "Americans to have an active voice in the decisions in the workplace that most directly affect their lives" (1973: 186).

As the task force concluded its deliberations, two of its members released the persuasive results of a massive study of worker attitudes (Sheppard and Herrick, 1972). The book, which was whimsically entitled *Where Have All the Robots Gone?* yielded a pessimistic but suggestive portrait of American workers' dissatisfactions. The reference to disappearing "robots" had to do with a shift—particularly among younger workers—from relative contentment—assuming bread-and-butter demands were met— to dissatisfaction having to do with unfulfilled needs for respect and esteem, the opportunity for learning or advancement, and the availability of meaningfulness, variety, and substance in the work itself. Sheppard and Herrick highlighted the finding that "the labor force as a whole considered job characteristics to be more important than the economic benefits derived from the job. The highest-ranked item among all age groups was interesting work" (1972: 118). Younger workers, especially,

> placed substantially more importance on the interesting nature of the work, on their opportunity to develop their own special abilities, and on their chances for promotion. They were less concerned than their elders with being asked to do excessive amounts of work, whether or not their transportation arrangements were convenient, and whether their jobs allowed them to forget their personal problems. With regard to pay, job security, and fringe benefits, age seemed to make no difference: all age groups seemed to be equally interested in the economics of work. . . . [But] while the greatest satisfaction gap among workers over 30 had to do with pay, among younger workers it concerned

their lack of opportunity for self-development. (The issue of pay placed second.) The third and fourth areas of greatest discrepancy among young workers (the interesting/or uninteresting/nature of their work, and their chance to do the things they believed they did best) also resulted from high values and low realities in job-content areas [Sheppard and Herrick, 1972: 118-119].

Younger workers were generally more dissatisfied than older workers; those *least* satisfied tended to be blue collar rather than white collar, black rather than white, more educated, female rather than male, married rather than single, and more poorly paid. Though the trend was clearly alarming, the reasons for the young workers' dissatisfaction suggested (as they did to the *Work in America* task force) the direction of a solution. Sheppard and Herrick pointed out that

if . . . young people draw the line and demand that their unions reorder bargaining priorities and that their employers give them a voice in reshaping their work lives, then . . . we may see at long last an extension of our democratic principles to the workplace [1972: 120].

Sheppard and Herrick explored the prospects of "an extension of . . . democratic principles to the workplace" by conducting a survey of corporate managers and union officials. The interest in the questionnaire was high: Half the returns were personally prepared by corporation presidents and international presidents of unions. Of the managers, 50 percent answered "yes" to the question, "Would you be willing to consider an experimental or demonstration project (in other words, job enrichment) in your establishment?" Two out of three management and union respondents deemed it "very important" to improve workers' opportunities to "achieve and grow on the job." Union leaders, however, ranked " 'challenging work' low on their list of priorities (compared to pay, safety, etc.)" (Sheppard and Herrick, 1972: 180-181).

Several paradoxes emerged. Union leaders recognized worker concerns with job content, but in prioritizing their unions' goals, "rated pay first and job content either last or next to last." Another surprise was that "contrary to the folk wisdom which says that both management and the trade union movement are strongly negative to the idea of labor participating in management decisions," the survey showed that both groups were favorably disposed to increased involvement of workers in decisions that affect their work (Sheppard and Herrick, 1972: 182-183). Managers seemed sympathetic though they were not attuned to worker dissatisfactions; unions were receptive while appearing to be "stuck" with their bargaining table priorities.

Sheppard and Herrick's data implied both good news and bad news; the good news was "that all groups involved are remarkably positive towards humanizing work"; the bad news was that while "both groups recognize the fact that there is a problem . . . neither considers it to be of the same order of magnitude as do the workers themselves" (Sheppard and Herrick, 1972: 190-191).

Deepening Discontent?

The question (deepening discontent?) is the subheading of a report (Cooper et al., 1979) that summarized the views of 175,000 workers surveyed over almost three decades. The report concludes that "discontent among hourly and clerical employees seems to be growing" (Cooper et al., 1979: 118). More significantly,

> The work force itself and what it demonstrably values are indeed changing: all parts of the work force are beginning to overtly articulate their needs for achievement, recognition, and job challenge . . . hourly and clerical employees' satisfaction with pay does not offset either their high level of job dissatisfaction or their feeling that they are not treated with respect as individuals. In contrast, managers feel that they get intrinsic satisfaction from their jobs, not just good pay [Cooper et al., 1979: 118].

The brunt of the workers' demand is recent, in that "since 1975, the majority of hourly and clerical employees have not rated their companies favorably on treating them with respect as individuals" (Cooper et al., 1979: 123). The dissatisfaction is specific, in that "esteem-related items seem to account for the recent downturn in overall job satisfaction, while extrinsic items, such as satisfaction with pay, do not." Since "the changes are . . . ubiquitous, pervasive and nontransient," the implication is that "employers must now begin to change their patterns of

responsiveness to accommodate these changes in employees'
values and expectations" (Cooper et al., 1979: 124).

Why the recent shift in worker expectations? The 1973 *Work in
America* task force speculates:

> From a workforce with an average educational attainment of less
> than junior high school, containing a large contingent of
> immigrants of rural and peasant origin and resigned to cyclical
> unemployment, the workforce is now largely native-born, with
> more than a high school education on the average, and affluence-
> minded. And, traditional values that depended on authoritarian
> assertion alone for their survival have been challenged.

> Simplified tasks for those who are not simple-minded, close
> supervision by those whose legitimacy rests only on a hierarchical
> structure, and jobs that have nothing but money to offer in an
> affluent age are simply rejected. For many of the new workers, the
> monotony of work and scale of organization and their inability to
> control the pace and style of work are cause for a resentment which
> they, unlike older workers, do not repress [1973: 18].

The task force conducted its own surveys of workers and found
that "perhaps the most consistent complaint reported has been
the failure of bosses to listen to workers who wish to propose
better ways of doing their jobs. Workers feel that their bosses
demonstrate little respect for their intelligence. Supervisors are
said to feel that the workers are "incapable of thinking creatively
about their jobs" (Special Task Force, 1973: 37). The feelings
relate to a perceived management presumption that workers are
paid to work, while managers are paid to do planning, and that
the two roles should remain separate.

Quality Control: A Concern of Workers or Managers?

In a recent New York *Times* "op" insert (April 9, 1980), an
assembly-line worker addressed the worker's view of quality (or
nonquality) production. He wrote,

> When I'm asked, "How can you build those death traps?" I
> patiently respond that the manufacturers take the position that
> auto workers are contractually barred from designing the cars and
> have no control over the quality of materials or the methods of

construction. We have little say about how much we are expected to do in the minute or so we work on each car.

Assembly-line jobs are repetitive, dreary, boring and draining. They require little or no initiative and allow for little or no creativity. Yet I have always tried to do my best because there is more self-respect in doing even this type of job well than in doing it poorly and because otherwise it would be impossible to get through the day.

The worker (writing under a pseudonym) questioned a prevailing popular assumption that American workers are unproductive because of a decrement in "work ethic." The problem—he felt— was the unwillingness of management to allow workers to express any work ethic, in the form of a concern with (and pride in) work. Suggestions for improvements and complaints about shoddy parts or defective equipment are thus not encouraged but ignored or stifled. Quality control tends to be relegated to inspectors and foremen, whose reputations hinge on getting the work out, rather than on producing quality commodities.

Workers who are expected not to think about work must find different subjects to think about. Runcie (1980: 108-109), a sociologist who worked on a car assembly line, reports that "you become adapted to the flow of the job and begin to find other things to do with your mind. Some workers try to find shortcuts to make the job even easier. Others read books, magazines or newspapers in between cars. Still others (I was one of these) try to calculate how many cars have already been completed and how many more are still to come."

Non-work-related thinking is apt to affect one's work. Runcie confesses that "one time I realized I was doing my job to the rhythm of an aria from an opera I had heard the last weekend. Another time I found myself a thousand miles away, driving an imaginary automobile down a highway I had not been on for years. How many chassis went by during my mental lapses—and whether I even did my job—I don't know and never found out" (1980: 109). Worse, some "workers often block out monotony and boredom with alcohol and drugs"; others play games with parts and equipment, or may pretend illness to gain a day's respite. Over half of a sample of workers surveyed by Runcie agreed they "have to take a day off every once in a while" (Runcie,

1980: 110). At General Motor's ultramodern Lordstown plant, workers traded jobs to ward off monotony; when management objected, the workers struck. In a group interview of Lordstown workers they were asked why they "doubled up." They responded,

> Dickerson: Inventiveness. One way to explain the thing is that anytime there's a human need, there's always an invention, or a way to get around it.
>
> McGarvey: I'd say inventiveness definitely. I was explaining to my father what the line was like. He said, "Well, why don't you push a broom?" He doesn't understand that pushing a broom is a priority job out there.
>
> Lawrence: Yeah—it gets you off that line.... I'd also tell people on the outside, "Listen, if you had a job paying four dollars an hour, you and your buddy, and you're each going to carry a package"—I bring it down to very easy words so the average man can understand—"You're going to get paid four dollars an hour to each carry a package up the steps and down. Well, isn't it a little easier for you to break your back and carry two packages up and down for half an hour and your buddy resting, and then let him take over and you rest your back? If you want to go get your drink of water or go call your chick, you got the simple freedom to go, see?"
>
> And then they understand it a little bit more. I mean, they would say, "Hey, yeah, that makes life a little easier." That's all we want [Kreman, 1974: 149-150].

In Runcie's plant, the workers had a personal interest in quality control. Runcie reports that "one thing that bothers most workers about their jobs is what they call 'bad stock,' material that does not meet specifications or that is in some way defective, which causes the worker to fall behind" (1980: 111). Where workers complained, they found supervisors unresponsive. Runcie writes that "I have seen engineers ignore comments from workers that could improve the production of individual jobs" (1980: 114).

Management was similarly unresponsive to mundane features that affect work, such as clutter and lack of cleanliness. Another feature of work climate with which managers were predictably unconcerned was their own management style. Runcie points out that practically all workers are confronted with impersonality. When a new worker enters some department, the first question the supervisor asks is, "What's the social?"—meaning the worker's social security number. It seems that no one cares what your name is, only your number. Workers are often referred to as "heads," not people, as when one supervisor calls another and asks if there are any extra heads that can be sent over to help out [1980: 114].

The Numbers Game

Runcie concludes that "the workers want changes at the plant, but they are not certain what the mechanisms for the changes should be" (1980: 114). Runcie's factory had a work reform (Quality of Work Life) program (see Chapters 7 and 8), but most of the workers had never heard of the program. Those who had mistrusted the impersonal, bureaucratic flavor of distant committees. What the workers felt they needed was a vehicle for affecting their immediate environment:

> To workers quality of work life is not an abstraction; it affects their jobs. If a workbench is too close to a pillar, if a hose connection is loose, if the work area is too cold, if a pair of gloves is not available in the morning, the quality of work life is diminished. Once these problems are eliminated, workers would be able to enjoy the luxury of deciding the degree to which they really want to be involved in either overall company decision making or in simply choosing the color for the walls.

> Accompanying the individual nature of the QWL problems is the fact that, while many workers know what it is they do and what their own job title is, most do not really know how their jobs fit into the whole. Some additional orientation for all workers—new and old—might increase their feelings of belonging to the company [Runcie, 1980: 115].

Runcie felt that his fellow workers not only cared about their jobs, but "do care about the company well beyond the paycheck they bring home each week" (1980: 115). They felt, however, that no one cared that they cared. They felt treated with disdain, and subserviently to technology, in the sense that "the technology of the assembly line fosters the idea that the people should be like the products rolling off the line. All workers should think the same, act the same, do the same things" (Runcie, 1980: 115).

Against the backdrop of this perceived message, workers' resistance may not be aimed at the managers' goal (output), but at the way it is defined and imposed. A situation can arise (as at Lordstown) of competing prescriptions for getting the job done, with the clash leading to stalemates or paralysis.

The most tangible source of regimentation in human service settings is a "paper organization," which consists of (1) detailed documents (regulations, prescriptions, lesson plans) that circumscribe work, and (2) routinized documents (reports, records) that testify that work has been done. The more seriously the paper organization is taken, the closer a human service setting approximates an assembly line. The client assembly line (in which managers and/or workers "play it by the book") is the sort of setting in which the adjustment of practice to paper is rigid. In such settings, clients become a processed commodity. The hospital patient may be left in pain because "Doctor hasn't prescribed pain killers"; the welfare recipient may be denied benefits and the offender may be violated because regulations provide inconsequential (but tangible) excuses. The system highlights safety of staff, depersonalization, anonymity, lack of responsibility for action, and standardization of product.[1]

In the client assembly line, human services are quantified as units that can be managerially prescribed, monitored, and controlled. For purposes of quantification, superficial or formal attributes of services (usually common denominators that self-consciously ignore quality issues) are highlighted. Agency mission statements ignore such facts, but in-house communication—and budget justifications—often emphasize them. The syndrome is the familiar "numbers game" in which quotas (number of home visits, interviews, admissions, discharges) are stressed despite sermonizing and propaganda claiming a concern for quality service.

Status offers no protection from assembly-line thinking. A scholar at a major university, for instance, may encounter an administrators' assistant who operates

an automated system designed to collect, process, and report faculty instructional workload. It is not a faculty activity analysis, because it is concerned only with the instructional component of a faculty member's work. We recognize our faculty conduct research, advise students, provide support to the community, engage in public service, but we have found it necessary to collect and describe the instructional components of a faculty member's effort [Kopf, 1981: 7].

The administrators' phrase "we have found it necessary to collect" reflects the assumption that managers must be concerned with quantifiable productivity. The human impact of this assumption (to which we return in Chapter 9) is alienating. It invites antibureaucratic feelings among human service staff and their clients.

Antibureaucratic sentiment has recently taken a variety of forms, from the revolt of welfare recipients and the "student revolt" of the sixties (whose nemesis was mass production in education and the ubiquitous IBM card) to crises among prison guards and among staff nurses in hositals.

A midwestern paper (Grand Rapids Press, August 10, 1981) gives a police example under the headline "Morale Faltering, Friction Building as Police Decry Lax Administration." The paper describes "friction between (police) officers and administrators (that) has resulted in low morale and seriously damaged job performance."

According to reporters,

Several officers complained that commanders penalize those who show initiative and reward others who go through the motions on patrol.

"They don't care how many crimes you solve," said one patrolman, "as long as you write traffic tickets. There's not that much emphasis on arrests. That all has to be self-motivated."

Said another patrol officer: "It makes you less willing to get involved because everything extra you do is another chance of doing something wrong."

As in the various surveys we have discussed, the protest described in the story is reported to be centered among younger, more educated workers:

"You're given an order and expected to stick by it no matter what," Ostapowicz said. "It was the old World War II mentality."

"But this was a smart breed of cat coming in, bright young college-educated people who might not have a problem following the order, they're just asking why it is important."

The production model that workers in all sorts of organizations resent is typified by quantifiable indices of work. In the police example, strong objections arose to quotas for traffic citations (see above), and a second conflict is described as one in which

"hard feelings escalate when officers are obliged to feed data into an ill-conceived, multi-million dollar computerized record keeping system called SPARMIS (Standard Police Automated Resource Management Information System)."

A sore point for young police officers was the demand that "things should go by the book." The issue here is not whether to produce (e.g., arrest), but whether to follow predefined production goals. The concern is with an ethic that reduces the worker's right to on-the-job judgments and to discretion in deciding what to do and/or how to do it.

If this predefinition-of-production issue is forced, workers may retreat (as in our example) into disgruntled lethargy. The resulting nonproductivity of workers may be wrongly attributed to their indolence or congenital rebelliousness or lack of work ethic. Retreat is in fact *antithetical* to what these workers want from work, and as such involves compromise or sacrifice (see Chapter 11).

The Postindustrial Morass

The malaise among today's workers has been diagnosed as a terminal case of postindustrial "blue-collar blues." The term *post*industrial is somewhat faddish. Bell (1976: ix) points out that the concept owes its popularity to the "vogue of 'future schlock,' in which breathless prose is mistaken for the pace of change." But trends, however exaggerated, converge, and they change the nature of the worker and the spectrum of work the worker must do. Most relevantly,

In a pre-industrial world, life is a game against nature in which men wrest their living from the soil, the waters, or the forests, working usually in small groups, subject to the vicissitudes of nature. In an industrial society, work is a game against fabricated nature, in which men become dwarfed by machines as they turn out goods and things. But in a post-industrial world, work is primarily a "game between persons" (between bureaucrat and client, doctor and patient, teacher and student, or within research groups, office groups, service groups). Thus in the experience of work and the daily routine, nature is excluded, artifacts are excluded, and persons have to learn to live with one another. In the history of human society, this is a completely new and unparalleled state of affairs [Bell, 1976: xvi-xvii].

The transition from goods production to service production is not smooth. Unlike old soldiers, blue-collar industrial workers do not just fade away; unlike fruit flies, the "new" generation (the information-centered service worker) does not arise full blown to take his or her predecessor's pace.

In three decades, the service sector has increasingly taken over in most advanced economies, and new jobs tend to be white-collar jobs. There are now women in the work force, members of minority groups, part-time workers, young workers, highly educated workers. Turnover is high, and leisure time (authorized and unauthorized, voluntary and enforced) is sharply on the increase. There is generally financial security among workers, which reduces dependence on work as a means of livelihood. There is increased mobility and galloping urbanization. There are in the long run more social services—ranging from hospitals to prisons—and there is greater need for social services. Such needs are a mixed bag, including higher aspirations (such as expanded demand for education) and greater deficits (drug use, crime, emotional disorders, and the like). In the work place, unionization is prevalent, productivity increments are declining, and worker discontent is rife.

Such trends (and others) are intertwined, and future historians might enjoy unraveling them. For the present, what we must do is cope. This means—among other things—that we must align the "new worker" with a "new type of work setting." In facing this task, it matters little whether we stress organizational need (the demand for sophisticated and productive workers) or personal needs of workers (the demand for humanized work settings). In the long run, the pursuit of one goal leads us to achieve the other.

In this book, our concern is with organizational responsiveness to workers' (and clients') needs. We have therefore defined the problem in terms of new workers and their dissatisfaction and alienation, motivations and aspirations. Our point so far is that today's worker accepts less, expects more, and wants something different than his or her predecessor wanted. This fact strikes us as clearly diagnostic—as posing a problem—and as prescriptive—as implying the core of a solution. We shall in the remainder of this section deal with the first issue, and later (in the remainder of this book) turn to the other.

Overt and Latent Agendas

There are two ways of reading this book. The most direct way is at face value, as a survey of work-centered change strategies that is aimed at students of human service organizations (schools, hospitals, prisons, and the like). The reader will find the survey unobstructed and illustrated with examples, including a very detailed, fleshed-out case study. The aim of the examples is to show what can be done and how it can be done, to provide a feel for the process, and to anticipate problems one may encounter.

The overt agenda follows the outline of the book. Part I (The Problem) suggests the necessity or desirability of change. We have begun this section with a broad spectrum view, which we shall narrow to portrait dimensions. We shall next (Chapter 3) take a closer—more "diagnostic"—look, drawing on some management theory that most students find helpful. Chapter 4 returns to the human service setting, and to social context variables that help us understand it.

Part II (The Prospect) describes two trends—job enrichment and quality of work life—in the contemporary change spectrum. We describe each movement from its literature (Chapters 5 and 7) and apply or extend the view to human service settings (Chapters 6 and 8). The trends show us what can be done, and suggest that the time is ripe.

Part III (The Prescription) deals with two themes we regard as central to planned organizational change in human services. One of these themes is a major one—participation—and we deal with it as a general theme (Chapter 9) and as a component of the change process in practice. Our second theme is action research.

This theme is more specialized and has to do with a mode of participation we see as helpful (Chapter 12).

The last part of the book (The Demonstration) describes a participatory, science-informed change effort in a human service organization (corrections) that uses quality-of-work-life technology to arrive at products yielding further quality of work life and job enrichment. The components of this technology are described with special emphasis on the process of implementing participation products. Our last chapter deals with extensions of the approach.

A second way of reading what follows is as the fleshing out of a personal view or "model" of change. The view is social-psychological. It sees the sources and remedies of worker discontent and of self-limiting adaptations in the work place and the way it is managed. The view is a bias that shortchanges larger contextual (structural) factors and individual psychological ones. It is also an expression of faith (not totally misplaced, we hope) in the potency of self-actualizing involvement in group-based inquiry and in democratic decision making.

NOTE

1. All these attributes have been diagnosed by Merton (1957), who reviews consequences of bureaucratization, or what Max Weber called the "exercise of legal-rational authority." For Weber, the components of legal-rational authority consisted of the power of rules and the stress on efficiency and the prizing of emotional neutrality in encounters among bureaucrats and between bureaucrats and clients. Merton (1957: 199) contends that regulations are supposed to help get the organization's job done, but become ends in themselves. "This emphasis," he argues, "develops into rigidities and an inability to adjust readily. Formalism, even ritualism, ensues with an unchallenged insistence upon punctilious adherence to formalized procedures." An example from the client's perspective is the proliferation of red tape. The "bureaucratic virtuoso" is the person "who never forgets a single rule binding his action and hence is unable to assist many of his clients" (Merton, 1957: 199-200). Just as important is bureaucracy's stress on depersonalized relationships, which "produces conflict in the bureaucrat's contacts with the public or clientele" (Merton, 1957: 202). One problem is precategorization of problems that the client sees as individual or unique. This "impersonal treatment of affairs which are at times of great personal significance to the client gives rise to the charge of 'arrogance' and 'haughtiness' of the bureaucrat" (Merton, 1957: 202). The impression is undergirded by the bureaucrat's penchant for self-appointed spokesmanship (usually unappealable), which ultimately leaves the client no recourse since (unlike in private organizations) there are no rival unemployment services, police departments, schools, or prisons to which a disaffected client can take his or her business.

CHAPTER 2

ALIENATION AND BURNOUT

Human service workers who become disgruntled or disillusioned often think of themselves as being "stressed" or "burned out." Blue-collar counterparts of such workers have no penchant for self-diagnosis, but the diagnosis of their fate has been taken out of their hands by Karl Marx. Marx, anticipating the postindustrial consequences of preindustrial antecedents, predicted that most workers would feel "alienated" from their work.

In his view of alienation, Marx focused on the distance created between the workers and their work if there is no consciousness of a product, no sense of completion, no ownership, no involvement, no spontaneity, pride, or creativity:

> What then do we mean by the alienation of labor? First, that the work he performs is extraneous to the worker, that is, it is not personal to him, is not part of his nature; therefore he does not fulfill himself in work, but actually denies himself; feels miserable rather than content, cannot freely develop his physical and mental power, but instead becomes physically exhausted and mentally debased. Only while not working can the worker be himself; for while at work he experiences himself as a stranger. Therefore only during leisure hours does he feel at home, while at work he feels homeless. His labor is not voluntary, but coerced, enforced labor. It satisfies no spontaneous creative urge, but is only a means for the satisfaction of wants which have nothing to do with work. Its alien character therefore is revealed by the fact that when no physical or other compulsion exists, work is avoided like the plague. . . . Finally, the alienated character of work for the worker is shown by the fact that the work he does is not his own, but another's . . . the worker's labor is no more his own spontaneous activity; but is something impersonal, inhuman and belonging to another. Through his work the laborer loses his identity [Marx, cited in Josephson and Josephson, 1975: 87-97].

To the extent to which work becomes meaningless and tyrannical, man must seek sources of satisfaction *outside* work. This fact was no consolation for Marx (who saw nonwork as providing only "animalistic" need satisfaction), nor has it impressed a wide range of experts—including the NIMH task force—who point to work as the core of human functioning because it can yield meaning and a sense of purpose or accomplishment.

Seeman (1959) provides an insightful description of the connotations that coexist in the term "alienation." One such connotation stands out in Marx's view of the industrial worker: It is the assumption (for Marx, the discovery) that one is powerless. To feel powerless, according to Seeman, means to feel that one cannot affect one's fate.

The survey results we have reviewed in Chapter 1, particularly those relating to younger workers, contain variations on the powerlessness theme. The arbitrariness of supervisors is a deeply felt issue for workers, as is the notion (particularly salient for the Lordstown strikers) that the centers of union and management power are remote and unresponsive. In the extreme, workers see themselves regarded as extensions of rigid systems devised by desk-bound managers, whose output is gauged in terms of numbers, with utter disregard for quality. Workers' opinions, even when they relate to work, are cavalierly disregarded.

In human service work, the target of feelings of powerlessness is often the worker's *client*, who is seen as obdurate and/or recalcitrant. Client stereotypes differ, of course. Stereotyped students are antagonistic and intractable, welfare recipients dependent and demanding, offenders unregenerable, patients uncooperative. Given such perceptions, worker ministrations must be confined to ritualistic wheel spinning, with few, if any, results. A perceived contributory cause in this picture is invariably "the system," which withholds resources and erects barriers to effectiveness.

A related concern is meaninglessness, the worker's conclusion that he or she does not know what is expected of him or her. This concern applies nicely to organizations that provide workers with competing messages, and to the manager who never tells the workers what ends their work serves, or when they have done what they are supposed to have done. The first issue relates to complexity, because complex organizations are likely to give rise to mixed messages. Conflicting demands can originate with layers of management, between management and union, between the organization and its surroundings. The human services are redolent with dissensus. "The book" one allegedly follows is always different from prevailing practice, and managers differ in their compliance with (or fondness for) regulations. Confusion also arises when humane and "hard-nosed" philosophies are simultaneously espoused—sometimes by the same spokesmen—and when prevailing rules change—usually suddenly and in midstream—as crises unfold.

Meaninglessness is *particularly* a feature of organizations in transition—which describes most work settings at some point. Shrinking resources and competition demand readjustments. Where organizational adjustments originate from above, the result is often felt at the working level as confusion and cross-pressures.

The second issue relates to *feedback*. If one does not receive feedback one does not know whether one's contribution is considered worthwhile by others. This experience transcends mere meaninglessness, and it suggests an alienation dimension (the feeling of not being appreciated) that is not on Seeman's taxonomy, but that is a prevalent concern of disaffected workers.

A third of Seeman's "meanings," that of self-estrangement, is the most obvious theme in worker surveys. The issue relates to "the loss of intrinsic meaning or pride in work," to "the inability of the individual to find self-rewarding—or in Dewey's phrase, self-consummatory—activities that engage him" (Seeman, 1959: 790). We have seen that the bulk of workers' expressed concerns and the bulk of their resignation or resentment are vested in this area.

Burnout

The discovery of alienation in the human service industry is recent. Compared to the concern with alienation generally, the literature on burnout has wide popular appeal. *Time* magazine called burnout "a syndrome verging on a trend." According to *Time*, burnout is

> faddish and indiscriminate, an item of psychobabble, the psychic equivalent, in its ubiquitousness, of jogging. . . . Part of the problem resides in the term itself. It is too apocalyptic. . . . The term perfectly captures an American habit of hyperbole and narcissism working in tandem: a hypochondria of the spirit. The idea contains a sneaking self-aggrandizement tied to an elusive self-exoneration . . . it is a declaration of bankruptcy—necessary sometimes, but also somewhat irresponsible and undignified [Morrow, 1981].

The same thought is expressed by Seymour Sarason (1980), who writes that "some use (burnout) as an excuse, some as a badge of honor, and others as a negative symptom of our times and a fast changing society. Like so many other catch phrases it encapsulates a kernel of truth wrapped in attractive language."

We are cautioned not to discard the baby with the bath water. Cary Cherniss (1980b) starts a monograph admitting that "for better or worse, burnout *has* become faddish."[1] He adds, however, that

> it would be unfortunate if those interested in improving the human services dismissed the subject simply because it has become so popularized. For burnout in the human services does exist. It is a common reaction to job stress, and it reduces the motivation and effectiveness of many human service providers. Burnout also is a complex, social psychological phenomenon that deserves more serious study than most writers have given it [Cherniss, 1980b: 9].

The term burnout was coined (in 1974) by Freudenberger, who repeatedly captures the "burned out" image with vivid descriptive passages.[2] In a recent book, Freudenberger tells us that

> If you have ever seen a building that has been burned out, you know it's a devastating sight. What had once been a throbbing, vital structure is now deserted. Where there had once been activity, there are now only crumbling reminders of energy and life. Some

bricks or concrete may be left; some outlines of windows. Indeed, the outer shell may seem almost intact. Only if you venture inside will you be struck by the full force of the desolation.

As a practicing psychoanalyst, I have come to realize that people, as well as buildings, sometimes burn out. Under the strain of living in our complex world, their inner resources are consumed as if by fire, leaving a great emptiness inside, although their outer shells may be more or less unchanged [Freudenberger with Richelson, 1980: xv].

Three similes are critical. One is that of a "throbbing, vital (pre-burnout) structure"; the second is a sequence of "inner resources . . . consumed by fire"; the third is a postburnout shell with "a great emptiness inside." The first point is that those who burn out are "vital" to start with, that they are "people who are dedicated and committed to whatever they undertake" (Freudenberger with Richelson, 1980: 19). Presumably burnout candidates are not deadbeats but idealists, men and women who at first see work as a consuming missionary enterprise.

The second point is a corollary. It is that "when trouble sets in, it is usually a result of *over*commitment or *over*dedication" (Freudenberger with Richelson, 1980: 19). Workers suffer because "there are many circumstances beyond the helper's control . . . not every alcoholic can be saved and certainly not every medical patient," which means that "unless an individual has strong compensating factors in his life, he can fall victim to the constant onslaught of despair his patients bring him" (Freudenberger with Richelson, 1980: 152). The phrase "compensating factors" implies that work is taken excessively seriously; in this view, "if the worker has been looking (in work) for the kind of personal fulfillment he should be finding elsewhere, he will quickly begin to burn out" (Freudenberger with Richelson, 1980: 153).

This version of burnout dynamics is psychoanalytic (Freudenberger is a psychoanalyst) and it has been widely adopted. A very different version (also offered by Freudenberger) is sometimes neglected. This version—which Freudenberger calls "functional burnout"—is closer to our views about blue-collar alienation. In Freudenberger's words,

Both government and private corporations have become so big, people feel dwarfed and inconsequential within their framework. Far from working in an autonomous or intimate situation, employees have become microscopic dots. . . . They work with faceless colleagues on splintered projects of which they have never been given a comprehensive view. . . . It is one thing to be a cog in a wheel, but quite another not to know where the wheel is going. Without a sense of destination or completion, it is impossible for workers to feel pride or even interest in their work. Since they don't know exactly how they fit into the picture, the tasks they perform come to be seen as arbitrary, and in short order the distancing process takes over" [Freudenberger with Richelson, 1980: 163-164].

The "distancing process" describes the notion that the worker gives up, becomes cynical, avoids clients, goes through motions, and "does time" on the job. Freudenberger's view is that *partial* retreat is salutary. "You may have to forfeit some of your ideals," he argues: "you may have to compromise some of your work standards" (1980: 177). He writes that "while it's true that reducing one's involvement may lower the quality of work, compromise is a better solution than Burn-Out. . . . Although it's not easy, it *is* possible to reach a happy medium between cynicism toward your work and thankless idealism" (1980: 177).

Overload versus Underchallenge:
Two Models of Burnout

A recent book (Pines, Aronson, and Kafry, 1981) begins with two vignettes. One describes nurses in a cancer ward whose burnout is ascribed to the fact that they "become involved—and then their patients disappear." Pain and fear, moreover, also make cancer patients "less than considerate, grateful, responsive patients" (Pines et al., 1981: 4). In response, nurses "begin detaching themselves emotionally from their patients (Pines et al., 1981: 4). As cancer nurses discover their own callousness and contemptuousness for patients, they feel guilty and ashamed, "but attempt to mask the symptoms from one another. . . . [Most] tried to look crisp,

efficient, sometimes even ebullient on the
1981: 5). The result is pluralistic ignorance, w
Chapter 4: Nurses see advertised cynicism ai
but "what they *don't* see are other nurses h
anguished and guilty" (Pines et al., 1981: 5).

A contrasting example is that of burned-out d
theirs "seems like a relatively easy, lucrative, relatively
profession" (Pines et al., 1981: 6). What dentists are is victims of
dreary detail; they spend their time poking, excavating, and
cementing disembodied teeth in disembodied mouths. Dentists deal
with clients, but do not relate to clients as people. Among other
things, dentistry "makes it difficult to communicate (other than to
gasp, groan, or emit an occasional 'uh huh' through lips swollen
with novocaine)"; moreover, patients "are not very likely to utter
sounds of approval even if it were physically possible and even if
they were in a frame of mind to do so" (Pines et al., 1981: 7).
Unsurprisingly, dentists (particularly, burned-out dentists) describe patients with "adjectives like 'sullen,' 'uncommunicative,'
'uncooperative,' 'uninterested,' etc." (Pines et al., 1981: 8).

One is led to conclude that there are two kinds of burnout, that
"people burn out not only from being overstressed with a great deal
of work to do but that they can also burn out from being
underchallenged, from having less to do than they have training to
do; from not really feeling well utilized" (Pines et al., 1981: 35).
There are some experts who emphasize the first type of burnout.
Maslach (1976: 16), for example, writes that

> hour after hour, day after day, health and social service
> professionals are intimately involved with troubled human beings
> . . . they are often unable to cope with this continual emotional
> stress and burnout occurs. They lose all concern, all emotional
> feeling, for the persons they work with and come to treat them in
> detached and even dehumanized ways.

By contrast, Karger concludes that

> the routinization of public welfare is complemented by increased
> specialization and the creation of continually narrower job
> descriptions . . . accountability is achieved through daily logs,
> regulated breaks, and performance objectives. The assumption is

orkers are selling their labor rather than their skills. . . . Even n private welfare we see "numbered contact hours"—a designation referring to quantity rather than quality. . . . The workplace in a large public welfare bureaucracy—with its large rooms filled with long rows of cubicles—appears more like a bureaucratic assembly line than a private environment in which to discuss personal matters. The atmosphere is one that leads both the worker and the client to feel insignificant. The client is objectified as a problem that must be processed as the line grows longer [1981: 279-280].

Such views have different implications for solutions and remedies. The first (overload) model seeks to *lighten* workers' emotional burden with time out, catharsis, vacations, extracurricular interests, and relaxation. It prescribes the *sharing* of feelings in "support groups," workshops, and seminars. This view has shaped a burnout ("stress reduction") industry, which furnishes packaged interventions that (1) sensitize workers to their own burnout, (2) cause their frustrations to surface, and (3) ameliorate despair.

Such interventions can backfire when the "overload" diagnosis does not fit, and when burnout results from work fragmentation, poor supervision, and "assembly-line" routine. In settings such as these, a subjective (worker-centered) approach exonerates bureaucratic responsibility for the problem, and teaches workers to adjust. Such an approach may be ameliorative, but *only in the short run.* In the long haul, burnout-related talk reduces the motivation of workers (and their managers) to remedy the causes of burnout through organization-centered interventions such as those we describe below.

Dehumanization: Cause or Symptom?

Maslach (1976: 16) suggests that "in many cases, professionals who have burned out from stress and can no longer cope begin to defend themselves not only by thinking of clients in more derogatory terms but even by believing that the clients somehow deserve any problems they have." Concerns of clients are made light of, and clients are classified as superficial, dependent, and manipulative. Personal contacts are reduced. Caseloads are perceived (and dealt with) for their nuisance value. A tongue-in-cheek portrait of the stance is offered by Erickson, a chief probation officer. Erickson suggests, among other things,

> Always write while conversing with the subject, and continue to make and receive telephone calls. Interrupt your dialogue with him to attend to other important matters, such as obtaining the daily grocery list from your wife or arranging to have your car waxed. Apologize repeatedly and profusely for these necessary interruptions and appear to be distracted, weary, and slightly insane. Having experienced the full treatment, it is unlikely that the probationer will subsequently try to discuss with you any matters of overwhelming concern. You should henceforth be able to deal with him on an impersonal paper-pushing and button-punching basis, if indeed he tries to report any more at all. . . . If despite this initiation the probationer should still try to seek you out for advice, assistance, and interpretation of his rules, you can counter with, "Sorry, but that's not my decision to make." When he asks permission to travel two miles outside the district to visit his elderly, ailing father for Christmas, tell him that you will first have to consult with the judge, police, district attorney, and possibly the dogcatcher. . . . Play the obedient and powerless functionary. Confide to him, "I'd probably let you do it but 'they' are liable to object," or, "I really feel bad about revoking you and sending you to prison, especially on your birthday, but they made me do it" [1977: 37].

Erickson (1977) echoes one explanation of burnout when he tells colleagues:

> When personal or professional problems are bothering you, lay them on a convenient probationer; it's not healthy to bottle up your frustrations. Don't take any crap from the characters on your caseload. You can maintain your position of authority through the timely use of sarcasm and/or multisyllabic professional terminology.

"Dehumanization" in practice is bureaucratic processing. At minimum it becomes unclear to what extent the worker adopts prevailing routine or peer group fashions rather than reacting against job-related "stress." More serious is self-fulfilling prophecy, because any client who is dealt with as an assembly-line object may become (if he or she is not) ungrateful, surly, uncommunicative, recalcitrant, and nonamenable. Such a client becomes a source of stress (burnout) to the Frankenstein who created him or her.

The chicken-egg problem becomes troublesome when complaints ring true, and a third option (clients *are* inhuman) compounds "dehumanization" and "self-fulfilling prophecy" explanations. A prematurely retired teacher reports that

> right up to my final day of teaching last January, my teenage pupils arrived late, cheated on tests, forgot their supplies, fought with each other, smoked in the restrooms, sneaked out of class. I had been a teacher long enough to regard this behavior as normal. I expected teenagers to be teenagers, which means that they whisper to their classmates, make obscene gestures to kids across the room, design paper airplanes, mark on their desks, complain about homework, and distract me at every opportunity. I could handle that.

> What I encountered in recent years was much more disturbing, even frightening. In increasing numbers, teenagers have begun using their ultimate weapon against the school, the teachers, and themselves: They are simply refusing to do the work that leads to learning [Bardo, 1979: 252].

Such assumptions are hard to test. Bardo (1979) claims (believably) that she began by expending inordinate efforts to disconfirm her assumption of student resistance to learning. In an alienated setting (a slow learners' enclave, for example) efforts by workers may be prematurely discouraged. Cherniss, Egnatois, and Wacker (1976: 433) note (as have others) that burned-out staff promotes pessimistic views of clients' change potential:

> One new mental health professional told us how he initially had been troubled by the lack of progress in many of his clients. His methods simply were not working. However, his co-workers and supervisor helped him "to see" that the problem was not caused by

his technique or lack of ability in using the technique. Instead, the "problem" was in the clients. They did not respond to treatment because of a combination of cultural and psychodynamic factors that they brought with them into therapy.

Burnout consultants see the problem in this fashion but offer no remedy beyond helping workers to reconceptualize the change paradigm ("clients are not *really* hopeless targets of change; such feelings are the result of burnout"). No technological assistance or change prescription is furnished to improve the performance of workers or to effect change in the client. There is thus no reason why client recalcitrance should not reassert itself and produce more burnout.

Burnout is an individual *and organizational* problem. To address a problem of this kind, one must view it in more full-blooded terms than as a personal reaction of burned-out workers. This is noted by Sarason, who writes that

> there is another and more insidiously fateful consequence of these catch phrases, and that is that their metaphorical quality directs attention away from the structure of the social contexts in which the phenomenon occurs. What are the characteristics of these contexts in which the phenomenon occurs? What are the characteristics of these contexts in which burnout appears to be frequent? Why do contexts vary in this respect [1980: viii]?

Sarason makes his comment in a foreword to a book. It is this book (Cherniss, 1980a) to which we must direct some attention.

The Burnout Transaction

A crucial fact about burnout—as Sarason implies—is that you find it disproportionately in some organizations and rarely in others. This suggests that (1) pressures that originate in organizational settings and (2) impinge on all or most people working in such settings (3) can create a common fate or shared problem for a group, which (4) is mutually reinforced as workers compare notes (Chapter 4), and (5) produces a climate or "group culture" that facilitates the individual worker's burnout. It is not surprising that a whole setting can seem to burn out, in the sense that Monday's shared enthusiasm becomes Friday's anomie. Herbert Freudenberger talked about this phenomenon as "group Burn-Out" or "communal Burn-Out." He refers to the campaign staff of an unnamed governor who were charged with policy planning, and "fell to it in high spirits, calling a meeting for that very evening. By midnight, when they finally adjourned, they had compiled an agenda . . . they resolved to be ready on time, even though they realized they would have to give up their evenings and weekends" (Freudenberger with Richelson, 1980: 172-173). The group's work was ignored, and in reaction, "by the summer of that year, all seven (staff members) had resigned to take jobs in the private sector." Interestingly enough, "the governor was startled by the rash of resignations and never connected them with disillusionment over his failure of commitment to the issue. He chose, instead, to deliver diatribes on the undependability and ingratitude of 'that generation' " (1980: 174).

Cherniss (1980a: 5) provides a human service example involving a "group home for youth [that] had an exciting, innovative program" and a staff among whom "there was a tremendous dedication to the teenagers, who were seen as having great potential to change and grow." Over time, though, the climate changed: "Staff members rarely worked a minute over their regular shifts and became furious if they had to stay a few minutes longer because someone on the next shift was late. At staff meetings, they began to ask how much physical force was permitted in dealing with disruptive behavior and why tranquilizers were not used more to help control the youths' behavior" (Cherniss, 1980a: 6). What had happened (among other things) is that "staff members were irritated by what they considered to be insensitive and inept administrators . . . red tape . . . the lack of administrative support" (Cherniss, 1980a: 5-6). Shared work experiences and job attributes (intrusive supervision, routinization, lack of recognition, and the like) can "turn off" motivated workers and thus make burnout likely.

According to Cherniss (1980a), young professionals employed by public organizations such as schools, social agencies, and legal aid offices often become disillusioned during the first year of employment, and "the extent of burnout seemed to be strongly influenced by the nature of the work setting." Specifically, "those (young professionals) who worked in extremely demanding, frustrating, or boring jobs tended to change more negatively than those whose jobs were interesting, supportive and stimulating" (1980a: 5). Cherniss's study is critical because—as he puts it—he was "especially sensitive to the structure of the job and work settings, including its role, norms, traditions, patterns of authority and control, organizational climate, and so on" (1980a: 12). This sort of approach makes it possible to trace *transactions* between environmental pressures or climate features and changes in work motivation.

We know that the motives with which workers initially approach the same job may differ. Some of us, for example, have a greater need to feel competent, or are more likely to blame ourselves (i.e., feel incompetent) when we fail. Even the worker who feels most self-assured, however, can discover that his or her supervisors may demand too much too soon, deny support, and be critical (or insufficiently appreciative) of his or her performance. Settings can also interact. Our experience (graduate school) may ill prepare us or "set us up" by generating unreasonable or other-worldly expectations. Such relationships between our experiences or motives and settings are "transactions."

Among organizational components of stress transactions, "bureaucratic interference" looms large. The problem includes administrative style (authoritarian), operating procedure (red tape), and job definition (segmented). Personal expectations, of course (such as rebelliousness and intolerance for routine), are still at issue, as is skill and motivation. There will always be workers who resist destructive climates, who swim against bureaucratic tides, "crowd the system," or circumvent it to find challenge or autonomy and meaning for themselves, while others give in, grouse, or leave the field. We have seen that tolerance for clients' recalcitrance varies, as does the explanation for how one's ministrations are received. Teachers may blame students for non-learning or change their teaching strategy. They may also blame the school ("bureaucratic interference") or themselves ("problem of competence"). Some of these strategies are likely to produce burnout (detachment, cynicism, and the like); others are not.

In human service settings, the impact of "bureaucracy is . . . the greatest enemy of professionalism" because "in several respects, the 'professional ideal' and the 'bureaucratic ideal' are completely incompatible" (Cherniss, 1980a: 58). Bureaucracy not only circumscribes the professional, but also affects the services that may be delivered to people. It tends to place the professional "in the middle, often torn between the demands of bureaucracy and client" (Cherniss, 1980a: 63). Different options (e.g., advocacy) may be open, but to exercise such options means to embark on an obstacle course that carries risk of disappointment and finally, burnout.

The most serious risk is for the professional to "adapt" and to become *part* of bureaucracy, thus joining an enemy he or she cannot beat. Cherniss writes that

> Contrary to what they had expected, many new public professionals find that they must perform the functions of the "street-level bureaucrat," an individual who, while providing service directly to the public, is also expected to perform a bureaucratic function. They are the ones who categorize the clients and process the forms in ways that enable public bureaucracies to function. In the typical public bureaucracy, people cannot be provided with service until they are transformed into clients. This is accomplished by matching certain client characteristics with the fixed categories of service defined by the bureaucratic system [1980a: 67].

One problem with burnout is that the way people adapt when they burn out makes work even more unattractive. Many burned-out workers react by reducing "effort and involvement in [their] work," which obviously "may simply make things worse, for the less effort one puts into one's work, the less fulfillment one is able to get out of it" (Cherniss, 1980a: 69). To reverse such a cycle requires *self*-stimulation or calls for job enrichment programs such as those we shall describe in Chapter 6.

A standard prescription for burnout is the "support group," in which problems are shared and one gets the benefit of whatever reassurance is provided by awareness of a shared fate. Such support makes sense because burned-out workers often feel lonely and isolated, and sometimes ashamed and guilty. What matters, however, is the *direction* of support and the *content* of group discussions. Group sessions dominated by unhappy people can easily become "gripe sessions." They can promote added despair. Problems that everyone complains about seem to become irremediable and unsurmountable; outside forces become omnipotent and individuals impotent. The result can be "even more burnout, whether or not the gathering is euphemistically called a 'support' group" (Cherniss, 1980a: 233).

The problem is not with the concept of "support group" but with the connotations of "support." People get helped by learning to recognize and label their own feelings, and by learning to deal with frustration. But if sources of frustration remain undiagnosed, there is no "support" for the notion that contextual conditions can be changed.

Catharsis can be followed by constructive thinking once the air has been cleared of accumulated feelings. When the sources of burnout lie in bureaucratic management, organization-centered problem solving is more relevant than frustration sharing, and too much of the latter may make the former difficult or impossible. When sources of burnout are mixed (as they usually are), the most parsimonious strategy promotes problem solving with as much (or as little) "support" as the emotional climate, or the shape of alienation, demands.

There is no prescription for "support problem-solving" groups of this kind. Such groups must be more than—and different from— what is usually meant by support groups. They must contain both burned-out and un-burned-out members (if the latter exist). They must be problem centered as well as feeling centered. They must be run with a more complex technology, have more administrative support (so products stand a chance of implementation), and must require harder work from members.

Unfortunately, burned-out workers tend to like the more person-centered model because it portrays them as sensitive, overdedicated victims of thankless crusades. Such victims can demand compensation. In one police department, for example, "disability pensions for psychological stress are up 67 percent for the first six months of this year (1981), compared to the same period in 1980 . . . 'stress pensions' now outnumber all other pension awards combined—including those for orthopedic injuries, common in police work . . . last year alone, the total cost for 37 stress-related disability pensions was $37 million" (APA Monitor, 1981).

Managers like the notion of personal "stress." It makes them pay for burnout, but the burnout condition becomes "a God-given consequence of running an organization, [which] is less troubling than the idea that workers are acutely unhappy with their job conditions and your outdated management style" (Toch, 1980: 27).

NOTES

1. One consequence of the popularity of the burnout concept is that the prevalence of the phenomenon is overestimated. A recent survey was designed to highlight burnout among teachers, but found almost none. The report listed among *lowest* ranked items (1 on a scale of 0-7), "I haven't really cared what happens to some students," "I have worried that this job is hardening me emotionally," and "I have treated some students as if they were impersonal 'objects.' " Among highest ranked items were statements testifying to a commitment to teaching and to feelings of accomplishment gained from work with students (New York Teacher, 1981).

2. Safire (1982) traces the prehistory of the concept. He points out that the phrase " 'to burn oneself out'—applied to people, in the manner of a fire dying for lack of fuel—entered the slang lexicon around the turn of the century." Safire also mentions that "in 1917, the poet T. S. Elliot bemoaned 'the burnt-out ends of smoky days,' followed two years later by Fanny Hurst's 'a tired, a burned-out, an ashamed smile.' "

CHAPTER 3

SHAPE OF THE WORK PROBLEM

One trend in the literature—which includes the work of Karl Marx—is that of romanticizing preindustrial work conditions, presenting these as the "guild" era in which self-employed, free-spirited artisans created and marketed ingeniously designed commodities, an activity that filled them with justifiable pride. The fun of such creativity was spoiled, according to myth, when artisans began to be herded into efficient conglomerates by greedy entrepreneurs, and when they were given minute tasks to perform, subservient to mechanized fragmentation, and coordinated by bureaucracies.

The portrait holds as long as we equate preindustrial work conditions with those in Cellini's workshop[1] or in other unrepresentative enclaves in which specialized and prized craftsmen created luxury commodities. But most work throughout history has been performed under dawn-to-dusk sweatshop conditions, which were hardly ameliorated by the fact that workers made whole products, e.g., frantically baked mud implements, and that they had the dubious privilege of squatting in bazaars hoping for customers with incomplete table settings. It is also a sleight of hand to exclude from the "worker" category the vast armies of slaves and peasants who made up the bulk of the population, and who toiled at the margin of a very precarious subsistence. Thousands of men and women died mining and transporting rocks for the pharaohs. They were clearly "workers," but made minimal contribution to the genesis of "products" (pyramids) and rarely lived to see the results of their labor.

Be the situation as it may, the advent of the "managed worker" is a comparatively recent development. For our purposes, we can trace this worker, and the system into which he or she fits, to the impact of Frederick Taylor. Taylor is the key figure in the history of work because he articulated the role of manager in industrial organizations, and thereby defined the role of the manager's counterpart, the worker.

Taylor (1947) has been described as originating the machine-shop version of "classic management" theory.[2] At the time, his approach was called "scientific management," in part to escape the immodest connotations of the term "Taylorism." The ideas of Taylor were manifold, but our interest lies in his notion that workers' activities must be predesigned or "planned" in detail, and that this function (design, planning, "thinking") must be performed by different people than those engaged in work (see Foreword).

Taylor did not claim that workers were incapable of exercising ingenuity, but he maintained that workers tended to hoard any ideas they had, and he also felt that work reform must derive from studies of work. Studies of work excluded workers, who could not work and observe work simultaneously. The most crucial of Taylor's concerns had to do with the notion that the steps involved in getting an organization's job done had to be standardized to maximize efficiency. It was the manager's job to divide work into segments, to ascertain the most economical steps and procedures required to get each job segment completed, and to direct ("teach") workers their contributions, as well as to monitor and reward compliance. Management, in Taylor's first machine-shop experiment,

> meant the building of a large, elaborate labor office where three college men worked, besides their clerks and assistants, planning the work of these workmen at least one day in advance. . . . It meant, then, building a big labor office and playing a game of chess one day in advance with these 500 men, locating them just like you would locate chessmen on your board. It required a timetable and a knowledge of how long it took them to do each kind of work [1947: 39].

Taylor talked of "matching" workers with jobs, but the role he envisaged for personnel selection was modest. Since Taylor thought that all job tasks must be simplified as much as possible, he merely recognized gradations in simplicity. He told a group of congressmen, for instance, that shoveling is a great science compared with pig-iron handling. I dare say that most of you gentlemen know that a good many pig-iron handlers can never learn to shovel right; the ordinary pig-iron handler is not the type of man well suited to shoveling. He is too stupid; there is too much mental strain, too much knack required of a shoveler for the pig-iron handler to take kindly to shoveling [1947: 50].

Though this passage implies that Taylor had little concern for worker morale, he felt that workers should be delighted to have managers arrange their jobs, because efficiency ultimately accrued—in the form of wage incentives—to the benefit of workers, who were bound to prize productivity when their paychecks arrived. The routinization of work might be stultifying, but sensible workers should be pleased to pay this small price, recognizing its merits, or (minimally) its inevitability:

Now when through all this teaching and this minute instruction the work is apparently made so smooth and easy for the workman, the first impression is that this all makes him a mere automaton, a wooden man. As the workmen frequently say when they first come under the system, "Why, I am not allowed to think or move without someone interfering or doing it for me!" The same criticism and objection, however, can be raised against all other modern subdivisions of labor [Taylor, 1947: 125].

From the preceding chapter, we know that Taylor's assumptions about the worker's gratitude have proved shortsighted. Some of Taylor's more practical followers—including executives of "scientifically" managed companies—suggested more active concern with worker morale, but Taylor reacted to their advice impatiently. He wrote

I am very much interested in your statement that shop committees should be selected by the workmen of your Chicago Link Belt Company to discuss rates, etc. I think you are making a great mistake in doing this. I do not believe that there is the slightest dissatisfaction among your men [Copley, 1923: 428].

In the long run, the workers' "dissatisfaction" could no longer be ignored, and the "great mistake" Taylor refers to proved to be the dawn of a new approach to management, which we shall explore in the next sections of this book.

Motivating the Worker

Taylor's formula for motivating workers was to pay them more when they produced more. To state the case more accurately, Taylor's formula was to pay workers more if *as a result of following management instructions to the letter*, they had produced more. Taylor assumed that workers work in order to get paid, and that (within limits) better pay would translate into harder work.

In its extreme form, the classic management perspective comprised an unflattering image of human nature and conceived of mankind in its natural state as basically lazy. "There is no question," wrote Taylor, "that the tendency of the average man (in all walks of life) is toward working at a slow, easy gait.... There are, of course, men of unusual energy, vitality and ambition who naturally choose the fastest gait, set up their own standards, and who will work hard, even though it may be against their best interests. But these few uncommon men only serve by affording a contrast to emphasize the tendency of the average" (Taylor, 1947: 30-31).

The management perspective fathered by Taylor held that workers are motivated for leisure, but unmotivated for work. Taylor claimed that he had "timed a naturally energetic workman who, while going and coming from work, would walk at a speed of from three to four miles per hour, and not frequently trot home after a day's work. On arriving at his work he would immediately slow down to a speed of about one mile an hour. ... In order not to do more than his lazy neighbor he would actually tire himself in his effort to go slow" (Taylor, 1947: 31-32).

Several decades after the advent of the Tayloristic approach, Douglas McGregor—a psychologist who revolutionized organizational theory—summarized the psychological assumptions held by most "Tayloristic" managers. He characterized these assumptions as a coherent theory about human motivation, which McGregor called "Theory X." The Theory X Manager treats his workers *as if* he believed that the average human being has an inherent dislike of work and will avoid it if he can.

Because of this human characteristic of dislike of work, most people must be coerced, controlled, directed or threatened with punishment to get them to put forth adequate effort toward the achievement of organizational objectives.

The average human being prefers to be directed, wishes to avoid responsibility, has relatively little ambition, and wants security above all [McGregor, 1960: 33-34].

McGregor outlined a sharply contrasting set of assumptions about worker motivation, which he called "Theory Y." The manager subscribing to this perspective, according to McGregor, acts as if he assumed that

the expenditure of physical and mental effort in work is as natural as play or rest. . . .

Man will exercise self-direction and self-control in the service of objectives to which he is committed.

Commitment to objectives is a function of the rewards associated with their achievement.

The average human being learns under proper conditions, not only to accept but to seek responsibility.

The capacity to exercise a relatively high degree of imagination, ingenuity, and creativity in the solution of organizational problems is widely, not narrowly, distributed in the population.

Under the conditions of modern industrial life, the intellectual potentialities of the average human being are only partially utilized [McGregor, 1960: 47-48].

McGregor did not maintain that workers are *necessarily* accurately viewed (or dealt with) in Theory Y terms. Traditional organizations often produce the sort of workers who are congenial to them, and for such workers the advent of a Theory Y regime might come as an unassimilable shock. In traditionally managed organizations, the worker might require weaning or graduated transitional experiences before he could assimilate or could constructively deal with autonomy and challenges. According to McGregor, the *first* commodity workers must be furnished is security, which is the requisite of freedom.

McGregor's view is compatible with a psychoanalytic portrait of human development, but it rests more heavily on the self-consciously optimistic motivational sequence envisioned by Abraham Maslow (1954), who studied the psychological evolution of healthy, creative men and women. Maslow's thinking—with or without its translations by McGregor—fills textbooks of management, and it undergirds the prescriptions for management reform that were born in the 1960s and have been expanded in the 1970s.

Unlike Freud, Maslow did not dichotomize motives into basic drives and "higher" motives, nor did he assume that the latter are derived—in sublimated form—from the former. Instead of Freud's inaccessible Id, perpetually pressing for its pound of flesh, Maslow saw man's basic need level as the basement of a pyramid with a functioning psychological elevator. As one floor is reached, the next one is aspired to. The average person progresses from specific desire to satisfaction of desire and from satisfaction to new desire, redirecting energy to "higher" functions as "lower" ones lose their hold. The crucial implication, which McGregor called "of profound significance" to organizations, is that "a satisfied need is not a motivator of (worker) behavior" (Maslow, 1954: 36).

We can assume that within organizations—except concentration camps—people are not motivated by hunger or other phys-iological drives. Workers have mostly graduated to other needs, which have to do with (1) safety, which means tenure, predict-ability, and structure (job security, steady income, pension schemes) followed by (2) sociability or geniality and group support.

Higher on the Maslow/McGregor need hierarchy than the social needs of workers are motives McGregor labeled "egoistic needs." McGregor characterized these motives (which Maslow called esteem needs) as "the needs of greatest significance to management and to man himself."

Precisely following Maslow, McGregor (1960: 38) subdivided esteem motives into

(1) Those that related to one's self-esteem: needs for self-respect and self-confidence, for autonomy, for achievement, for competence, for knowledge.

(2) Those that related to one's reputation: needs for status, for recognition, for appreciation, for the deserved respect of one's fellows.

Maslow's interest lay in the next step of his hypothesized progression, the penthouse of his motivational edifice. Here, as McGregor (1960: 38) notes, "are the needs for realizing one's own potentialities, for continuing self-development, for being creative in the broadest sense of the term." For the expression of these needs "the conditions of modern industrial life give only limited opportunity."

The Theory X manager views workers as governed by the needs that hunger for pay, fringe benefits, and congeniality, in roughly that order. These commodities entice leisure-oriented humanity to do what must be done to keep civilization alive. The view is illustrated in New York *Times* (March 28, 1982) advertisements seeking to entice engineers to join the space age. One such ad reads,

> As an engineer at . . . Aircraft, you'll surround yourself with the benefits of a climate and location that lets you enjoy it all—the arts, educational opportunities and the great outdoors. Every day. All year round . . . with easy access to beach, desert, and mountains. . . . Make the Great Escape that could last a lifetime.

Another ad (featuring an endomorphic lobster) refers to "career opportunities," but goes on to read,

> And if that doesn't give your appetite a whet, how about sitting down to a boiled live lobster, sailing against the wind, or stopping by a quiet spot where mountain streams are all that remains of winter snows [New York Times, March 28, 1982].

Another advertisement queries,

> Engineers—thinking about a move to Southern California? then why not consider the "best" area? . . . located in the beautiful . . . Valley, has been twice named by . . . Magazine as the best place to

live in the greater Los Angeles area. Nearby are located some of Southern California's other prestigious living areas. . . . The best programs, the best careers, and the best living, all merge at . . . [New York Times, March 28, 1982].

The Theory Y manager feels that men and women have "graduated" from lower needs to those centering on esteem, the need to make a significant contribution—one that is worthwhile and appreciated—and the desire for self-actualization (challenge, creativity, exploration). Such needs can be met through the type of work that permits their satisfaction. In New York *Times* ads, Theory Y managers address a different version of would-be employees. One advertisement asks such persons,

> Who will spearhead the next major advance in computer technology? It could be you at . . . . We've undertaken an exciting task at. . . . It is expected that the end product will set the standard for many . . . applications through the end of the century.
>
> The complexity of the systems we are now planning requires more than progressive thinkers. You must be able to perceive the project on varied planes. You must be bold enough—imaginative enough—to redefine problems when solutions prove elusive. And you must be team-minded enough to interact with specialists in other disciplines; to spread insights; to sharpen each select view; and to retain the goal as the driving force behind your work [New York Times, March 28, 1982].

Another Theory Y employer points out that "like the popular cube puzzles, there are engineering problems that have millions of solutions, but only one right answer. That's why we need gifted engineers with special talents." A third company promises "*challenges* that creative minds thrive on. *Freedom* to innovate—expand intellectually, and most important, to truly work at the cutting edge of technology" (New York Times, March 28, 1982).

McGregor's Split-Level Hierarchy

The two essential attributes of Maslow's scheme are (1) the *developmental* premise, which describes a process in which, when some needs are satisfied, we become oriented toward other needs,[3] and (2) the concept of a need *hierarchy*, which implies the interdependence and continuity of motives.

McGregor remained faithful to the first assumption by emphasizing that workers have a personal history that relates to the satisfaction in infancy of basic safety and social needs. The Theory X appeal to "lower" motives of Maslow's hierarchy could translate workers back in time, and could make them feel and behave like children. The experience of such workers, as McGregor saw it, was one of *dependence*, which relegates managers to a nurturant role, and makes them the targets of childlike rebelliousness. Sudden liberalization could backfire, because—like enforced or premature adolescence—it faces workers too suddenly with an adult (autonomous) role for which they are unprepared. The other side of the coin is that continued Theory X management of workers whose lower needs have been met stunts the progression of those who are ready to graduate to adulthood and who are interested in doing so. Such workers are no longer motivated by pension plans. They do not respond to the "carrots" of Theory X, and see the "sticks" of supervision as an affront to their personal integrity as chronological and psychological adults.

McGregor accepted Maslow's hierarchy, but by combining half of it under Theory X and the other half under Theory Y, he unwittingly and irrevocably subdivided the complex scheme into two mutually exclusive categories, those of (1) motives primarily centered on security and material rewards (compatible with a carrot-and-stick management approach), and those of (2) motives centered around self-esteem, recognition, and desire for achievement (compatible with a worker-centered management approach). This view of worker motivation was similar to others introduced into the work-related literature by influential theorists, most notably the key contribution of Frederick Herzberg (1956, 1966).

Herzberg's concepts are more data based than those of McGregor. They derive from an analysis of statements made by workers (mainly white-collar workers) when they are asked to describe the high and low points of their work lives. The surveys yielded overlapping sets of concerns, but the most important

finding was that the *good* days that are remembered by workers—
the positive critical incidents—involve satisfactions they derived
from the work itself, while the *bad* days—the negative incidents
they reported—feature *dis*satisfaction with pay, working
conditions, and other external incentives.

The practical significance of this fact is tied to the classic
management emphasis on non-work-related satisfactions
embodied in the Theory X approach. Theory X managers respond
positively to worker safety needs by providing clear-cut
instructions; "softer" versions of Theory X emphasize insurance,
pension plans, and vacations in scenic places. Making work
congenial through "human relations" can satisfy social needs; pay
responds to the basic need level, and pay increments and
promotions massage lower ego (status) needs.

All material rewards, Herzberg notes, are *necessary*, but they
are not *sufficient* to produce happy workers. Their absence makes
workers disgruntled, and their presence is a requisite (a "hygiene
factor") for a healthy organization. Different rewards must be
created to "satisfy" workers or to "motivate" their work. These
rewards are "intrinsic" to the job, rather than being "extrinsic" to
it. They involve opportunities for workers to satisfy their esteem
and actualization needs by using their capabilities, finding work
meaningful, experiencing results, getting recognition, learning,
growing, and exploring.

Some details of Herzberg's scheme hinge on the use of his survey
procedure, with its emphasis on dissatisfiers at work. When other
techniques are used to poll workers, extrinsic incentives show up
as sources of satisfaction, but of *a lower order* than intrinsic
incentives. The essence of the distinction, though, remains
inviolate: For most workers, the intrinsic rewards of work—those
neglected by traditional managers—are the dominant concerns
that emerge in surveys of attitudes, values, satisfactions, and
dissatisfactions at work (see Chapter 1).

Alienation Revisited

The above implies that we can conceive of intrinsic and extrinsic
rewards as higher- and lower-order satisfiers; another possibility is

to emphasize the *dis*satisfying or frustrating consequences of *withholding* the two categories or rewards. It is the latter formula that reminds us of alienation as it was defined by Marx and more recently described by Melvin Seeman (1959; see also Chapter 2).

Self-estrangement is a clear-cut consequence of Tayloristic, Theory X management, of the emphasis on hygiene factors to the neglect of esteem needs and workers' potential for actualization. If work means, in Seeman's (1959: 790) terms, "to be something less than one might ideally be if the circumstances . . . were otherwise," the feeling defines the sense of having climbed part-way through Maslow's hierarchy only to discover—reluctantly and with varying degrees of bitterness—that one can go no further. It is in *this* sense that Herzberg's satisfiers become dissatisfiers—or rather, "alienators," and that we can speak (as in Chapter 1) of a "postindustrial syndrome."

The "syndrome," like all syndromes, is made up of "symptoms." In this case, we call the symptoms "alienation." Each alienation theme points to needs that have been frustrated in work settings. Powerlessness denotes squelched autonomy needs, meaningless-ness suggests frustrated cognitive[4] and/or safety needs, self-estrangement tells us about unrequited needs for esteem and actualization. The composite picture catalogs ways in which personal growth and fulfillment have been stunted along the Maslow/McGregor hierarchy.

The final question is whether Marx was right—and Taylor wrong—from the start. Is the *post*industrial syndrome the *industrial syndrome* come home (belatedly) to roost? The facts, tentatively, argue otherwise: Among discontented workers, older workers are relatively happier. One assumes that with echoes of the depression alive in their mind, their lower needs can be resuscitated. Youth builds on the Maslowian basement of its elders. Feeling safe, young people expect more and want more. Today's younger workers are a far cry from Taylor's recruits fresh from Ellis Island, or from Ford's southern migrants escaping from plantations—and starvation—to Detroit. Sources of alienation, as Marx suggests, may be centuries old, but workers had to grow to discover disjunctures between their needs and settings, their aspirations and rewards. Having discovered such disjunctures, they feel alienated, and this experience and its consequences are probably here to stay.

NOTES

1. Even artisans were poorly off. Cellini himself was a slave driver. He drove his apprentices to exhaustion and admits that he kicked and punched them when he was angry.

2. Classic management is often referenced to Max Weber, whose description of bureaucratization captured the sociological imagination. Weber, however, was not an innovator. Taylor was, as were other entrepreneurs at the turn of the century; the advent of classic management is a joint product of their separate and independent contributions. A random example is a biographer's observation about the famous chef, Georges Auguste Escoffier:

> His reforms, down to organization, were radical. In the kitchen chaos of the old regime, for example, one cook took fifteen minutes to prepare Eggs Meyerbeer. Under Escoffier's system of specialists, an *entremettier* baked the eggs; a *rottisseur* grilled the kidneys; a *saucier* whipped up the truffle sauce, and a gourmet was rendered ecstatic in only a few minutes [Frizzel, 1961: 126].

3. A modified version of Maslow's model is provided by Alderfer (1972), whose needs (existence, relatedness, growth) move in a diverse progression. Alderfer assumes, for instance, that if relatedness needs are not satisfied, both relatedness and basic needs will be alive, and that unsatisfied growth needs may lead to pursuit of relatedness as well as growth.

4. Maslow (1954) writes of two types of "cognitive needs"; the first is the desire for knowledge (the need to know), and the second the desire for meaning (need for closure).

CHAPTER 4

CYNICISM:
THE HUMAN EQUATION

Work dissatisfaction, of course, is never an individual reaction. Some workers grouse and others grouse back. Coffee klatsches and gripe sessions spread alienation, and at times, as at Lordstown, collective expressions of protest occur. At the core of most blue-collar discontent, however, we find "the job"—its boring, stultifying character, its intrinsic sterility and fragmented, authoritarian cast. This cause-and-effect sequence is less clear cut among teachers, social service workers, and prison guards in that *perceptions* of the job are socially reinforced to a greater and more complex degree than are perceptions of factory work. This fact is of importance in considering remedies and solutions. Of even greater importance is the subculture component of resistance to human service work reform, which we shall discuss below.

Concern with group reinforcement of worker reactions to their jobs has inspired recent research. A study by White and Mitchell (1979) shows the potential of ingenious experiments that simulate organizational realities. The goal was to show that positive and negative comments of fellow workers and "enriched" and "impoverished" attributes of the job interact. The job was preparing data for processing, with varying responsibility for doing the job. Stooges made loud comments reflecting content and discontent with work conditions. The legitimate workers' satisfaction level reflected the advertised gripes and grunts of simulated fellow workers; even more dramatic is the fact that productivity levels varied with the fake social climate. Enriched jobs could produce unhappy workers and low levels of production (despite very accurate perceptions of the job) where the script of stooges called for mild grousing. This fact is doubly impressive because, as White and Mitchell (1979: 8) note, "The effect of the comments of an unknown co-worker in a short work session would intuitively seem to be less important than the comments of a co-worker with whom one works 8 hours a day, 5 days a week, because the ad hoc nature of the present groups probably produced far less social pressure to conform than could be expected by members of a long-term integrated work team."

The issue of "social pressure to conform" in workplaces is a time-worn issue, and there has been consensus among experts on the ability of workers to shame other workers into working less or to inspire them to work harder. Taylor's concern was with worker resistance to production pressures, and it took the Hawthorne studies (Roethlisberger and Dickson, 1961) to highlight group support for work involvement. In these studies, which were conducted in the early thirties, traditionally managed workers sabotaged production quotas that were imposed on them, and a relatively leaderless group of workers exceeded goals they had determined themselves. The Hawthorne findings suggested that organizations have group-based underworlds that are beyond the pale of management, and that can be supportive of or destructive to management goals. As a result, Hawthorne-inspired reform efforts—"human relations" and "organizational development"—tried to create responsive managers who could link the "formal" (manager-run) to the "informal" (autonomous work culture) organization from the "top" down.

Human service settings have more complex underworlds than assembly lines. One way of describing this complexity is to think of staff as having a "subculture" with a developed ideology, such as the anomic, anticlient perspective of the burned-out workers we have described. Membership in a burned-out subculture would entail consensus on beliefs such as "clients are at best grateful," "this place is a zoo," "everyone here goes through useless motions," and "I once cared, but I don't now."

Staff subcultures are ingroups; the public, clients, and management are outgroups. Defending the ingroup against outgroups places a premium on solidarity and dictates sharply controlled communication across ingroup borders. While all sorts of workers (and most other human groups) reject informants, subcultural definitions of "finkiness" are consequently especially generous and strongly felt. William Westley (1970: 111-112) makes this point when he describes the police subculture, and tells us that "secrecy and silence are among the first rules impressed on the rookie. 'Keep your mouth shut, never squeal on a fellow officer, don't be a stool pigeon,' is what the rookie has dinned into his ears; it is one of the first things he learns." Westley himself was concerned with police violence and to a lesser degree, with police corruption. Bad officers, he notes, are a minority, but secrecy norms of the locker room protect such officers from exposure. The subculture's commitment to keeping the game going transcends its professional concern for rendering lawful service to the community and lowers the quality of its members' productivity. The subculture is not antipublic but pro-subculture. In the process, it supports its more reactionary members *as if* it agreed with them.

For administrators to single out bad officers is not only very difficult, but the strategy seems bound to increase solidarity in the subculture and make its members angry. Pointing an accusing finger at some makes the rest feel vulnerable. The experience cements the image of a threatening outgroup, which now incorporates the reform manager as its spearhead (Toch, 1976).

Westley's portrait may be extreme, but peer-protective codes have been located elsewhere. A Canadian corrections officer study (Karlinsky, 1979) describes such a code. Most of it is reminiscent of Westley, but the code also deals with officer/client relationships. The code contains a plank "which specifically refers to not being a 'con lover,' never doing favors for inmates as they are the enemy and can never be trusted" (Karlinsky, 1979: 130). The anticlient norm is presumed typical of guards and is paralleled by a "never talk to screws" norm ascribed to inmates (Wheeler, 1961).

The social distance norm is not a peer-protective measure in the same sense as the "no rat rule" and the "don't make waves" rule referred to by both Westley and Karlinsky. It is instead a cynical, burnout-promoting norm.

Staff subcultures in schools, welfare agencies, and mental health settings are known to generate pressures that prescribe cynicism. Holdouts in the staff subculture—mental-health-oriented guards, for instance, or client-centered social workers—feel restricted to low-visibility acts and to guarded expressions of their philosophy. Closet idealists such as the "inmate lover" or "bleeding heart" join rate busters and stoolies as deviants to be ostracized and objects of contempt. We infer that service enrichment schemes are also anathema unless they are self-consciously confined to innovation ghettos and are sharply circumscribed.

Pluralistic Ignorance

In many settings, the shoe of the reactionary subculture fits, in the sense that (1) subcultural "spokesmen" (very loudly) espouse client distance norms; (2) outside observers "observe" staff/client distance, and (3) workers who favor reduced distance feel disapproved of and/or squelched. Two situations are isomorphic with this view; one is that of a subculture that takes its alienation out on available clients who heartily reciprocate staff views. Where service organizations fit this model, they feature "keepers" and "kept" who play a nonstop game of cops and robbers.

Version 2 *looks* like Version 1. It may even *feel* similarly, in that (1) staff think clients reject them, (2) clients feel rejected, (3) staff view other staff as custodially oriented, and (4) clients see fellow clients opposing staff contacts. Under this surface, Version 2 describes an organization in which most staff *privately* favor reduced client distance and inmates *privately* prize staff services. This syndrome is *pluralistic ignorance*.

Subcultures can induce conformity; *imaginary* subcultures—in situations in which pluralistic ignorance exists—have commensurate conformity-inducing potency as long as the illusion of a make-believe majority exists. Where publicized burnout symptoms in organizations drive idealism and commitment into the closet, knowing how others feel can have a potentially liberating impact.

The Custodial Subculture: Fact or Fiction?

The concept of a police officer subculture is enshrined in the criminal justice literature, and so—by analogy—is the notion of a guard subculture (Duffee, 1974). The beliefs ascribed to custodial subcultures are proenforcement, in the sense of a subcultural premium placed on controlling "bad guys" firmly, and if/where necessary, by force. The presumed manly enforcer, for example, would be entitled to tell enforcement "war stories" to the admiring recruits of the subculture. Custodial subcultures in noncustodial settings would highlight locker room themes comparable to those of criminal justice settings. The subcultural parole officer would discuss sidearms, and the teacher, discipline.

Packard and Willower's (1972) work reflects a concern with custodial subcultures in schools. Packard and Willower write that "norms enjoining strictness towards students and the maintenance of social distance typically appear to mark the teacher subculture, and pressures for faculty members to exhibit a united front to guard against organizational problems resulting from pupil control breakdowns seem substantial." They add that "in such circumstances, persons may feel obliged to represent their views on pupil control so that they appear to support prevailing norms" (1972: 78).

The issue of feeling "obliged to represent [pupil control] views" arises in visible situations, in the sort of "on-stage settings where support for the common defense against pupil recalcitrance and defiance is affirmed" (Packard and Willower, 1972: 80). Where private views in reality are noncustodial, teachers suffer from pluralistic ignorance. Teachers hear teachers talk tough, and assume that they are tough, or at least, that they think tough. This would reinforce the desire to keep quiet about one's nontough beliefs and to reduce the visibility of one's nontough behavior. The findings of research depict such a condition, not only for teachers, but for principals, who act only slightly less "tough" than teachers.

The problem is more serious for prisons. Teachers, at least, are not labeled "custodial," but correctional officers through at least two centuries have been "keepers of keys," guards, or hacks. They have held this role by acclamation of members of the public, of social scientists, and of convicts. Recommendations for officer role expansion (President's Commission, 1967) have created *some* expectation of change, but the advent of civilian "rehabilitation" specialists (teachers, counselors, mental health staff) have preempted the most obvious directions of professionalization. What is left is the presumption that prison guards should do more than they traditionally have, so as to live up to their beefed-up labels (correctional officer or correctional counselor) and earn their newfound status.

Throughout, of course, the suspicion has been that officers *prefer* to be custodial, that they incline toward restricted inmate contact and prefer to count, escort, and watch inmates to acquiring more "enriched" functions, such as advising, counseling, and ameliorating inmates' adjustment to prison. This suspicion has survived evidence to the contrary, such as enthusiastic officer participation in the group counseling movement (Fenton, 1957), innovative small-scale experiments (Briggs and Dowling, 1964), and a variety of surveys—both formal (Lombardo, 1981; Teske and Williamson, 1979) and informal (May, 1976; Johnsen, 1979; Toch, 1978).

The myth is one of a custodial subculture that is said to favor narrow definitions of the officer's role, and to discourage officers from more meaningful work with inmates. To test the subcultural model, Kauffman (1981) asked prison staff to judge the actions of a make-believe officer faced with pro-inmate and anti-inmate choices, and then to estimate how many officers would approve/disapprove the mythical officer's decisions. Kauffman (1981: 288) reports that the officers tend to view their group opinion as homogeneous. "An average of 42% of the officers thought that almost all of their colleagues would respond in one way—*either* 'almost all' or 'almost none' would approve in a given situation." Such perceived homogeneity, Kauffman notes, hides dissensus in fact, because "the pattern . . . applies to the issues that lack clear consensus."

The *direction* of error, Kauffman points out, is that "officers who gave (inmates) unsympathetic responses were far more likely to perceive that they held the dominant view than were officers who gave sympathetic responses. And that this is true notwithstanding that on all but two of the situations the sympathetic response actually predominated" (1981: 289-290).

The implication is that inmates are not faced with a hostile guard force but with "a diverse body of officers who are more treatment and inmate oriented than they or others think" (1981: 290). Among the "others" deceived by the illusion are the inmates (human service clients) themselves and most students of prisons.

The Cop and Con Game

A custody transaction involves two complementary factions, the cops or "custodial subculture" and the cons or "inmate subculture." Cop norms have to do with social distance from cons, suspicion, an eagle eye for infractions, and an affinity for enforcing discipline. Con norms involve social distance from cops, suspicion, a penchant for infractions, and fear of "trouble" in the shape of cops.

Custody transactions that involve *real* subcultures are refractory to change, because the behavior of each subculture is responsive to activities of the other. A school in which students are bent on exploiting fellow students, on committing vandalism, and on inflicting mayhem will have a faculty dedicated to tight supervision and justifiably obsessed with discipline and safety issues. Each side invites and shapes the other: Teachers-turned-cops spawn students-turned-cons and vice versa, in a cycle of monitoring-evasion-discipline-sullenness, and so forth. "The feeling," as the saying goes, becomes "mutual," and the norms endorsed by each subculture reliably and validly reflect the problems posed by the other.

Even a residue of such warfare can demoralize both sides of the fence, producing spurious fear and groundless suspicion. Clients forced to act like cons suppress their desire for staff contact and for services, and exaggerate their antisocial (or at least, antistaff) dispositions; staff, in turn, downplay services and advertise safety concerns. Cloward (1955) called the client antistaff syndrome the "sour-grapes pattern." He observed this sour-grapes reaction as a prevalent client stance in a military retraining compound, and noted that

> many respondents privately expressed skepticism about the standardized bravado which characterized informal relationships. As one man said, "I hear them say, 'I wouldn't take restoration; I

wouldn't go back no matter what they did.' But that's a lot of bull. They just say that to act big and make people think they're tough. They don't mean it. They'll take anything to get out of here, but they don't think they have a chance, so they act like they don't want anything." But whether most prisoners genuinely subscribed to this sour-grapes pattern is of little importance; the fact is that it both persisted and was engaged in by a goodly number of them irrespective of their personal feelings. And the point is that extensive exposure to and participation in this sour-grapes pattern is but a prelude to the emergence of a more concrete and observable kind of behavior which I categorized as passive noncooperation [Cloward, 1955: 88].

Cloward's point about the sour-grapes pattern was that *a majority of clients secretly desirous of services could be intimidated by an antistaff minority into rejecting services.* Wheeler documents the existence of the same syndrome in prison settings. Two of Wheeler's (1961: 234) items have to do with the inmate's desire for staff services:

> Inmate Martin goes before a committee that makes job assignments. He is given a choice between two jobs. One job would call for hard work, but it would give Martin training that might be useful to him on the outside. The other job would allow Martin to do easier time in the institution. But it provides no training for a job on the outside. Martin decided to take the easier job.
>
> Johnson, an inmate, learns that the institution has a group therapy program for interested inmates. He thinks the program might help him understand his problems. He asks a member of the treatment staff if he can get into the program.

In the first Wheeler item, inmate Martin opts for a work assignment with zero rehabilitative potential; three out of ten (31 percent) fellow inmates agreed with Martin, but the average estimate of peer approval of Martin was 54 percent. Wheeler's other inmate hero (Johnson) joins a group therapy group; virtually all of Johnson's peers (99 percent) approve, but their *estimated* approval figure is 63 percent. This does not mean—Wheeler adds—that inmates are wild about therapy. "In the discussions following administration of the questionnaire," he writes, "many inmates were quick to mention that *they* didn't need therapy, but weren't opposed to it for those who did" (Wheeler, 1961: 236). The ascribed subculture stance, however, dictates unqualified opposition to therapy.

Wheeler studied staff perceptions of inmate attitudes and inmate perceptions of staff attitudes. He reports that "though the differences in actual expectations between inmates and staff are quite large, they are uniformly less than they are perceived to be by inmates and staff alike" (1961: 240). There is—Wheeler notes—an "overperception of conflict in the role expectations of staff and inmates" (1980: 248).

Discovering Pluralistic Ignorance

Phantom subcultures are as potent as real subcultures. Where they exist, very convincingly loud minorities become unchallenged spokespersons for silent majorities and discourage initiative among majority members. In agencies, staff and clients conform to custodial norms and admire or posture cop and con conduct to avoid ostracism. Unenthusiastically militant armies face each other across trenches, mouthing slogans and rattling sabers.

The first result of this situation, as Wheeler (1960) points out, is the "overperception of conflict." A related impact is the discouragement of collaborative activity, including reciprocated initiatives from staff to clients and vice versa, and uninhibited participation in service delivery or recipient roles. Teachers cannot afford to teach in such a climate, and students cannot afford to learn. Inmates are loath to display rehabilitative moves, and guards to further them. Client development is stunted, and staff contributions (which lead to staff development) are impoverished.

The ironic outcome of pluralistic ignorance is that conformity to illusory pressures stifles personal potential and retards social progress just as surely as does conformity to real pressures. It also makes majority members publicly untrue to themselves, which raises problems for them privately. A closet idealist buys the approval of cynical (or presumed cynical) peers at the expense of consistency in his or her self-image.

This fact is a liability, but *in planned change terms*, it is also an asset. It means that if pluralistic ignorance is exposed, the discovery can be a welcome experience, which helps the person achieve congruence. In settings such as those we have described, we can expect survey data to yield surprise, followed by widespread relief. Vulnerable inmates can more easily seek staff support, and new options are created for them by removal of informal taboos. Workers discover other workers who are clearly seeking to enrich their jobs. Perceived constraints to professionalization—including experimentation with new technologies—are removed.

Feedback of pluralistic ignorance data is a catalytic intervention. It frees the informal organization to consider change that might otherwise be resisted and offers autonomy to clients and staff who welcome autonomy and want it. In some settings, removing pluralistic ignorance may bring change. Elsewhere, it opens new change options. It leads to the discovery of *real* resistance to change, which must be faced and challenged. In such efforts, however, the interventionist now works side by side with men and women freed of *imagined* constraints, persons who can decide to be clients of change, or possibly agents of change.

PART II

THE PROSPECT

CHAPTER 5

THE NOTION OF "JOB ENRICHMENT": FROM CHORES TO CHALLENGES

Alienation has diverse roots. Among them is the perceived unrewarding nature of most people's work experience (Chapter 1). Many jobs turn their encumbents off rather than on, and men and women trudge to work for the sake of paychecks they expect but do not value.

As we have seen, part of the problem has been linked to the way in which work is subdivided, yielding simple, meaningless tasks that are doled out, one task per person, to workers. This mode of job design (work fragmentation) is efficient, and it allowed industrial pioneers—such as Taylor and Ford—to make mass production possible. *Technically*, the idea still works. In *human* terms, it does not. Students of organizations discovered this in the 1930s (when they encountered worker boredom) and confirmed it in the 1960s (through experiences with worker alienation).

The NIMH task force asked, "What does the employer gain by having a 'perfectly efficient' assembly-line if his workers are out on strike because of the oppressive and dehumanized experience of working on the 'perfect' line?" (Special Task Force, 1973: 15). Cooper et al. (1979: 124) answered that "employers must now begin to change their patterns of responsiveness to these changes in employees' values and expectations." The point was that new types of workers need new types of jobs.

But how to design more responsive jobs? The solution was made possible by Herzberg's linking of job attributes to workers' motives. Herzberg (1966) implied that "motivators"—intrinsic aspects of work (opportunity for achievement and recognition, interesting and challenging things to do, personal responsibility, chances for advancement and growth)—can be built into jobs. It happens that in fragmented jobs they are not built in. When boredom is reduced by summing work fragments (a strategy that is called job enlargement), more variety is built into work, but the experience does not really change. As Herzberg put it, "Two or three meaningless activities do not add up to a meaningful one" (1966: 177).

There are many listings of motivators, of desirable intrinsic attributes of jobs. When the goal is to make work more attractive to workers, lists usually contain recognizable variations on Herzberg's themes. An example is a Tavistock-inspired roster of "psychological job requirements." It includes:

(1) Adequate elbow room. The sense that [workers] are their own bosses and that except in exceptional circumstances they do not have some boss breathing down their necks. Not so much elbow room that they just don't know what to do next.

(2) Chances of learning on the job and going on learning. We accept that such learning is possible only when men are able to set goals that are reasonable challenges for them and get a feedback of results in time for them to correct their behaviour.

(3) An optimal level of variety, i.e., they can vary the work so as to avoid boredom and fatigue and so as to gain the best advantage from settling into a satisfying rhythm of work.

(4) Conditions where they can and do get help and respect from their work mates. Avoiding conditions where it is in no man's interest to lift a finger to help another: where men are pitted against each other so that "one man's gain is another's loss"; where the group interest denies the individual's capabilities or inabilities. . . .

(5) A sense of one's own work meaningfully contributing to social welfare. That is, not something that could as well be done by a trained monkey or an industrial robot machine. Nor something that the society could probably be better served by not having it done, or at least not having it done so shoddily.

(6) A desirable future. Quite simply, not a dead end job; hopefully one that will continue to allow personal growth [Emery and Emery, 1974].

Another example is the following three-item list:

There appear to be three characteristics which jobs must possess. . . . The first is that the individual must receive meaningful feedback about his performance. This may well mean the individual must himself evaluate his own performance and define the kind of feedback that he is to receive. It may also mean that the person may have to work on a whole product or a meaningful part of it. A second is that the job must be perceived by the individual as requiring him to use abilities that he values in order for him to perform the job effectively. Only if an individual feels that his significant abilities are being tested by a job can feelings of accomplishment and growth be expected to result from good performance.... Finally, the individual must feel he has a high degree of self-control over setting his own goals and over defining the paths to these goals [Lawler, 1969: 429].

Listings like these, or like Herzberg's original one, are prescriptions for "enriching" work. The strategy of putting these prescriptions into effect—of shaping jobs that are more challenging and meaningful—is called "job enrichment."

Job enrichment always increases a worker's contribution and arena of responsibility. A secretary's job is enriched when he or she is asked to reply to mail or originate correspondence. The enriched repairman is one who is given a "territory" and has a group of "customers." In many settings, job enrichment takes the form of work teams, which divide and arrange their work. Work teams substitute for assembly lines and produce complete products such as trucks or packages of dog food. In other words, enriched teams cover the entire work process, from soup to nuts. They need little supervision or quality control because they exercise such functions themselves.

Issues in Job Enrichment

Two controversies surround job enrichment, and we shall deal with them in Chapters 10 and 11. The first has to do with *how* to enrich jobs and the second with *whose* jobs to enrich. Jobs can be enriched from "above," by managers and experts. Enriched jobs can also be designed by the workers *on* the job, from "below." How far "below" is another issue. Some argue that lowest-echelon workers make unlikely targets for job redesign. Some—including us—would disagree.

Among employers who disagreed was Texas Instruments, one of the world's top manufacturers of electronic equipment. The organization is redolent with high-level professionals, but it was concerned about "the assumption that growth, recognition, achievement and responsibility are needs restricted to people with the more prestigious jobs and that people in low-skilled or unskilled jobs somehow have different values and motivations," and that "the poor guy who pushes the broom just wants to do the least he can get away with and take home his pay" (Rush, 1971: 39). In 1967, the company tested the hypothesis with a dramatic program exploring the limits of job enrichment as a strategy.

The Poor Guy Who Pushes the Broom

Texas Instruments began its experiment by hiring foremen for a prospective army of janitors and matrons (male and female cleaning personnel). Training for the foremen included a "workshop on participative management and the relation between work and motivation" (Rush, 1971: 41). The company then approached a cadre of cleaning persons (whose educational level was fourth to fifth grade) and informed them of the company's "belief in the importance of each employee's contribution to the total corporate effort" (Rush, 1971: 41). The matrons and janitors may have been puzzled until they were informed that their first task was to recruit other matrons and janitors. They responded by organizing a recruitment task force that "visited churches, clubs and community centers to tell the advantages of working with the company. They also developed a special recruiting brochure" (Rush, 1971: 41). Not surprisingly, the janitorial force soon expanded to strength.

The core program began with intensive indoctrination of supervisors highlighting the writings of Herzberg and McGregor (Chapter 3). Foremen chaired weekly meetings of janitorial "teams" to discuss cleaning problems and to work out appropriate solutions. The solutions usually consisted of new ways of doing the job.

Among innovations that were implemented by the cleaning persons were the following:

(1) Teams eliminated cleaning carts, installed supply cabinets, took responsibility for inventories, and placed their own orders to keep stocks up to date.

(2) Work groups divided and controlled their own work. For example, groups set schedules for "close downs" of washrooms to minimize unpredictability for workers who might urgently need sanitary facilities.

(3) Matrons dealt with a disinfectant that had "corrosive effects" and caused dermatitis. They negotiated with a "vendor who developed a new chemical to their specifications. The new cleaner was packaged in spray form, which cut cleaning time in half" (Rush, 1971: 43).

(4) Teams originated a new toilet bowl cleaner that proved "quicker and more effective" and "cut down bowl stoppages" (Rush, 1971: 43).

(5) Janitors and matrons took responsibility for inspections, which involved using a special rating form.

(6) Teams of matrons and janitors worked out task allocations that permitted joint cleaning of adjoining facilities.

(7) Most impressive, the workers became concerned with preventive maintenance. They embarked on an ingenious campaign "to educate and involve the users. For example, lead ladies take turns speaking to new hires as part of the company's employee-orientation sessions to explain their cleanliness goals and to solicit cooperation. Another approach: matrons and janitors with their lead ladies, photograph areas that are particularly untidy and dirty. These photos are circulated on production lines, in an attempt to elicit more concern and cooperation from factory, laboratory and office employees" (Rush, 1971: 44-45).

Predictably, the Texas Instrument plant became spotless, worker turnover plummeted, and substantial cost savings (estimated at $103,000 per year) were effected. More crucially, a group of workers that is prototypically undervalued was afforded the opportunity to think and contribute. What was previously a "dirty" job acquired richness and meaning and became a source of pride and creativity. We see vintage "grass-roots management" in the fact that the lowest echelon of a multiechelon organization had taken over standard *management* functions. As Rush points out,

> Employees [have undertaken] the responsibility for much of the planning and controlling aspects of their jobs, as individuals and/or as teams, as well as the "doing" of the job.... For example, the matrons do their own inventory and ordering of equipment and supplies (planning) and do their own inspections and cleanliness ratings (controlling).... Furthermore, group planning, evaluation, and goal setting are integral to the process [1971: 45].

Job enrichment opposes work fragmentation and the assignment of job fragments to workers. At Texas Instruments, groups were "held accountable for the over-all job; the means of getting the job done were left to the employees themselves" (Rush, 1971: 45). Groups can coordinate large (meaningful) jobs without needing control from above. Groups, however, are only one means to such ends. What matters is that *somehow* the work originates with the worker, makes use of the worker's skills, and has a meaningful product attached to it.

Opponents of job enrichment point to constraints limiting the enrichability of jobs. Texas Instruments undercut such arguments. There are many enrichment efforts that are better known and more widely publicized than that at Texas Instruments, but none that are more revealing. For if toilet bowls can acquire motivating potential, *any* job is more enrichable than we at first suspect.

Job Enrichment Through Job Enrichment

If job enrichment accomplishes anything, it increases work satisfaction, which means that the worker finds his or her job interesting, instead of regarding it as an obligation. As work gains in interest, it is done more thoughtfully. The sense of responsibility that goes with enriched work also motivates reflection.

What follows is do-it-yourself enrichment, meaning that most workers seek better (more effective and/or meaningful) ways of doing the job. Job enrichment sparks experimentation with job design, and even if initial enrichment is done from above, further enrichment comes from below.

Self-enrichment can be reinforced by building occasions for reflection—sessions earmarked for "reviews" or work study—into programs. There are many ways of doing this: They range as widely as Quality Control Circles (Japan) and network meetings of rank-and-file innovators (Norway). At Texas Instruments, weekly team meetings were occasions for job redesign.

Ideally, as we shall see in Chapter 10, the process starts by having workers design their jobs. A model for this process is provided by Emery and Emery (1974), who have been involved in diverse enrichment efforts all over the globe.

The Emery model involves a "participative design workshop," which begins with indoctrination about job enrichment. In workshops, workers

(1) analyze how the job is now done,
(2) assess how far this falls short of meeting human requirements,
(3) redesign for a better way of doing the job (if such is felt to be needed),
(4) work out how the new design could be implemented [Emery and Emery, 1974: 168].

Workshop participants may be a work unit (four, ten, even fifteen) or representatives of a larger force, e.g., an assembly line. Emery favors a "deep slice" (stratified) design, which samples every layer of a large workforce. Workshops include union representatives and one or more foremen. Top managers appear at the beginning and at the end. Managers support the effort and (if it succeeds) appreciatively consume its product.

The group's slogan is "more human jobs for all," and its goal is to arrange everyone's work to make it more challenging and meaningful. Help is provided by an outsider (such as Emery), who acts as facilitator and resource; the consultant *as facilitator* "can umpire, suggest, criticize. *As an external resource* he can help broaden the workshop's range of experience and deepen their analysis with social science concepts" (Emery and Emery, 1974: 171).

The first order of business in any workshop process is an "analysis" or psychological inventory of jobs as they are now done. This consists of reviewing all work or types of work, and rating the jobs against criteria of enrichment/impoverishment. In Emery's model, all jobs are rated in terms of the degree to which they provide opportunities for decision making, optimal variety, chances for learning, mutual support, meaningfulness, and chances for a desirable future. Ratings follow a "-, 0, +" (insufficient, adequate, ample) scale, or are done numerically (0-10):

> The advantages of this first analysis are firstly that any misconceptions of the nature of criteria are hammered out by the group and a common and well founded understanding is established. Secondly, this first task is usually sufficient for members of the team to become acquainted with each other if they have not worked together closely on site, and to work through first stages of group formation [Emery and Emery, 1974: 172].

The next job is to review work flow, inventorying skills deployed by each worker in a "skilling table" (which lists skills against workers). Job enrichment calls for more sophisticated work, and skills often require supplementation through training, which can be pinpointed in advance.

Design workshops need not involve an outsider, and the Emerys suggest that outsiders keep a low profile. The consultant solves problems when they arise. He or she also reviews the group's ideas for job designs for conformity to the enrichment model.

Enrichment-Related Data

Jobs cannot be redesigned without information, and the requirement holds no matter who does the designing or redesigning. In the past, the field was the province of engineers; the sort of knowledge that was deemed relevant had to do with nuts-and-bolts technical questions. Fred Taylor (see Chapter 3) was the first "industrial engineer." He innovated mechanical improvements (fast machines) and streamlined deployment of manpower. In connection with the second enterprise, Taylor invented time-motion studies. The resistance of workers to being researched by Taylor sparked a famous strike and a congressional hearing.

Taylor studied workers to discover how fast a pace they could work at without self-injury. His perspective is technology centered in that it sees workers as extensions of machines. Today this view envisages a "man-machine system"; Taylor's modern counterparts are "human engineers," "systems engineers," or "systems analysts." The systems concern—like Taylor's—is with efficient arrangements that can get the job done. People are means to ends. Their experiences, concerns, perceptions, rewards, frustrations, stresses, aspirations, satisfactions, and dissatisfactions are not accommodated in systems inquiries. A systems question, such as "How can police patrols be deployed to best effect?" or "How can intake be most effectively handled in a hospital?" is not concerned with the experienced impact of patrol patterns on officers doing the patrolling or on citizens being patrolled, or with the experience of the nurses "processing" patients or of the patients being processed.

Early inquiries into the *experience* of work were those of Mayo (1930), the progenitor of the Hawthorne (Western Electric) studies. Beginning in the early 1920s, Mayo studied fatigue and monotony and explored deep-seated resentments of workers. The Hawthorne research (Roethlisberger and Dicksen, 1961) began with a standard human engineering problem (optimal lighting and arrangements of rest). Western Electric turned to social and psychological issues because the psychophysical parameters they were researching proved inconsequential. Unlike Taylor's subjects, workers at the Hawthorne plant bloomed under the attention of investigators. They liked being observed at work, polled, and interviewed, and talked to about having their working conditions rearranged. Among factors that proved crucial in generating worker enthusiasm were (1) the researchers' interest in them as persons and human beings, (2) the research-related consultation of the workers, and (3) the exploration of concerns that originated with the workers.

Job enrichment is *centrally* concerned with how workers feel and with the "impact" of jobs before and after design. Enrichment research covers experienced job attributes, reactions to the job, values, and expectations. The seminal contribution is that of a group at Yale (Hackman and Oldham, 1980) who use an instrument called the "Job Diagnostic Survey" (JDS). The first sections of this instrument require the worker to describe his or her job along impoverishment/enrichment dimensions. The first item asks, "To what extent does your job require you to *work closely with other people* (either 'clients,' or people in related jobs in your own organization)?" The answers range from "very little; dealing with other people is not at all necessary to doing the job," to "very much; dealing with people is an absolutely essential and crucial part of doing the job." The relevant category is on-the-job opportunity for "dealing with others." Other items explore the at-work availability of task variety, continuous or "whole" tasks, job significance or importance, autonomy, feedback from the job, and feedback from others.

The next sections explore the worker's reactions to his or her job. One of these sections subdivides sources of satisfaction or dissatisfaction into Maslowian needs, ranging from "the amount of pay and fringe benefits I receive" to "the amount of challenge in my job." A different section asks for peer ratings of reactions to the job.

The instrument ends by exploring the workers' aspirations. Job characteristics are presented, and the worker ranks them from "Would like having this only a moderate amount (or less)" through "would like having this *extremely* much." Another method is that of paired comparison. The worker is asked, for example, whether he or she would prefer "a job where the pay is very good" or "a job where there is considerable opportunity for me to be creative and innovative."

An inventory of this kind tells the job designer *precisely* where he or she starts from the worker's (individual and collective) perspective. The designer knows how the job is experienced and how workers react to the experience; he or she knows what workers would like that they now do not have and how they would prioritize their aspirations. The data offer a "baseline" at the inception of design. Over time (if and when jobs are redesigned), repeat measures yield pictures of progress. The data not only tell whether jobs are enriched, but the extent to which workers have been satisfied and/or have changed their aspirations.

Job enrichment centers around job attributes that can be enhanced by rearranging the way work is done. The point of research is to tell us how badly enrichment is needed and how easily it can be done. The greatest need for enrichment and the greatest potential go hand in hand where jobs are acutely impoverished and where workers suffer and seek a better life. Where jobs are impoverished but workers feel resigned the need may be just as urgent but the task is harder. It may be tempting (as we see in Chapter 11) to work with already enriched workers in search of further enrichment. Such is not the import of research: Data do not define goals, but—given goals—they tell us what we are up against.

CHAPTER 6

JOB ENRICHMENT IN
THE HUMAN SERVICES

No matter how badly off human service workers are, their fate is less circumscribed than that of men and women who serve machines and are constrained by their technology. Admittedly, *some* "people work" is limited and confining. For example, "a correctional officer assigned to tower duty . . . requires 20/20 vision, the IQ of an imbecile, a high threshold for boredom and a basement position in Maslow's hierarchy" (Toch, 1978: 20). There is frustration, fragmentation, and routine in many jobs. Men and women sit in cubicles, conduct 15-minute interviews, and fill out forms; they service the needs of drooling, smelly, incontinent bodies; they drive through deserted streets or walk past rows of snoring figures; they watch, escort, and wait; they ask (or answer) routine questions and deliver canned instructions. Though top human service professionals have lacunae of impoverishment (doctors poke orifices, Nobel laureates join committees), the core of "professional" involvement lies elsewhere. Not so with lower-echelon staff, whose impoverished duties are emphasized as *core obligations*; enriched work (if any) being included as a negotiable option. Job specifications dictate that bedpans must be emptied, beats patrolled, clients "contacted," office hours logged.

Civil Service lists include among "activities, tasks and assignments" for New York correctional officers, for example,

- Checks inmate passes and records inmates' movements in and out of area.
- Counts inmates and fills out count slips.
- Watches for unusual incidents and reports any to his supervisor either verbally or in writing.

- Makes periodic rounds of assigned areas checking for faulty bars, gates, etc. and checks areas for daily fire report.
- Searches cells for contraband and logs any contraband found.
- Frisks inmates and fills out frisk sheets.
- Mans a perimeter security post such as wall or gate post or interior security post such as cage officer.
- Informs inmates of changes in rules and regulations and answers their questions.
- Attempts to stop minor incidents and may take direct action to break up fights, or other disturbances. May call for assistance from fellow officers.
- May fill out incidents or use of force reports.
- May, as a member of an emergency response team, respond to unusual incidents.
- With proper authorization, may use weapons, chemical agents, restraining devices or protective equipment in case of emergency.
- Reports unusual or disturbed behavior to supervisor or physician.
- If authorized and assigned the responsibility to do so, issues prescribed medication and checks to make sure it is taken.
- Announces sick call.
- Supervises bathing.
- Makes sure that inmates have proper clothing and gear by checking issue and instructs on proper use of equipment . . .

[New York Department of Civil Service, 1974: 51].

A worker whose job is defined in this way may do more than is required. He or she may console people, listen, advise, refer, tutor, mediate, intercede, protect; he or she may expend empathy and concern in helping people. Chances are that if he or she does so, his or her employers will not recognize and reward his or her involvements. Nor will they object to them unless the worker neglects mandated job components, such as cell counts, traffic citations, reports, or office hours. The point is that self-enriched workers are on their own. Some workers swim against the tide and seek to enrich their jobs; others find the lack of incentives overwhelming.

Emphasizing Human Contact

Hackman and Oldham (1980) list "dealing with others" as an enrichment-relevant attribute. This *by definition* means that human service workers (if all else is constant) have more enriched jobs than non-human-service workers. It also means that enrichment varies with the emphasis that workers (or organizations) place on "dealing with others." In agencies and institutions such as schools, prisons, or hospitals, custodial emphasis (see Chapter 4) increases the social distance between workers and clients. Custodial norms impoverish jobs unless workers choose to defy the norms. The same holds for caretaking norms, which convert clients into physical bodies to be washed, examined, or moved about.

An impoverished job tends to be a "burned-out" job. It is "just a job," meaning that it is only performed because it leads to pay and fringe benefits. Clients are uninviting, and one deals with them (not necessarily callously, but always with indifference) because one is paid to do so. As a result, there is no satisfaction in learning about people's problems (task variety), the solving of problems (task identity), client responses (feedback), responsibility for solving problems (autonomy), or chances for having impact (task significance). By contrast, the same worker is "enriched" if he or she finds clients interesting, challenging, and responsive.

Impoverished jobs are self-enriching if the workers refuse to relegate client contacts to an officially predefined low priority. Subprofessionals often "opt out" of realms hypothetically preserved for professionals. The stubbornness with which other lower-echelon workers insist on doing "people work" (and gaining pride from it) is a testimonial to the potency of their higher-level Maslowian needs, since they must "stretch" job definitions to do what they do. This point is illustrated by a study of psychiatric attendants in North Carolina (Simpson and Simpson, 1959) in which each aide was asked why he had taken a job as attendant and why he kept the job. Answers were coded as "extrinsic" or "intrinsic." Intrinsic reasons included "interest in understanding mental illness through contact with patients, humanitarian interest in patients' welfare, satisfaction of working with people rather than things, and affection or sympathy for patients" (Simpson and Simpson, 1959: 390). Extrinsic reasons ranged from salary levels and friendships to convenient transportation.

Extrinsic reasons predominated (to the tune of 82.6 percent) among initial attractions of the job, but dropped to less than 50 percent (46.5 percent) as reasons for staying. The attendants had developed an "occupational self-image . . . which places heavy emphasis on the importance of the attendant in patient care" (Simpson and Simpson, 1959: 390). The point noted by Simpson and Simpson (1959: 392) is that "the attendants . . . tend to stress activities directly connected with patient care as most important, although housekeeping tasks such as cleaning floors and making beds may be more time-consuming."

Colarelli and Siegel (1966: iv) note that attendants who are allowed some enrichment, "have been the eyes, ears and hands of the doctor; they have acted as middlemen between patient and doctor. Their presence has permitted one doctor to treat many patients. They have reported faithfully their observation of the patient and have carried out prescriptions and treatment. Because they have served this function so well, for most patients the mental hospital has become a place of hope." Self-enrichment among workers enriches the delivery of services to the organization's clientele.

This fact becomes important as we review *Ward H*, a classic report by Colarelli and Siegel (1966). Ward H aspired (1) to improve the lives of chronic patients in a mental hospital, and (2) to enrich the jobs of psychiatric hospital attendants. The way these two goals relate is touchingly described by Colarelli and Siegel:

> How do you change the static hopelessness of these patients? How does one humanize them and their treatment? How does one relate to them as persons? How does one stop the process of dull, unending routinization of the personality? A possibility is to

provide them with a model—someone lively, fully human, spirited; someone who cries, laughs, struggles with life. Let us put this person near them. Perhaps through identification, through learning, the patient will come alive.

Who will serve as our model? Let's put the aide in this role. We see our aides at parties and in their personal lives and know that they are spirited and vital. Why aren't they their own vigorous selves at the hospital?

It is hard for them to be themselves. They are middlemen; their function is to be an extension of the doctor. But while this arrangement works for many patients, it doesn't seem to work for these lost ones. So instead of making the aides middlemen, let us make them headmen. Let us give them patients and tell them that they are totally responsible for those patients and their treatment. If the aides want help from the staff they can ask for it, but the treatment is up to them and we confidently expect results.

The aides will have something to struggle over—their own patients. Whether they make mistakes or not, let us trust them and encourage them to be themselves, to find out what they are. Let them make their own mistakes; their pain will be their own, but so will their triumph. If we can do that, we will have our model.

Yes, but how do we do it? Why not apply the same logic as before? If a model will help the patients, perhaps a model will help the aides. Why don't we relate to the aides in the same way that we want them to relate to the patients? Why don't we struggle with them, make them our problem, commit ourselves to them? Maybe they will learn to do the same with their patients [1966: iv-v].

The strategy of Ward H involved assigning aides their "own" patients and making them responsible for programming the patients' lives. The arrangement struck the ward's doctors and nurses as predictably strange, but with the experimenters' support (and their clout), the aides ultimately overcame professional resistances. The program proved successful, and both the patients and the attendants blossomed. The most dramatic finding was the transmutation of aides along Maslowian lines. The aides moved — sometimes from needs for safety—to concern with self-actualization. Clinicians did pre- and posttesting of attendants and reported that the post-group appears to have a relatively higher drive level or achievement motive. There is a definite tendency on the part of the post-group to want to . . . accomplish tasks requiring skill and effort. . . . The group has shifted toward questioning past precedents, traditions, norms and standards. . . . The group appears to be leaning toward doing things which may in the past have been considered to be unconventional or different. The group also appears to have a much stronger need for independence, freedom and a position which gives them more prestige, control, respect and status. . . . There is also a general drop in the need for order in the postgroup. This may reflect a moving away from being overly concerned with minute, routine, mechanical, repetitive details and a stronger concern for the general aspects of their environment. . . . There is a definite maverick flavor to the postgroup. . . . It is the type of group who will now challenge authority [Colarelli and Siegel, 1966: 181-182].

The suggestion is that where job enrichment takes hold, personality—at least work-related personality—changes to match. The process is probably irreversible, in the sense that Theory Y managed workers may become resistant to Theory X management. The potency of successful job enrichment is such that the strategy cannot be deployed lightly or "experimented with." The trip up the workers' Maslowian hierarchy may be one way, and aspirations that are raised must be reckoned with. The price of retreating is disillusionment and potentially bitter alienation among workers and clients.

Congruence Between Worker Aspirations and Organizational Expectations

Ellsworth and Ellsworth (1970: 7) point out that "even in programs that have temporarily succeeded in utilizing aides in ways that are clearly recognized to be therapeutic . . . the probability of maintaining such utilization over a prolonged period of time has proven to be extremely low." The problem lies with the failure of the professional staff to appreciate the contributions of enriched aides and to respond to evolving aspirations.

The Ellsworths have reported three experiments that brought job enrichment to psychiatric aides, with remarkably positive results. In the first experiment (Fort Meade, South Dakota), "the aides reported themselves as most actively participating in hospitalized schizophrenic patients, and became the primary decision makers in team meetings" (Ellsworth and Ellsworth, 1970: 8). Follow-up studies of patients showed enduring increments in their hospital and community adjustment. A second study involved nineteen psychiatric units in five Veterans Administration hospitals: "Those units that had the lowest rehospitalization rates were generally those in which psychiatric aides reported themselves s most actively participating in treatment planning and decision making" (Ellsworth and Ellsworth, 1970: 8). In a third VA study, "psychiatric aides were found to succeed with those patients the professional staff largely abandoned. . . . For twenty-eight of most chronically hospitalized locked-ward patients in Ward 8 . . . the aides assumed primary responsibility for planning and carrying out a token economy program. Based on the aides' creativity and ingenuity, the locked ward was opened, the patients improved significantly within two months, and twenty of twenty-eight were able to leave the hospital within one year. No locked doors have been used in this ward since January 1967, despite the fact that newly admitted patients are assigned in equal rotation to all three psychiatric wards" (Ellsworth and Ellsworth, 1970: 8).

Despite such documented successes, job enrichment programs have been abandoned and new ones successfully resisted. In nonenriched settings,

> both the professional staff and the aides seem to perpetuate (the aides') role through their own expectations and attitudes. We professional staff observe the aides doing the routine things we expect them to do, which reinforces our belief that this is all they are capable of doing. When we ask them to take an active part in team meetings, or to work therapeutically with patients, we often find aides hesitant or seemingly disinterested. One problem, then, may very well be that our own expectations regarding the aides' role have also become the expectations that the aides themselves have adopted [Ellsworth and Ellsworth, 1970: 9].

The issue may hinge, according to Ellsworth and Ellsworth, on assumptions about the relevance of academic training. Though "most (professionals) found . . . that much of what we were taught had no relevance whatever in preparing us to work effectively with other people," and despite "recent indication that graduate training may actually *reduce* one's therapeutic effectiveness," there are no models of alternative (experiential) roads to knowledge. This makes it hard to think about how to go about designing a support system (and an incentive system) for the professional development of nonprofessionals. Ellsworth and Ellsworth write that, as a start,

> Anyone who wishes to be effective in creating a therapeutic role for aides must become involved with the setting in which the aide works. Unless the setting clearly communicates an expectancy for the development of therapeutic role relationships between aides and patients, and unless there are meaningful rewards for altering role relationships, the psychiatric aide will most likely not increase his therapeutic effectiveness in working with patients [1970: 10].

Opportunities must be created for aides "to learn new skills and try different approaches with patients." It is critical to assign "meaningful rewards," including respect and the recognition of colleagueship—which means, for example, that "the professional staff should make every effort to actively seek out aides for advice, and to follow it if at all possible in order to communicate to the aide the importance of his role." Administrative supports for new roles are also critical, and these include "increased authority in decision making and planning, and increased responsibility for patient rehabilitation" (Ellsworth and Ellsworth, 1970: 11).

Support systems for job enrichment are hard to build and even harder to maintain. Supervisors must see themselves as colleagues or (as in Ward H) as models. Established habits (including ways of relating to patients) must be up for grabs. Doubts and insecurities related to unsettled roles and to roles not yet defined must be surfaced and confronted. Most critically, issues such as "Who is competent?" and "Who is in charge?" must be dealt with. For professionals this means (1) communicating confidence they may not feel in skills that are unrelated to academic backgrounds and job descriptions, and (2) relinquishing cherished prerogatives such as diagnosing, planning, and deciding what is to be done to people.

Where such issues are faced and resolved, the solutions are always informal, and they are typically labeled as "experimental." This means that the enriched components of lower-echelon jobs have no tenure. What the administrator or professional giveth, he or she taketh away under pressure, such as in the face of complaints, personnel changes, or budget constraints. Most typically, persons outside the support system (professionals or administrators) prevail by invoking traditional structure. Client improvements are no help, because agencies are not judged in terms of quality of their services. Ellsworth and Ellsworth (1970: 12) conservatively state that "one should clearly recognize that the effectiveness of patient treatment has become only one of many priorities of the mental hospital." Among other priorities are structural ones (including streamlined bureaucracy), which job enrichment programs compromise.

Structure as Resistance

The President's Commission on Law Enforcement and Criminal Justice (1967) endorsed a job enrichment model known as "team policing." A prominent rationale for this model is that of John Angell (1971), who linked police bureaucracy to low morale. In drawing his nexus, Angell cites Max Weber, who is quoted as having said, "It is horrible to think that the world could one day be filled with nothing but these little cogs, little men clinging to little jobs and striving toward bigger ones. . . but what can we oppose to this machinery in order to keep a portion of mankind free from this parcelling out of the soul, from this supreme mastery of bureaucratic way of life?" (Weber, cited in Angell, 1971: 191).

Angell blamed the Tayloristic management of police for the prevalent feeling among officers that they were "cogs in a machine" instead of having "a sense of pride and self-importance" in doing police work (Angell, 1971: 191). One problem was that "the generalists or patrolmen tend to become nursemaids to the specialized officers such as investigators, and juvenile and traffic officers" (Angell, 1971: 192). Another problem was that of "feelings [among officers] about their inability to affect their own working conditions . . . the continued utilization of classic autocratic managerial techniques by traditional managers only increases employee hostility and dissatisfaction" (Angell, 1971: 192-193). The result, according to Angell, is low morale *plus* the inability of managers to affect the behavior of officers on the job.

Angell's alternative is team policing, "a flexible, participatory, science-based structure," the guts of which are "teams of generalists (patrolmen) decentralized to work in a small geographic area" (1971: 194-195). Team members have equal rank, no "formally assigned supervisor," and leadership is "expected to develop situationally as the circumstances dictate" (Angell, 1971: 195). Team members elect (and reelect) their own leaders, decide how to deploy their resources, and work collaboratively with others. In this connection

> a team will be expected to work closely with the community of its area. Each team should be responsible for maintaining a community office that will be its local headquarters. Informal meetings involving team and community members should be held periodically to discuss the policies, procedures, problems, and conduct of the community and police. Attempts should be made in these meetings to get consensus on various police responsibilities and procedures [Angell, 1971: 196].

Teams draw on specialists (available from headquarters), request information (ditto), and work with other teams. If there are conflicts, they are ironed out in "intraorganizational communications and training programs and meetings" (Angell, 1971: 196). Teams are assigned to areas "where the citizens have relatively homogeneous value systems" (Angell, 1971: 198). Team members are selected for compatibility and are subject to reassignment; if necessary, teams can be broken up and new members assigned. A coordinator who is responsible for such assignments must be skilled in human relations and should be selected with rank-and-file and community input.

Specialists who are invoked by the team would be working for the team; however, they have freedom to make professional judgments, and might evaluate the team in their area of expertise. This arrangement increases the professional standing and prestige of the generalist without damaging the status of the specialist. It recognizes that the generalist is important and has the intelligence needed to make decisions about his job. On the other hand, the importance of the specialist is recognized and rewarded. Since this plan permits hiring from outside the organization, highly skilled persons could be selected for specialized jobs, thus saving the organization training expenses [Angell, 1971: 201].

Angell foresaw sources of resistance to team policing. Among these was the reluctance of officers "to accept increased responsibility and to deal with it realistically"; team members might also be "constantly frustrated by the ambiguous, unstructured, insecure nature of their jobs" and the fact that they would "need to learn to accept and deal with the problems inherent in such an environment." Managers would also have to adjust, but "democratic ways are never tension-free or easy" (Angell, 1971: 203).

After reviewing several case studies, a Police Foundation research group (Sherman, Milton, and Kelly, 1973: 61-62) concluded that "the support or resistance of non-team members was probably the most critical factor in determining the success of team policing." Team problems often began at the planning stage, in which "outsiders"—civilian "experts" took over proposal drafting and tended to talk only to the "chiefs" (Sherman et al., 1973: 62). Police departments, including middle managers (and sometimes top managers) were served up fully shaped programs, funded, approved, and sometimes about to be implemented. This sometimes sparked immediate revolt, but the opposition more typically bided its time and subverted the program later.

A refreshing exception to such sequences was the Holyoke (Massachusetts) planning process:

> In Holyoke, after the team members were selected, the outside consultants then made it clear that the patrol officers, not the consultants, were responsible for developing the experiment. The consultants limited their own role to suggesting options and furnishing specific information. In this case, planning became training.... Subcommittees of patrol officers were formed on such matters as uniforms, equipment, how to perform an investigation,

and the rules and procedures for the team. Once the officers were convinced that the program was their own, they took the initiative. They made some quick decisions on equipment by contacting vendors directly. The decision to wear blazers was reached after the uniform subcommittee had arranged for fashion-show presentations. Another subcommittee developed a new team policy and procedures manual, which spelled out its policymaking process and the functions of the team chairman and various committees [Sherman et al., 1973: 64].

Holyoke illustrates the potential market for police job enrichment. Angell's scheme was explained to the officers by two consultants (Angell himself and M. R. Galvin). Of thirty *randomly selected* officers, twenty-five immediately volunteered.

Teams typically have strikingly high morale, and the jovial informality one encounters in team storefronts stands in contrast to the austere tension one experiences in precinct houses. Teams contain middle managers, but they are hard to identify. Civilians (mostly children) wander in and out of offices, and officers seemingly just come and go. Efficiency is not advertised, but this fact is deceptive. Statistics showing increases in arrests and decreases in offenses can usually be produced to document reliably team achievements.

The problems encountered by teams are similar to those of the psychiatric aides. Difficulties typically originate *in* the organization, but *outside* the enclave. Managers excluded from the planning—or from the process itself—complain or "send out the word through informal channels of communication that this crazy team idea was a hoax." Appeals to structure are effective. It is axiomatic that "the view that the rules and regulations are sacred and unchangeable subverts not only team policing but any changes at all" (Sherman et al., 1973: 92).

Another source of resistance lies among nonenriched officers. According to the Police Foundation group, "In most cities studied, the larger patrol force—those not involved in the team project—objected to team policing. . . . The first pilot teams formed new elites. The patrol officers had learned to accept the old elite forces (e.g., detectives) but they were not eager to accept the new ones. . . . Also, to outside patrol officers, the community aspects of team policing smacked of appeasement of hostile minorities" (Sherman et al., 1973: 93). Other problems (e.g., the inflexibility of centralized dispatching) may look small, but the lessons we draw remain substantial. Experiments (such as police teams) are uncomfortably embedded in inhospitable organizations (such as traditionally managed police departments). Ingroups and outgroups are inevitably out of phase, and the outgroup (1) has been around longer, (2) is much larger, and (3) can invoke precedent.

The Enrichment Ghetto

It follows that experiments require vigilant protection from their contexts. Dangers may not be obvious to enthusiastic worker sectarians and intoxicated client constituencies, but crowded storefronts and soaring arrests do not protect against nagging contrasts between traditional and experimental networks. Success, in fact, may accentuate contrast. An enriched enclave is viewed, *for similar reasons*, as showcase and malignant growth.

For innovation ghettos, survival hinges on administrative autonomy with a pipeline to top management. The arrangement has assets and liabilities. It attenuates the jurisdiction of hostile managers and removes the sting of peer disapproval. But top managers come and go and financial resources dry up. During crises, experimental ghettos are uniquely vulnerable. Survival spells return to "basics" and regression from concern with selfactualization to one with survival (safety).

The problem we have noted is one of reversibility or irreversibility of retrenchment. Hope does not really lurk eternal; once it is dashed, it resists being invoked again. Twice impoverished jobs are alienating jobs because workers have risked trusting and committing themselves, and they have (however justifiably) been betrayed. If "burnout" has any meaning, it is a condition that we invite when we promote "hit-and-run" enrichment, leaving newfound friends and colleagues to a predictably inhospitable fate. Job enrichment is strong medicine; it is never lightly administered or casually prescribed, but requires thought, planning, and diagnosis that is based on relevant, systematic data.

CHAPTER 7

THE NOTION OF "QUALITY OF WORK LIFE": HUMANIZING THE ASSEMBLY LINE

Classic management left a twin legacy that many organizations are trying to undo: job impoverishment or work fragmentation, and bureaucratic autocracy, which is the "chain of command" that extends from administrators, who plan and make decisions, to workers who do not. The strategy we reviewed in Chapter 5 addressed work fragmentation, because its main point was to increase the "horizontal loading" of the worker's job to give it richness and meaning.

Another strategy, quality of work life (QWL), targets the conventional autocracy of the organization and seeks to soften it. The QWL concern—humanizing the organization through "vertical loading"—has roots in a diffuse movement called organizational development (OD), which at first extended the benefits of democracy to upper echelons of organizations, making managers more responsive to each others' needs (and presumably, to the needs of workers), and promoting a collaborative, problem-solving ethic in management (French and Bell, 1978). In QWL, the same process starts at the bottom with the worker, and democracy spreads upward. Where OD-softened management shows receptivity to QWL, democracy becomes a pincer movement enveloping middle management, which becomes a source of resistance.

What is quality of work life? QWL leaders admit that the phrase is not particularly self-defining. "As a name," writes QWL spokesman Ted Mills, "quality of work life is somewhere between a bummer and a disaster . . . it suggests visions of happy workers having a picnic, instead of working any more" (1979: 24). The problem Mills describes is not solved by overambitious characterizations of QWL goals, including Mills's contention that

"QWL is actually the sum of all . . . various attempts to label a general new direction for work, working and work organizations in the 20th century" (1979: 24). Were this definition to stand, QWL would become, in the words of Gilbert and Sullivan, "the embodiment of everything that's excellent."

In less enveloping terms, Irving Bluestone, the United Auto Workers' vice president who shares paternity (or maternity) of QWL, describes the aim of the approach as "bringing the democratic values of society at large into the plant." Bluestone explains that "this means that the worker must have a greater control over his destiny in the plant, over his job and over his workplace. To do that he must be given the opportunity to participate significantly and meaningfully in the decision-making process" (Herrick, 1981: 27). A QWL-involved manager (Al Warren of General Motors) argues that "it fundamentally comes down to extending adulthood to the work place. . . . We're talking about creating an atmosphere that makes employees feel their ideas and their help in making better decisions are needed" (Herrick, 1981: 27).

One way of defining QWL is in relation to collective bargaining. During contract negotiations, unions represent the interests of workers in furthering vital bread-and-butter concerns—concerns that are vested in the lower reaches (basic and security) of the Maslowian hierarchy of needs. Management representatives at the bargaining table seek to place limits on organizational responses to worker concerns, and a constructive resolution (the contract) defines the compromise that is achieved between conflicting "bids" of workers and managers.

Though collective bargaining is democratic, it is circumscribed and divisive. No matter how much a union may be concerned with the professionalization of its workers, union leaders cannot voice these concerns during contract negotiations, nor can unions help managers shape meaningful jobs for union members or help create opportunities for the personal growth or (worse) the self-actualization of workers. Managers are typecast as ogres in that their role is to *curb*—or at least, to modulate—the satisfaction of worker needs. A manager who is steeped in McGregor and

Herzberg becomes transmuted—when he or she is faced with worker representatives—into a Theory-X figure who is fated to belligerently quibble about the minutiae of extrinsic job attributes.

In this sense, QWL machinery was mainly created as an expansion of options. QWL is seen as a forum for collaborative worker/management responses to the "higher" (non-bread-and-butter) needs of workers. The QWL process lives side by side with the bargaining table. (For this reason, "contractual" issues become "off limits" to the QWL process.)

Given the union/management partnership implicit in QWL, there is stress in the model on not endorsing management goals that would make QWL programs a carrot approach to raising worker production. In this respect QWL differs from "quality circles" in which democracy is billed as a way of building better mousetraps. A *Time* (January 28, 1980) introduction to quality circles begins:

> Like the jowels of an aging Hollywood star, U.S. productivity is sagging . . . experts increasingly believe a primary reason is that remote corporate bureaucracies have isolated workers from all decision making, turning many of them into uncaring automatons. To change that, more and more U.S. companies are returning the responsibility for solving factory floor problems to the factory floor itself. On the premise that the workers often know best, the firms are forming "quality circles."

By contrast, a *Business Week* (May 5, 1980) exposition of QWL reads

> For all its success, traditional collective bargaining in the U.S. may be failing to deal effectively with problems in the workplace that cannot be solved simply by raising pay. . . . [Unions and companies] will set up "labor management participation committees," made up of rank-and-file workers and supervisors, as far down as the department level in selected plants. The purpose is to see if these committees can find ways to satisfy the needs of workers—by giving them a voice in improving job environment, work schedules, production processes and the like—and to help management cut costs.

QWL advocates strongly disclaim productivity as a goal of QWL programs, but do *not* deny that QWL may raise productivity. Mills sees the point as one of decency being a shorter road than a straight line. He writes (1979: 27):

In a kind of curiously illogical logic, as QWL advocates believe, if managements of any kind of enterprise become *honestly* concerned for the real needs and aspirations of their employees, and can convince their employees it's a real and continuing concern, and prove it, then a strange phenomenon occurs: they get productivity increases from their people without even asking for it, as a byproduct or payback of that growing concern. In other words, by inverting priorities of basic management concerns from organizational needs to employee needs, the organizational needs will actually be better served.

Irving Bluestone similarly maintains that:

A quality of working life program must place its greatest emphasis on creating job satisfaction and enhancing the dignity and human development of the worker. It must afford the opportunity for the worker to exercise greater control over the work place by participating in the decision-making process. Management will reap the advantage [Herrick, 1981: 28].

A more jaundiced union official (William Winpisinger) questions the premise that QWL priorities are taken seriously by managers:

I've never seen any of them (managers) get too excited about making the life of a worker any easier if it didn't mean something for them. But I'm sure that, if they perceive the quality of working life as satisfying their motives, they are going to get into it in a hurry [Herrick, 1981: 28].

This view is not a rejection of QWL, but implies that unions and managers may sponsor the same program for different reasons.

Adversariness and Adversity

While managers may see QWL as a roundabout way of motivating workers to produce, unions may have "unofficial" concerns of their own. One such concern has to do with the extreme disaffection of union members, which extends to the unions themselves. When unionized workers grieve supervisors and employers, the union (a) becomes overloaded with complaints, and (b) derives the "backwash" from unsatisfactorily resolved grievances.

The classical union stance has been adversary, and unions have gained stature from effective militancy. When militancy reaches the point of diminishing returns, unions often look silly; the fact that employers also look silly carries little consolation.

The scenario is well illustrated in the General Motors plant at Tarrytown, the site of a QWL venture that ultimately encompassed 3,800 employees. According to Robert Guest (1979: 77), "Frustration, fear and mistrust characterized the relationship between management and labor [at Tarrytown]. At certain times, as many as 2,000 labor grievances were on the docket." Opposing sides in the conflict were caught in a spiral of reciprocal defensiveness; the no-win nature of this game can be deduced from retrospections of company and union officials.

Guest quotes the following managerial recollections (1979: 77):

> We were instructed to go by the book, and we played by the book. The way we solved problems was to use our authority and impose discipline.

> We were very secretive in letting the union and the workers know about changes to be introduced or new programs coming down the pike.

Guest's union officials sound similarly jaundiced (1979: 77):

> There was no trust and everybody was putting out fires. The company's attitude was to employ a stupid robot with hands and no face.

> When I walked in each morning I was out to get the personnel director. . . . Every time a foreman notified a worker that there

would be a job change, it resulted in an instant '78 (work standards grievance).

I was expected to jump up and down and scream.

The point that such reminiscences make is, in Guest's words, that "workers were mad at everyone. . . . Not only did workers view the company as an impersonal bureaucratic machine; 'they number the parts and they number you,' but also they saw the union itself as a source of frustration" (Guest, 1979: 77). Tarrytown's younger workers had especially antibureaucratic and antiunion attitudes. The plant manager recalls that

> It was during this time that the young people in the plant were demanding some kind of change. They didn't want to work in this kind of environment, the union didn't have much control over them, and they certainly were not interested in taking orders from a dictatorial management [Guest, 1979: 78].

A situation such as this makes it unsurprising that when the Tarrytown plant manager suggested experimenting with worker democracy (QWL), Tarrytown union officials were warmly sympathetic.

The Tarrytown Version of QWL

QWL programs may start with a commitment by top managers and top union official to the *concept* of participation. The *content* of participation programs, however, (the details of who is to be involved and what is to be discussed) tends to respond to work-related problems faced by the organization. (If there are no problems QWL programs may take extracurricular forms.) Tarrytown had problems, and the most immediate concern in the plant in 1971 was with an impending reshuffling of its men and machines. Guest reports that

> at first, the changes were introduced in the usual way. Manufacturing and industrial engineers and technical specialists designed the new layout, developed the charts and blueprints, and planned every move. They then presented their proposals to the

supervisors. Two of the production supervisors in Hard Trim, sensing that top plant management was looking for new approaches, asked a question that was to have a profound effect on events to follow: "Why not ask the workers themselves to get involved in the move? They are experts in their own right. They know as much about trim operations as anyone else" [1978: 78-79].

The point of participation at Tarrytown (at least, in 1971) was to seek "advice" in planning changes in technology affecting workers. The substantive premise was the assumption that workers will foresee nuts-and-bolts problems that would escape engineers or administrators, who per force deal in sweeping vistas. The philosophical premise is that those affected by changes in a democracy should react to changes before they are "sprung." A pragmatic version of this argument is that participation *prior* to implementation reduces resistance *after* implementation.

The Tarrytown experience—replicated in many QWL projects—is that worker expertise is invariably underestimated. This holds even for those (like the Tarrytown supervisors) who felt that "they (the workers) are experts in their own right." The reason for the underestimate is that expertise is associated with the doing of the work rather than the planning of work-related conditions. The manifestation of expertise in sessions that deal with charts and diagrams, with sequence, motion, space, and resources is therefore unexpected. At Tarrytown, "The supervisors were impressed by the outpouring of ideas: 'We found they [the workers] did know a lot about their own operations. They made hundreds of suggestions and we adopted many of them' " (Guest, 1979: 79).

In 1974 Tarrytown hired a consultant. The role of such a person—which QWL consultants feel is a critical one—has to do with group dynamics and communication. There are several issues involved: One is that managers and workers are used to shouting across and pounding tables. They must now learn to collaborate with each other, which involves listening, influencing, and arriving at rational solutions to consensually defined problems. It also means that former adversaries must learn to trust each other, must surface reservations, must work through anxieties and defenses. More mundane is the coordinating function, which consists of scheduling and running meetings. The goal here is to circumvent whatever tendency groups have to build up short-term enthusiasm (the honeymoon effect) that quickly fizzles out. Inspiring sustained motivation—such as through successful experiences—is different from building interpersonal competence. Consultants versed in the latter (such as T-group trainers) may be helpless when faced with the need to orchestrate activity so as to sustain interest.

The most important task of a consultant is to arrange his or her own demise by "training trainers" who can carry on after he or she leaves. This involves building teams that possess skills and can disseminate these to successive generations of workers and managers.

An effort of this kind culminated at Tarrytown on September 13, 1977, when 22 QWL trainers, who had been trained by two QWL coordinators, unleashed a self-designed training module on 3300 workers—a process that took fourteen months of day-and-night training to complete. Groups of 25 assembly-line workers were paid for a 27-hour diversified experience, which involved "learning three things: first, about the concept of QWL; second, about the plant and the functions of management and the union; third, about problem-solving skills important in effective involvement" (Guest, 1979: 83). The trainers presented a variety of data to the workers, using self-prepared "printed materials, diagrams, charts and slides." In addition, workers "were shown how and where they could get any information they wanted about their plant" (Guest, 1979: 84). The involvement of trainees was heavy in the core of the training program, which consisted of problem-solving exercises. Again, the quality of worker output was a surprise. Trainers reported that "once the participants opened up they threw a lot at us." Guest notes that "although they [the trainers] understood intellectually that participation is the basic purpose of the QWL program, . . . [they] had to experience directly the outpouring of ideas, perceptions, and feelings of the participants to comprehend emotionally the dynamics of the involvement process" (1979: 84). During the third of three training sessions, the workers usually took over completely and carried the ball themselves "with a minimum of guidance and direction from the two trainers" (Guest, 1979: 84).

The Tarrytown QWL model is one that centered on work-related concerns. From the first, the workers' attention was focused on technology and on the resolution of dilemmas that are related to technology. Guest points out that in the QWL program "hourly employees (were) substantially involved in working out thousands of 'bugs' in the operations," and "hundreds of small problems . . . were solved on the shop floor before they accumulated into big problems" (1979: 85).

Managers brought the organization's problems to the union and to the QWL groups instead of solving the problems unilaterally. The result of such democratization of management was a unified organization with a sense of shared purpose. The union reported lower absenteeism and fewer grievances. The management view was that "we used to fight the union, the worker, and the car itself. Now we've all joined together to fight the car" (Guest, 1979: 85).

The Bolivar Version of QWL

If Tarrytown represents "quality of *work* life," there are other organizations that have instituted "quality of work *life*" programs. In such programs, the emphasis is less on democratizing the management of work than on letting workers experiment with rearrangements of the physical, social, and organizational climate of their workplace.

The climate emphasis is prominent in the best known of all QWL ventures, which was begun in 1973 at Harman International Industries in Bolivar, Tennessee. Bolivar, like Tarrytown, had serious morale problems. According to Macy (1979: 529) "Workers whispered to each other about their complaints, and managers stewed inside."

Surveys showed "that 70 percent of the [Bolivar] workers had ideas about improving their jobs which they kept to themselves" (Macy, 1979: 529). The QWL philosophy was to let workers brainstorm in no-holds-barred fashion, instead of limiting them to strictly job-related isues. The president of Harman, Sidney Harman, had been (among other things) head of an experimental college. Michael Maccoby, his consultant, was a psychoanalyst committed to "stimulating the fullest possible development of each individual's creative potential" (1975: 49). This principle—which Maccoby called *individuation*—"directs the Work Improvement Program beyond . . . the sociotechnical efforts to improve the quality of working life. . . . No one is forced into a mold. As a result, the program has satisfied individuals who do not want enlarged jobs, career advancement, and 'meaningful work' within the plant, as well as those who do" (Duckles, Duckles, and Maccoby, 1977: 389).

Many of Bolivar's QWL projects were only marginally work related or were completely extracurricular. The best-known Bolivar project was the "Harman School," in which workers teach workers, though professional teachers and sometimes students are drawn from the surrounding community. The school covers work-enriching subjects (e.g., accounting), but it also deals with more esoteric content (such as dancing and music) that is of no conceivable relevance to the job. School-time derives from official work-time that is liberated through increased productivity.

Bolivar also has a worker-edited newspaper that serves the plant and community. Workers have made all sorts of fieldtrips, including to the Volvo plant in Sweden, where they garnered QWL pointers. Under Swedish influence, Bolivar has experimented with work teams and other group arrangements. In such ventures, the experience itself is often seen as the goal.

Typical of the mind-expanding philosophy of Bolivar is a "proposal from the pre-assembly core group" to the effect that "each employee participating will spend 3 to 4 hours one day with the foreman during the shift, following him everywhere, watching, asking questions, and receiving an explanation of what is happening." Following this tourist phase, "each employee who wants to continue would get practical experience in several aspects of supervision" (Duckles et al., 1977: 393).

The foreman involved in the project was eventually transferred, and his old job was rotated for a time among group members. However, a second foreman was shortly hired. The consultants noted that "the original intent of the experiment was not to do away with the supervisor. The participants in the experiment, while disappointed that they could not fully supervise themselves, have gained an understanding of the processes in which they are involved, and dialogue about the work continues to take place" (Duckles et al., 1977: 397-398).

The structure of QWL at Bolivar revolves around "core groups" that include union officials and one supervisor. These QWL groups discuss any problems that are of concern to them and study them as systematically as they wish, sometimes with the help of data. The groups are authorized to originate proposals for change. Any reform ideas that transcend the shop floor and/or that require added resources or structural changes are transmitted to a higher-level committee for study (the consultants' job includes writing up the proposals for transmission). The supervisory committee is called the Working Committee and it consists of plant management and union leadership. Consultants are the link between the core groups and the working committee. Except for this feature, the committee structure is common to most union/management QWL experiments.

The Role of Surveys in QWL Experiences

Maccoby saw as one aim of the Bolivar project, "through the survey and study . . . to help people learn about themselves and to stimulate critical, independent thinking about alternatives" (1975: 49). The Harman pre-QWL survey mapped discontent at the plant and suggested the potential of participation in terms of workers' ideas for work improvements.

Surveys are standard for QWL projects. There are pre-, during, and postsurveys, and their focus is on attitudes and feelings, particularly toward the larger workplace (the organization) and the immediate work setting (Carlson, 1978). QWL surveys map work climate, over time.

Ideally, the pre-QWL climate should be rotten. A bad work climate documents the need for the QWL program and gives the QWL groups something to talk about. Surveys are ideal for this purpose because they combine cues to self-knowledge (peer group opinions) with vistas of remediable conditions (gripes).

A rotten pre-QWL climate makes a perfect baseline measure, because there is no way to go but up. Subsequent surveys make good "feedback" because (a) they map progress in areas diagnosed as trouble spots, and (b) reward groups with tangible (data-based) indices of success. Ideally, program-concurrent surveys should yield *mixed* pictures, which discriminate achievements in progress, as well as unexplored opportunities. In large organizations, "mixed" climates equate with natural experiments in that comparable settings serve "experimental" (QWL) and "control" (no QWL) functions.

If "post surveys" show congenial climates, they provide ideal measures of QWL success. As a commodity, a decent climate appeals to management and the union. Climate is not "productivity" (which is unacceptable as a QWL goal), but is correlated with productivity (which helps "sell" QWL).

A less tangible virtue of survey data is that they promote responsiveness to workers' needs. The act of surveying shows that an organization cares;[1] the use of surveys as a *basis* for programs gives programs a people-centered goal; surveys as *measures* of programs gauge impact in terms of humanization. In this sense, surveys get close to quantifying the unquantifiable—they map the "quality" in the "quality of working life" programs.

NOTE

1. The GM QWL survey is entitled "The Quality of Your Work Life in General Motors"; the instructions tell the workers, "This survey is aimed at getting your ideas about what it is like to work here. We are trying to learn more about the quality of work life where you work. The purpose of this survey is to measure the attitudes, opinions and work climate of GM organizations from the employee's point of view" (Carlson, 1978: 25).

CHAPTER 8

HUMANIZING CLIENT ASSEMBLY LINES

If the task of QWL is to explore "alternatives to hierarchies" (Herbst, 1976), then this task can be visualized more easily where workers are workers and managers are managers than it can be in the more confusing world of human service settings, where people's roles are often blurred and the borders between roles are sometimes diffuse.

In blue-collar settings, management clearly manages. However, in human service settings, many executive tread softly (or inconsistently) in dealing with their subordinates. One reason for their diffidence is the "professional" status of their workers; another is the nature of the workers' tasks, which may be difficult to monitor and which often call for delicate judgments and complex decisions.

The characterization does not imply that classic management is absent from human service settings, but suggests that managers must *also* learn to let their workers exercise professional autonomy. Police and correctional officers may wear uniforms, for instance, and they are viewed as quasi-troops in quasi-military organizations. But officers on their beats or in their tiers see few supervisors; their work gives them awesome power and they make decisions with fateful and explosive consequences. Such work cannot easily be second-guessed, nor can it be anticipated in detail. The same fact holds for discretion that is routinely exercised in classrooms, hospital wards, or in enclaves in which clinicians (psychologists, social workers, and the like) diagnose problems and provide counseling and other services to clients.

The management dilemma gives rise to paradoxes and hypocrisy. For example, a nurse may one day be ordered about, and the next (after a union organizer arrives), may be enjoined to be Florence Nightingale, whose life-preserving mission makes her a "partner" and a prized member of the hospital "team." A social worker or teacher may be disciplined by a supervisor who is transformed into an instant "colleague" during professional seminars, conferences, and workshops.

The emphasis and deemphasis of roles has to do with shifts in the caste system that was built into the organization at its inception. This caste system is sometimes undisguised, as in the military, where the officers are "gentlemen" (and presumably gentlewomen) by act of Congress, and the enlisted personnel are not. The aristocracy of military officers is certified by their private accommodations, tastefully served food, exclusive social arrangements, and so forth. By contrast, members of the lower military caste are crowded into dormitories, are fed plain and wholesome cafeteria meals, are clothed in unresplendent uniforms, and are peremptorily and impolitely ordered about by members of the officer caste.

Sharp distinctions between managerial and worker castes have their origins in socioeconomic class differences. These at one time were perfectly correlated (and are now imperfectly correlated) with educational opportunities available in society. College as a requisite for membership in the manager caste (which was emphasized by Taylor, who was himself a dropout) preserved and buttressed—but also rationalized—assumptions about ingrained capacities to lead and to follow.[1]

In human services the professional/subprofessional distinction rests on skills acquired through higher education. The relevance of academic preparation is sometimes safely assumed. Elsewhere, however, the correlation is an article of faith that subordinate castes call into question.

Increments in the average educational attainment of workers has contributed to their rise in expectations (see Chapter 1). Such expectations function differently in a blue-collar/white-collar/factory caste system than they do in a self-styled meritocracy. Many human service managers are former workers (police officers, nurses, teachers, prison guards) who were promoted on merit or after "putting in their time." Others are generalist managers (hospital administrators, court administrators) who supervise professionals.

In both situations, castes are modified or diluted. The promoted manager's past can haunt him or her because it blurs the discontinuity he or she must seek to emphasize and his or her workers may wish to deemphasize. The generalist manager interfaces with craftspeople and specialists (from his or her perspective, "prima donnas"), whose expert judgments circumscribe (or seek to circumscribe) his or her managerial jurisdiction. More complexity is added where organizations contain professionals and subprofessionals (each with their own hierarchies) subsumed under generalist managers.

Probably the best-known QWL experiment in a human service agency is one that targeted the hospital crisis. The experiment was, for the most part, a failure—it was aborted after three years, thanks to a mismatched consultant and the indifference of the hospital medical staff—but the crisis is increasingly manifest. A New York blue-ribbon group that was charged with considering the "nursing emergency" studied job dissatisfaction and concluded that the solution lay in "increasing (the nurses') role and recognition." This solution involved, according to the task force, "allowing nurses to participate in decision-making policies relating to health care and also to take part in the formal committee structure of health care facilities" (Albany Times Union, April 15, 1981). The prescription of the task force dovetails with recent developments in a number of hospitals. One of these hospitals has advertised for new staff with a letter signed by its nursing executive (who happens to be a nurse), which reads

> Come share our bold new venture in nursing! . . . I believe that as a primary patient care provider, the nurse has the right to participate in decision-making affecting the patient's welfare and wellness. The nurse's input should be encouraged at all levels—on the unit, in the division and within nursing administration.
>
> The practice of nursing should be a constant learning experience. The challenge of problem-solving and decision-making stimulates growth, maturity and self-confidence.
>
> A nursing program based on a dynamic participatory leadership style kindles motivation and fosters true fulfillment on the job.
>
> Nurses . . . should be listened to, treated with dignity and respect. . . . I believe that, with our new environment, the career-motivated nurse can flourish here at . . . [New York Times, April 4, 1982].

Another hospital advertises for nurses under the banner "The Decision is Yours." The recruitment message reads:

> . . . a major . . . teaching hospital in the . . . area, offers you, the professional Primary Nurse, the opportunity to make decisions.
>
> They are your patients from admission to discharge. And the decisions involved in the planning, assessing, implementing and evaluating their care on a 24-hour basis is a primary concern of yours. At . . . , you will have clinical specialists as consultants on complex nursing problems. And you will be backed by a nursing service that provides an avenue for you to question, discuss and review nursing practices.
>
> But the final decisions come back to you—the professional Primary Nurse.
>
> It takes a special kind of nurse to practice at . . . .
> That is your first decision [New York Times, April 4, 1982].

Several pages later, the Peace Corps assures its prospective nurses that they can find themselves

> Responsible for the health of 10 rural villages in Costa Rica.
> Responsible for a regional dispensary in Nepal.
> Responsible for a well-baby clinic in Africa.
> Responsible for a mobile health unit in Oman.
> Responsible for new training programs for local nurses in Fiji [New York Times, April 4, 1982].

Opportunities such as these do not describe formal QWL programs, but they point to ventures that share the essential QWL goal and its core process. They describe organizations in which the hierarchical caste system is diluted because low-echelon personnel have power and make routine policy decisions.

QWL Experiments in the Schools

Unlike nurses, teachers are currently in oversupply. The crisis in the schools is not one of turnover, but of teacher morale. Solutions are often targeted at this symptom, which is defined as "burnout" or (more prevalently) as "stress"(see Chapter 2). The proposed remedy entails sharing distress and using strategies designed to reduce subjective frustrations. Addressing sources of frustration, such as the role definition of teachers and the "Theory X" management of schools, is a less popular option.

Among the more unusual reforms in education is a government-sponsored, union-run experiment called the "Teacher Involvement Project" (TIP) in the San Jose (California) school system. This program is described by Crockenberg and Clark (1979), who point out that its rationale, "the argument that teachers would become more effective in their teaching if they participated more extensively in school decision making," has been a goal of for decades. They cite a 1913 proposal that argued that "since teachers do the everyday work of teaching and understand the conditions necessary for better teaching . . . [they] should have a voice and a vote in the determination of educational policies . . . [and] a share in the administration of the affairs of their own schools" (American Teacher, cited in Crockenberg and Clark, 1979: 115).

The San Jose TIP was established in 1974 under a grant from the National Institute of Education to the California teachers' union. The goal of the program was "to train classroom teachers to participate with their building principals in identifying and resolving local school problems and to sustain that involvement by implementing formal decision-making procedures at each school site" (Crockenberg and Clark, 1979: 115). The procedure used was analogous to the QWL strategy at Tarrytown (see Chapter 7) in that teacher-change-agents were recruited and were trained to conduct workshops for other teachers and administrators. These workshops dealt with research and planning. Groups were taught "how to determine specific decision-making interests of their faculties, how to establish priorities among the areas chosen, how to determine the degree of faculty involvement considered appropriate in each high-priority area, and how to formalize self-governance" (Crockenberg and Clark, 1979: 116).

Teachers in the schools were polled about their preferences for areas to get involved with, and they overwhelmingly chose "curriculum content and philosophy" followed by "instructional methods and grouping." Their preferred concerns were professional concerns that had to do with the goals, quality, and form of services rendered to clients—with "the everyday world of teaching" referred to in the 1913 article. In wanting to think about their teaching, and in wanting to determine (as a group) what to teach and how to teach it, the TIP teachers implicitly diagnosed the intrusion of academic administration into areas that (1) do not require management or (2) profit from it.

Once the TIP teachers were liberated from gratuitous circumscriptions of their judgments and choices, they worked more effectively. The San Jose project data yielded "evidence that students in the TIP schools experienced a greater increase in their test scores during the time of the project than did students in comparable non-TIP schools" (Crockenberg and Clark, 1979: 118).

Why does quality of service improve with participation? For one, decisions "are simply more likely to be implemented if teachers participate with administrators in formulating those decisions" (Crockenberg and Clark, 1979: 118). Participation also unleashes worker creativity; TIP incentives included grants to schools "to fund proposals for curriculum and instruction improvements drafted and approved by the faculty councils of those schools" (Crockenberg and Clark, 1979: 117). Participation also (1) brings to the surface obstacles to performance in the form of difficulties that have been swept under the rug, (2) provides a sense of mission and collective sense of ownership, (3) yields self-respect, as one's views are respected and decisions are based on them, (4) creates new knowledge by pooling workers' experiences and judgments, (5) provides group support for the tackling and resolution of problems, and (6) decreases the climate for burnout.

The Spark that Refused to Die

The San Jose project succumbed to a tax payers' revolt (Proposition 13) that repolarized union management relations around issues of survival. A similar fate *almost* befell the Parkway Program (the first "school without walls") in Philadelphia. This program was not a QWL program, but outdid QWL by granting teachers almost unqualified autonomy. Parkway is a mini senior high school system that enrolls 1200 students in various parts of Philadelphia. There are five "units," each with nine teachers and a head teacher. A support staff (eight additional teachers, the principal, and other staff) is located elsewhere. The five units, each teaching some 250 students, are independent. Unit teachers "are collectively responsible for planning the schedule, devising all courses and curricula, counseling students, choosing and ordering texts and materials, finding classroom space in neighborhood buildings, maintaining close contact with parents, and extending the curriculum to incorporate community learning opportunities" (Lytle, 1980: 700).

The Parkway Program is described as having been "designed to provide professional satisfaction to the faculty" (Lytle, 1980: 700). Working relationships among teachers are close, their supervision is minimal, and their creativity and innovativeness are encouraged. Students (chosen by lot, with no special qualifications other than interest) enjoy autonomy as well. Lytle writes that "much of the custodial dimension of schooling is eliminated, since students are responsible for themselves during free periods, travel time, and lunch time" (1980: 700). Despite this freedom (or possibly partly because of it) the students' performance exceeds Philadelphia norms. Students enter Parkway with "representative" backgrounds and achievement test scores, but they excel on tests upon graduation. They also disproportionately go on to college or find jobs. The suggestion—as with TIP— is that teachers freed of excess management teach more effectively.

During 1978, Philadelphia was forced to undertake massive layoffs of teachers, including in the Parkway Program. Parkway lost 26 teachers and acquired 16 new teachers who were assigned "against their will" (Lytle, 1980: 700). Lytle reports that the new teachers showed amazing resilience. They "assimilated quickly. They designed courses they'd never taught before, organized extracurricular activities, and got involved with every dimension of the school" (1980: 701). When the 1978 crisis passed, ex-Parkway teachers requested to be returned to Parkway. Remaining vacancies "were filled by teachers who had originally been assigned to Parkway against their will but who now chose to remain. Of the remaining 11 teachers . . . all but one indicated in discussions with the principal that they would have preferred to remain at Parkway rather than going on to another school" (Lytle, 1980: 702).

Clearly, there is congruence between workers who have unfulfilled higher-level Maslowian needs (see Chapter 2), and opportunities that are provided by high autonomy settings. Parkway's unattractive physical conditions (which are flagrantly unresponsive to basic needs) and Parkway's absence of structure (violating safety needs) proved inconsequential, while the program's autonomy increased morale and motivated performance. Lytle tells us that

> one teacher who had taught in Philadelphia for over 30 years (including five years in a special school for the gifted) explained that he'd never before had the experience of planning a curriculum that directly addressed the needs of the students. . . . Another teacher . . . commented . . . "I have been given the chance to try out some things I've always wanted to do. . . . I found a feeling of congeniality. . . . A third teacher with over 25 years experience in conventional senior high schools and a reputation for being a hard-boiled taskmaster was given a silver tray by his homeroom class as an anniversary gift. He'd never before had a group of students who were so appreciative and supportive of him [1980: 702].

The last scenario is revealing, because it confirms that the custodial orientation that is conventionally ascribed to "burnout" (see Chapter 2) or to subcultural forces (see Chapter 4) can be a consequence of classic management, and that settings that liberate staff can enrich the relationship between staff and clients. In this sense, client advocates and staff unions share common goals. As noted by Lytle, "Improving student performance through increasing the psychic rewards of teaching has, of course, been a continuing goal of collective bargaining" (1980: 702). QWL in human services differs from QWL at General Motors. In the former, productivity *can* be a goal, *provided* it means worker-defined quality service rather than the ritualistic "numbers games" that are often played by administrators.

Staff Democracy and Client Democracy

Another difference between a GM plant and a school is that the base of GM's pyramid is the worker, whereas in schools, teachers (and elsewhere, other front-line staff) are authority figures for clients. It is thus usually the client who is the *real* bottom of a human services hierarchy.

Should participatory democracy extend to clients? This question is difficult to answer, especially in the abstract. QWL offers no guidelines, and simple extrapolations (no matter how humane or how philosophically consistent) can prove silly. For one, contacts between some workers and clients are transitory and constrained, and the contexts of such contacts (e.g., between officers and suspects) cannot plausibly be democratized. Elsewhere—in hospital settings such as intensive care units—clients are preoccupied with their problems. There are other human service recipients—patients in back wards or small children—who seem to be too impaired or too immature for participatory involvement.

The third objection—that of excessive impairment or immaturity—brings out a problem that (upon reflection) applies elsewhere. Many criteria we advance to exclude people from participation sound factual, but they are not. They are judgments, and they can become self-fulfilling, as did Taylor's assumptions about the laziness of workers and their incapacity for planning. We are reminded of McGregor's point that the *assumption* of worker capacity and potential (Theory Y) can *produce* worker capacity and potential.

The literature is redolent with instances in which Theory X management has produced clients who are virtual vegetables. More importantly, the record pinpoints Theory Y regimes that have regenerated clients whose vegetablelike dependence was produced (or was exacerbated) by Theory X assumptions.

Induced incapacity and engineered recovery have occurred among institutionalized senior citizens (see Chapter 17) and among psychotics committed to asylums. The hospital literature is particularly rich, and Albert Bandura has noted that

Over the years there have appeared numerous sociological studies of the psychiatric hospital . . . each of which documents the debilitating effects that prevailing institutional practices have upon inmate populations. . . . Throughout the period of institutionalization, the patients' behavior is closely regulated and accommodated to fixed hospital routines. Under these types of organizational contingencies, initiative, self-reliance, and self-determination, which are necessary for attaining satisfactory independent adjustment outside the hospital, are generally extinguished, whereas the more docile patient-role behaviors bring about the greatest rewards and promotion in graded ward systems [1969: 261].

Psychotics in hospitals become not only "more docile" over time, but also more disturbed. Wing (1969: 145) points out that "the longer the patient has been in the hospital, for example, the less likely he is to want to leave or to have any realistic plans for a future life, outside."

The most convincing study about environment-induced deterioration was done in England (Wing, 1969). Public hospitals were broken down into categories, depending on the degree to which they regimented their patients. The most regimenting hospitals (Type C) budgeted their patients' time, gave them no leeway for self-initiated behavior, locked them in wards, garbed them in standard issue, and allowed them no possessions or means of self-adornment. One out of four patients in such (Type C) hospitals proved "mute or almost mute," compared to 14 percent in Type B (medium regimentation) settings and 6 percent in Type A (minimum regimentation) asylums. A follow-up study of Type C hospitals showed that "it is the patients whose social environment has most improved (particularly by a decrease in the time spent doing nothing) who are clinically better" (Wing, 1969: 151). In other words, when the hospital makes an effort to involve patients in self-initiated activity, their level of pathology decreases.

A number of token economy experiments (reviewed by Bandura, 1969) have rewarded psychotics for emerging from their shells. The patients are generally given tokens when they engage in elementary self-help, or when they report to work. Their manifestations of helplessness—such as insisting on being washed, clothed, or fed—are discouraged. Their more engaging "symptoms"—such as hallucinatory conversation bids—are disregarded.

Tokens promote patient activity and also provide them with choice. When patients exchange their tokens they shape their own life-style, which can vary along dimensions such as privacy, activity, and personal freedom. More advanced patients can "bank" tokens, or can be furnished with "credit cards."

Some more sophisticated token economies feature watered-down or limited patient self-governance. Psychotics can be "paid" to meet in groups, and may be allowed to recommend decisions about work assignment, medication levels, and readiness or nonreadiness for furlough and release. The catch is that staff not only exercise vetoes, but can punish the patient groups for their work. Bandura reports that in one program

> The staff then either approved all recommendations made by the group, or rejected their recommendations. If warranted, the entire group could be rewarded or penalized by being raised or lowered one step-level, depending upon the appropriateness of the group's decision-making behavior [1969: 270].

A different version of patient involvement is that of the hospital therapeutic community (TC; Jones, 1953). In wards that are democratized as TCs, staff roles are fluid, and the staff's chain of command is attenuated. The assumption is that leadership passes from hand to hand and that it can be exercised—given the right circumstances—by anyone. Decisions facing the TC—those that affect the lives of staff and patients—are discussed in community meetings or in meetings that are convened when crises arise. More specialized concerns are dealt with by smaller groups or by committees. Sometimes staff get together to conduct "process reviews" and plan future interventions.

In the TC, staff and client democracy seem to serve different ends. Patient groups are "laboratories"; they are experiences in living (or "living-learning") for persons who have chronic difficulties relating to others. The staff's democracy makes patient experiences possible by insulating the TC from the chain of command in the larger organization and providing lack of structure (flexibility) internally. The TC's autonomy and its intimacy make it a miniworld in which people's interpersonal difficulties can surface and solutions to problems can be discussed and rehearsed.

In practice, lines between staff democracy and client democracy are less neat. Jones (the TC's founder) has argued that

> the two segments of the community (clients and staff) are inseparable. I'm tired of talking about "treatment" and "training." To me they are all the same process. I think that often you are treating the staff and being treated by the clients. The two terms can be lumped together into learning as a social process [Jones, 1980: 105].

The "social process" Jones refers to is a collective and an individual process. For Jones (1976), a hierarchical arrangement is one in which structure takes over, communication is ritualized, and initiative is squelched. This ensures that neither the organization nor the people in the organization will change or grow. The alternative is what Jones calls the open system, "a system that ... is open to learning and change" (1976: 40). "Open" means that (1) the organization responds to problems and solves them, and that (2) people who make up the organization learn, grow, and improve.

Grass-roots management is critical because it requires "that action planning will involve those people who are to carry out the plan, or at least their chosen representatives. This means that every individual who is involved in the action will have an investment on the outcome, because it is in part 'his plan' " (Jones, 1976: 41). How does this apply to the TC? If we waive distinctions between staff and clients, TC relationships are symbiotic. Each TC member can enhance (or reduce) the quality of the experience for others and can affect the TC culture; each stimulates others and defines the learning climate.

The TC undermines its context, the total institution (Goffman, 1961), a place in which staff are "keepers" and patients "inmates." The myth has it (see Chapter 4) that in such settings clients and staff face each other in trench warfare or uneasy truce. Total institutions are in reality "closed" because they warehouse people, which is a static (no-change) goal for a human service organization. It is also stultifying for individuals (staff and clients) whose energies are wasted in suspiciousness and reciprocal alienation. This class warfare is not unlike pre-QWL collective bargaining, and the issues are similar. As with early advances in the labor movement, progress (expanded due process and grievance machinery, client "unions," and the like) polarizes the two sides further, or leaves their enmity in place.

The advent of QWL-type rapprochement—even tentative modes of collaboration that fall short of the radical option of the TC—can "unlock" or "open up" a system. Where joint problems are addressed through joint planning, the products (innovative solutions) offer expanded collective and personal goals to staff and clients.

As this is written (or read), a student/faculty group in a school unveils antivandalism measures or designs a curriculum; in a prison, inmates and guards plan a father/son day, a picnic, or an "open house"; somewhere in town antirape measures are being shaped by assistant prosecutors and affected citizens. Future scenarios that we could envisage may shock and surprise us. They may include inmate/staff-designed jail improvements, staff/patient innovations in hospital care, and other collaboratively designed system changes forced by the bankruptcy of today's paralyzing stalemates that make everyone a loser.

The "grass roots" of an organization are its front-line workers and low-echelon staff. But as democratization at this level takes hold, its life is precarious. Grass-roots management must spread to survive. It must spread upward to neutralize middle management resistance and laterally (as QWL "networks") to lend itself support (Herbst, 1976). Other sources of resistance lie in clients. The ideal response is for grass roots to reach downward into QWL adventures that link workers and clients.

NOTE

1. Some observers predict exacerbations of the manager/worker caste system in organizations because there is increased emphasis on technology and formal or advanced education as a criterion of status. Merton describes such a trend when he writes:

Advances in methods of production . . . may enlarge the social cleavage between workmen and operating executives. It may produce a sharper *social stratification of industry*. As the complexities of the new technology make technical education a prerequisite for the operating executive, the prospect of workers rising through the ranks becomes progressively dimmed. To the extent that opportunities for higher education are socially stratified, moreover, managers come increasingly to be drawn from social strata remote from those of workers. Also, since technically trained personnel enter industry at a relatively high level, they have little occasion to share the job experience of workers at an early stage of their careers and tend, accordingly, to have an abstract knowledge about rather than a concrete *acquaintance with* the perspective of workers. Finally, with the increasing rationalization of managerial procedures, the relations between operating executives and workmen become increasingly formalized and depersonalized [1957: 565-566].

Merton concludes that these patterns "may in composite contribute to a secular trend toward growing tensions between the men who manage and the men whom they manage" (1957: 566).

PART III

THE PRESCRIPTION

CHAPTER 9

THE NOTION OF PARTICIPATION

Job enrichment and quality of work life are ambitious blueprints for redesigning organizations. They are also social movements that have "members" (consultants, executives) who promote, sell, and install programs. The "how-to-do" implications of the two models for agents of change who have limited influence and resources—persons such as grass-roots reformers in probation offices, slum schools, and hospital wards—are mostly propaedeutic, *except* for pointers, premises, or suggestions that they can abstract, borrow, and adapt to fit local conditions.

In this chapter we address the principal of these separable elements, the notion that front-line staff must participate in decisions that affect them. This element lies at the core of the QWL model, and it is compatible (as we shall see in Chapter 10) with job enrichment. But the concept is not *subsumable* under QWL or job enrichment, and it has been honored and practiced in remote historical times such as pre-Socratic Athens. (Socrates was a critic of participatory strategies and was convicted of blasphemy by a participatory criminal justice system). What distinguishes *contemporary* advocacy of participation from past theory and practice is not that the strategy is *new,* but that it is proposed as a remedy for new problems. It is in this context that the writings of Erich Fromm help to provide both historical and contemporary perspective.

Participation as Humanism

Fromm (1976) has deplored the rate of bureaucratization of postindustrial society, the consequences of which he sees as dehumanizing. By "dehumanizing" Fromm means that people come to be treated as statistics. The postindustrial trend— exacerbated by computerization—invites managers to play the "numbers game" (see Chapters 1 and 8), to quantify service at the expense of the substance or of the quality of service, so that clients take shape as "caseloads" or as other impersonal composites whose attributes are standardized to facilitate ritualized ministrations that subserve inflexible "rules."

Staff and clients suffer. Staff suffering (the Burnout Syndrome described in Chapter 2) takes less direct form than client suffering, because it consists of stultification and of uncaring, automated responses. The clients' reaction is passivity or passive aggression, which expresses—sometimes sullenly and sometimes volubly— how people feel when they are treated as objects.

Fromm's critique is partly of largeness in organizations but mostly of the formalization of roles and authority along classic management lines. Fromm argues that in bureaucracies, no one— including top management—has a stake in decisions, and everyone—including top management—is a slave (and "spectator") of routine. Since no person is responsible, no person cares and activity loses its meaning.

For Fromm, the antedote to bureaucratization is decentralization and democratization of decision making. By "democratization" Fromm does not mean votes and elections and delegated authority, but close deliberations in face-to-face groups, where consensus is reached about matters in which members of such groups have a stake. Face-to-faceness ensures that each member is known to each other member so that he or she acts and is perceived as an individual. Informed deliberations ensure commitment to group decisions. Consensus democracy, Fromm argues, produces "a social institution in whose life and manner of functioning every member becomes active and, therefore, interested" (1976: 181).

Fromm's concern with rehumanizing organizations has particular applicability to the understanding of staff/clients links in the human services. Fromm feels that when staff are treated like numbers, they will treat clients as numbers. In alienated settings in which staff feel used by their employers, they may even treat clients exploitively.

For Fromm, the consequence of bureaucracy is ultimately alienation. Though the concept for Fromm is a broad one, because he "seems to refer to almost everything of which he disapproves as an instance of 'alienation' " (Schacht, 1970: 147), his most unique worry is about people acting in nonautonomous ways, in the sense of doing things not because they want to, but because it is expected of them. Fromm agrees with Marx about capitalist workers not "owning" their work: A person cannot "own" his or her behavior, Fromm argues, when his or her contributions are not products of his or her own decisions but instead are shaped by bureaucratic prescriptions.

Participation neutralizes alienation because it interposes the workers' thoughts and volitions between the directives they receive and the way they act. Alienated workers complain that they are cogs in depersonalized machines and that no one listens to them. They feel lonely, unappreciated, manipulated, and impotent. To make workers care about their work, their settings must care about them, which means that organizations must provide occasions for workers to become known, to express their views, to think, and to make decisions. This solution is "humanistic" because it converts assembly-line production into *human* production, to output for which people are individually responsible and in which people have a personal stake. In this way, Fromm suggests that the automation of *people* can be separated from the broader automation process, which is a corollary of industrialization.

Participation and the Role of Management

Fromm and other antibureaucratic humanists of the 1930s anticipated trends such as the "youth revolt" of the 1960s and the QWL movement of the 1970s. In the youth revolt movement, Fromm's diagnosis (alienation) came to the forefront, and his prescription was lost sight of. This happened because ideologues of the movement expressed alieantion as they described alienation, and saw no escape (beyond alternative lifestyles) from an unredeeming "system" they deeply resented.

More detached observers, such as the authors of the *Work in America* volume we have already discussed, see alienation as a response to negotiable pressures. Like Fromm, the NIMH group argues the desirability—based on alienation data—of widespread reforms. They see hope in experimental programs such as QWL that create a participatory system that

> permits the worker to achieve and maintain a sense of personal worth and importance, to grow, to motivate himself, and receive recognition and approval for what he does. [That] gives the worker a meaningful voice in decisions in one place where the effects of his voice can be immediately experienced [Special Task Force, 1973: 104].

The NIMH group was more broadly concerned with resolving "a contradiction . . . between democracy in society and authoritarianism in the workplace" (1973: 104); Fromm has a less sanguine view of "society" and feels there is a need to decentralize decision making *everywhere,* with the workplace as a shining candidate for reform because of the importance work carries as an arena for self-expression.

Decentralization dilutes Fred Taylor's system in which executives plan and workers work. Neither Fromm nor the authors of *Work in America* thought that managers would lose under the change. The assumption is that resource development is not a finite pie, such that actualizing one person's potential diminishes that of another. The power of executives might be diminished, but their jobs could become more challenging in a climate in which new ideas proliferate and change is welcome. The experience would be that of the Bolivar foreman quoted in Duckles, Duckles, and Maccoby (1977: 399), who observed that "I've never had so much authority since I started giving it away." The point is that management autonomy can increase as routinization of management decreases.

What executives give up in open organizations is jurisdiction over details of the work process (the sort of planning prized by Taylor); however, "larger" decisions—decisions about how to react to forces outside the organization (such as legislatures and governing boards)—are not preempted. With participation, the manager can also expect reciprocity for whatever autonomy he or she provides. Where workers have a stake in the organization, issues such as budget allocation may invite more give and take and less of the sort of defensiveness that produces manager stress.

The other side of the coin is the diffusion of the management function (Frost, Wakely, and Ruh, 1974). The prescription "every man a manager" is drawn from literature about the Scanlon Plan, which was an early precursor of QWL. The goal the phrase refers to is that of maximizing the input front-line persons have in planning their contributions to the total output of the organization. To the extent to which the goal is achieved, central offices collect data and disseminate them, so that workers can discuss production issues within their areas of expertise and make recommendations for action. Centralized planning consists of collating recommendations and summarizing high points and areas of consensus. This procedure goes a long way toward addressing recurring resentment against "administrators behind desks far removed from where the action is" (front-office staff, generally) issuing "hair-brained edicts" that are considered impossible to implement.

Diffused management implies data sharing, a process to which we shall return when we discuss research (see Chapter 12). Diffused management also means an expanded function of coordination. What old line executives coordinate is actions, or worker behavior; what they do *not* coordinate is worker thinking, or plans of action. This new coordinating function can enrich management: It is delicate, probably challenging, and—in Fromm's terms—infinitely more "human" than bureaucratic planning.

Participation and Job Enrichment

Herzberg's (1978) views on work participation are of crucial interest because Herzberg is the dean of the job enrichment movement. This movement allows for participation but prescribes its shape. Herzberg's view is that "the way to motivate a human being to do a good job is to give him a good job to do"; that "work motivation results from employees loving their work" (1978: 44).

Herzberg has no problem with the concept of participation if it leads to workers "loving their work" because it is *their* work. Problems arise for Herzberg where workers design (or love) "bad" jobs:

(1) Herzberg feels that concerns with extrinsic job features can masquerade as involvement in work, though the job in fact remains unenriched. In making this point, Herzberg (1978) takes the more publicized European programs to task. He objects to team building in Europe as an end in itself, and notes that "a 'Mickey Mouse' job is a 'Mickey Mouse' job whether you have one person doing it or five doing it as a cooperative effort" (1978: 40). His main worry is about programs that involve the worker in creating congenial work environments. Herzberg observes that "no design of cafeterias, toilets or parking lots can make an uninteresting job interesting" (1978: 40).

(2) With respect to commitment, Herzberg asks, "To what is he [the worker] committed and why does he commit himself?" Involvement in the *process* of enriching jobs leads to involvement in jobs, *provided* jobs are *enriched*, and provided workers are *truly* involved. There is a need for quality control of participation, which for Herzberg means (a) ensuring that worker decisions are *informed* decisions, and (b) unscrambling peer pressure from genuine commitment. The second of Herzberg's points is an important one because Herzberg sees himself as an "individual" psychologist who must maintain his focus on the individual rather than on the group.

In the "typical" participatory program, the product—such as the innovative proposal for work reform—is collectively arrived at. Herzberg is anxious to divorce the benefit of this process for the group—such as the group's commitment to its product—from the benefit that can be derived by group members or by group beneficiaries, such as the persons doing the group-designed jobs. In Herzberg's view, involvement in work (like freedom) must be won day by day, and it derives from the worker's day-to-day relationship to his or her job. It is participation *on the job* that matters.

Herzberg's concern with participation—unlike that of QWL advocates—is with opportunities for autonomy that result *from* enrichment rather than with the worker having a voice *in* enrichment. The enriched job by definition offers the worker participation. Herzberg writes that "job enrichment, which reinforces the opportunity of the individual for psychological growth, leads naturally to more autonomy for the individual." He asserts that "tasks should be organized to give the individual worker maximum control over them"; and sees the worker "as an expert in some facet of his job." Authority lines are circumvented by the requirement that each worker be permitted "to communicate directly with personnel he must interact with in order to expeditiously complete a task." Herzberg also prizes "the opportunity to schedule one's own work," a goal that enjoins managers not to "pre-program a person's job" (1978: 40).

Job enrichment maximizes the management functions of workers. It prescribes jobs that are arranged so that the worker (the teacher, prison guard, or child care worker) can make unconstrained decisions about what to do, when to do it, and with whom, relying on recognized professional expertise, untrammeled by edicts, prescriptions, and schedules capriciously circumscribing autonomy. What participation means to Herzberg is making decisions about the job on the job. It does *not* mean (1) making decisions that help create jobs in which decisions are made, (2) a collaborative process of problem solving in groups or teams, or (3) helping shape QWL or organizational climate.

Herzberg warns against overconcern with groups and against underconcern with participatory opportunities offered by the job. For Herzberg, the latter is the "baby," and the former, the "bathwater." Herzberg sees "extrinsic" participation as bathwater, ultimately risking the loss of both form and content of participation.

A Mixed Model

Herzberg's exclusive concern with motivation through the job has earned the label "orthodox" job enrichment, compared to more eclectic approaches such as that of Hackman and Oldham (1980). The difference is one of emphasis. A case in point is the question, "Should workers participate in designing enriching jobs for themselves?" Like Herzberg's, Hackman and Oldham's answer is "maybe," but their concern—unlike Herzberg's—is with practicality ("yes, unless management can do it better"), rather than with principle.

The first of Hackman and Oldham's points is that "if consultants and managers do not have at hand all the information needed to assess the feasibility and desirability of contemplated changes, then a participative process may be more appropriate" (1980: 234). This point falls short of saying "if workers have useful knowledge to contribute, their expertise should be invoked." The latter argument is more appealing, but it risks becoming circular because workers with whom managers share data will have more to contribute than workers who are limited to their own *immediate* experience. There is also a difference between asking "Do we (managers and / or consultants) know enough about how to enrich jobs so we can do without worker input?" and "Can our perspective or our insight be improved (i.e., enriched)?"

The second question—which borders on a Machiavellian concern—is "Are top-town enrichment programs likely to be resisted?" What is here recommended is that "if the climate of the organizational unit is such that employee acceptance of management-installed work redesign will not be a problem, then a top-down approach might be favored on simple grounds of cost and efficiency" (Hackman and Oldham, 1980: 234). (Note that the criterion is *not,* "if employees don't care," or "if they prefer not to participate.") The third point is similarly (a) conservative and (b) paternalistic. It reads, "If . . . there are good reasons to believe that employee suggestions would focus on relatively trivial or work-irrelevant matters, then it may be preferable for managers to proceed with top-down installation—with the understanding that they may have to deal later with problems of employee acceptance and commitment" (Hackman and Oldham, 1980: 234).

All such points accidentally or deliberately ignore the self-fulfilling consequences of management behavior. The third point could be rephrased to admit that "managers who run gripe sessions under the heading of job enrichment will have 'reasons' to conclude that workers 'focus on relatively trivial and work-irrelevant matter.' " The same result would be achieved if managers were convoked by their subordinates into "participatory" conclaves with no-holds-barred definitions of group agendas.

Hackman and Oldham *do* introduce an issue of principle. This issue (which the three recommendations ignore) is whether democracy can be undemocratically arrived at. In practical terms, the question has to do with congruity between process and product, with "consistency between 'what we want to achieve' and 'how we are going to achieve it' " (Hackman and Oldham, 1980: 233). As McGregor (see Chapter 3) would observe, the top-down stance recommends Theory X approaches to the establishment of a Theory Y regime. The strategy is one that contains double messages. On the one hand, workers are told, "Managers want you to exercise autonomy and responsibility, to learn and to grow"; on the other, they are appraised of the facts that they are (a) mistrusted (Point 3), (b) disrespected (Point 1), and (c) bureaucratically manipulated (Point 2).

None of this implies that job enrichment *must* involve participatory initiation. What it suggests is the *desirability* of participatory design wherever enrichment goals are not impaired. This sort of model (a revised "mixed" model) recognized concerns of Herzberg, Hackman, and Oldham about misuses of democracy. It shuns a process with no product, or a trivial one. It does not equate process and product—as does Fromm—nor does it accept any old product (as do some QWL advocates) because the goal is to strengthen the process and/or promise future products.

Participation for What?

Worker participation is a many-splendored concept. It refers to goal setting by work groups, design of jobs, review and planning, teaming, job autonomy, policy input, horizontal or parallel organization, consultation, *Gemeinschaft*, power, and ownership. In opting for "participation" we become the blind men of the fable, grasping at the tail or trunk or leg of the "participation" elephant.

Our own hold on the beast has to do with the job and the way the job is defined. By participation we mean the opportunity for making decisions on the job and about the job. These decisions enrich the worker because they provide ownership (not literally, but psychologically) of the work he or she does. Ownership makes work more meaningful and interesting. The worker's clients benefit because they become objects of concern. His or her managers benefit if they share an interest in quality service. This is so because work that matters is done more carefully, rather than being rushed in frantic pursuit of numbers to satisfy accountants or traditional managers.

In blue-collar jobs, machines and routines limit the level of job enrichment. In human services, it is classic management that limits and participation that expands. The motions that are prescribed for us from above (those that *can* be prescribed) relate to custodial or caretaker functions. *More* management means greater emphasis on impoverished goals, and it means less personal motivation because job enrichment and the worker's role in goal setting are necessarily intertwined.

The point is that human services jobs (unlike other jobs) cannot be enriched without democratizing the workplace. Enriching a guard's or a police officer's job means expanding the prison's or police department's human service involvement, a task that cannot be accomplished by edict. In setting their own goals, workers set their organizations' goals, i.e., they "make policy." The reverse does not hold, because managers have no control over human service technology—over how the worker relates to clients—beyond the maintenance (custodial) level.

Liberal managers who come face to face with this disheartening discovery frequently compromise by creating localized "innovation ghettos." This means that some groups of workers (police teams, therapeutic communities, teacher task forces, and the like) have enriched jobs and make local policy while other workers are traditionally managed and do traditional work. There are virtues and liabilities to this arrangement. On the one hand, local reform comes in easily digestible chunks, and can be "tried for size" before it is adopted wholesale or disseminated. On the other hand, the larger culture and its classic management structure are apt to drown out the form and content of the miniculture and its democratized structure.

Another limited strategy is to confine participation to specific content areas or "projects." This strategy—often followed in QWL—permits a timid organization to get its innovation feet wet in strategically selected ways, or to try participation modestly for size. Payoff hinges on products and on follow-through. If managers like what they see, they may follow worker recommendations and try the process elsewhere. If participants feel responded to, they are likely to (1) participate again, and (2) feel increasingly more committed to the organization.

We have already emphasized that aborted participation—non-follow-through, one-shot experiments, or penny ante participation—may boomerang. Invoking the process can raise worker expectation. It can tap job enrichment needs, provide a taste for autonomy, whet desires for greater involvement. Such experiences cry out for more, or at least for closure. The antecedent of abortive experiences may be apathy, but its result is bitterness. In this sense, participation parallels the poet's view of learning: The participatory well nurtures and refreshes, but limited exposure to it is (or can be) dangerous.

CHAPTER 10

PARTICIPATION AND CHANGE

The question, "How much participation should there be in job enrichment?" (see Chapter 9) does not address the issue of participation and change because most change is not aimed at enrichment or concerned with it. Most planned change is designed either to accommodate pressures or to promote efficiency or both. The first type of change is usually reactive, and the second tends to be proactive. Some reactive changes cope with pressures that can hurt (e.g., "How can we accommodate that cut in our budget?") and other reactive change is more routine readjustment to impinging changes in the surrounding world (such as "We gotta do something about all these drug addicts they are sending us"). Of course, organizations have different thresholds for what they define as "crises" or routine pressures.

Proactive change is retooling and consists of enterprises such as academic curriculum revisions and model changes in cars. Change of this kind replaces routine with new routine aimed at new output or increments in output. *Pure* proactivity—retooling that is not at least partially responsive to pressure—is becoming rarer as change in the world accelerates. By the same token, accelerated change means that most reactivity is proactive, because the present one reacts to is apt to be history by the time one has reacted.

Participation in planned change means that people who are affected by a change have a hand in designing that change. The concept (participation in change) originates from the discovery that changes are apt to be resisted, and that people who resist can become quietly efficient because they resist as groups. This discovery was made by Taylor, who attributed group resistance to perversity and/or misunderstandings of his motives. Group-based resistance was more sympathetically reacted to by the Hawthorne researchers. Roethlisberger and Dickson tell us that

perhaps one of the most important ways in which the internal
equilibruim of a company may be disturbed is through the
introduction of technological change. In every organization there
are groups of technologists and specialists whose attention is
focused on the general problem of securing the effectiveness of
tools and machines for the purpose of manufacturing a better
product at the same or lower cost. . . . These changes in technical
organization, of course, have consequences in terms of the social
structure of a concern. They frequently result in the social
dislocation of individuals and groups and disrupt the
interpersonal relations which tend to give these individuals and
groups their feelings of security and integrity [1961: 579].

To defend against affronts to "feelings of security and integrity"
(and to prevent speed-ups, income reduction, and unemployment), groups of workers promote lethargy and other antichange
"norms." Mayo and his colleagues suggested that managers
respond with a form of variegated change salesmanship.
Roethlisberger and Dickson write that

in introducing technical change . . . it is important: first, that the
sentiments of the people directly affected be determined; secondly
that the sentiments of other people related to them be determined;
thirdly, that problems arising from the new pattern of
interpersonal relations be anticipated and understood; and finally,
that an understandable and acceptable explanation of the change
be made before it is introduced [1961: 580].

In this prescription, there is no mention of participation. The birth
of this strategy required that the prescribed empathy with workers
and the "understandable and acceptable explanation" be tried and
found impotent as a means to address and defuse group-based
resistance to top-down change.

Undermining Resistance to Change Through Participation

The Hawthorne-inspired manager was a human-relations-
oriented "nice-guy" who systematically appealed to his workers,
but was otherwise an unregenerate chain-of-command bureaucrat. His bureaucratic orientation was later diluted, as

organizational development (OD) made formal structure *at the top* unfashionable. As French and Bell (1978) point out, OD prized "collaborative management," meaning "a shared kind of management—not a hierarchically imposed kind." In actual practice, "the key unit in organization development activities (was) the ongoing work team, including both superiors and subordinates" (French and Bell, 1978: 15). Subordinates were typically the lower-ranking managers, though on occasion they included technical staff.

One reason why "reform" managers prized OD was that it inspired junior managers to generate good new ideas. The notion that one could similarly motivate rank-and-file workers did not occur to the managers. McGregor wrote at the time:

> One of the most important conditions of the subordinate's growth and development centers around his opportunities to express his ideas and to contribute his suggestions before his superiors take action on matters that involve him. . . . Participation of this kind is fairly prevalent in the upper levels of industrial organizations. It is entirely lacking further down the line [1944: 433].

OD owed a heavy debt to Lewin and his students. One set of demonstrations (Lewin, 1947) proved particularly influential. These studies aimed at breaking habits that inhibited experimentation and prevented change. One experiment involved housewives, and "the objective was to increase the use of beef heart, sweetbreads and kidneys." Lewin saw the task as difficult. He wrote that "if one considers the psychological forces which kept housewives from using these intestinals, one is tempted to think of rather deep-seated aversions requiring something like psychoanalytic treatment" (Lewin, 1947: 334). Lewin succeeded (with one-third of the housewives) in 45 minutes.

The Lewin study comprised three "experimental" and three control groups. Control groups received attractive lectures, complete with appeals to patriotism, nutritional charts, and enticing recipes. Only two ladies (3 percent of the sample) were impelled to prepare rognon meneure or some other exotic dish for their nonexotic husbands. Experimental housewives were involved *as partners* in the battle for gustatory innovation and culinary change. The groups considered why "housewives like themselves" might resist experimenting, which "led to an elaboration of the obstacles which a change in general and particularly change toward sweetbreads, beef hearts, and kidneys would encounter, such as the dislike of the husband, the smell during cooking, etc." (Lewin, 1947: 335).

In listing obstacles, housewives were engaged in *force field analysis,* which Lewin introduced as a step in planning change. The technique assumes that habit (nonchange) is a result of stable but competing forces. Some forces are allies of change (driving forces) and some are change opponents (resisting forces). Where habits we want to change are strongly motivated or truly matter, "pushing" (adding driving forces) causes people to dig in because the forces we add evoke resistance. As resisting forces build up, we get tension rather than change.

Lewin suggests locating resisting forces and evolving a strategy for dealing with them. This is what housewives in the sweetbreads study were engaged in doing, except that they were change agents (partners in the dietary war effect) and also change *targets*. They were involved *as groups*, which for Lewin is critical. Where a group resolves that kidney cooking is worth trying, it evolves a prochange force in the shape of an adventurous norm. This norm replaces the customary "meat-and-potatoes" norm of the Midwest. Lewin argues that "one of the reasons why 'group carried changes' are more readily brought about seems to be the unwillingness of the individual to depart too far from group standards; he is likely to change only if the group changes" (1947: 377).

Lewins's study and other demonstrations similar to it yielded a set of interrelated conclusions:

(1) a way of changing people is to make them participants in the change process;
(2) attention must be paid to resistance that the change is likely to mobilize; and
(3) if we fail, resistance becomes the norm of groups we try to change; if we succeed, we promote "prochange" norms that

generate peer pressure on our side of the issue rather than on the opposing side.

The Pajama Game

One of Lewin's students, Alfred Marrow, was crown prince of a pajama empire, and Lewin persuaded Marrow to apply social science in business rather than to propagate it in academia. One result was the transmission of Lewin's change-participation findings from the laboratory to a real-life factory. Research was done in the main plant of the Harwood Manufacturing Corporation, of which Marrow was president. Workers were young, rural, poorly educated, and mostly (80 percent) female. The plant was unionized, paid very well (at piece rate), and was extremely "progressively" managed. Despite such facts, modernization was resisted, and when jobs were changed workers resigned in droves, acted out, groused, and slowed down to a snail's pace.

The application of Lewin (Coch and French, 1948) began with three experimental groups. For a control group, management (the production department) modified the job; the control "group was told that the change was necessary because of competitive conditions, and that a new piece rate had been set. The new piece rate was thoroughly explained by the time study man, questions were answered, and the meeting dismissed" (Coch and French, 1948: 251). As had happened before, "resistance developed almost immediately after the change occurred, such as conflict with the methods engineer, expressions of hostility against the supervisor, deliberate restriction of production, and lack of cooperation with the supervisor. There were 17 percent quits in the first forty days. Grievances were filed" (Coch and French, 1948: 522). The group was also found to have increased its cohesion around a new common enemy (management) and a new common goal (resisting top-down change).

One experimental group (pajama folders) was shown two garments that had been produced one year apart and was asked to identify the garment that was 50 percent cheaper. The fact that this could not be done defined the problem for the workers, and they resolved as a group "that a savings could be effected by removing the 'frills' and 'fancy' work from the garment" (Coch and French, 1948: 251). Management then proposed a study of the job, a redesign of work, and special training for a group of workers who would then train others. The worker-trainers were convened separately, and "immediately presented many good suggestions" (Coch and French, 1948: 251). The new job was redesigned (the trainers referred to it as "our job") and the worker-trainers trained the rest of the force in new pajama-folding methods. Groups 2 and 3, which were smaller, participated together as a whole group. Coch and French note that "in the meetings with these two groups, suggestions were immediately made in such quantity that the stenographer had great difficulty in recording them" (1948: 521-522).

All groups did well, but "direct participation" groups (2 and 3) did better than the first group ("representative participation"). Control subjects were later regrouped for participatory change and also did well. Their attitudes and group norms shifted from resistant to congenial and change supportive.

Lewin's studies are scientifically priceless, but their goal was arguably unenlightened. Lewin's sponsor (the Food Habits Committee of the National Research Council) was concerned with undermining resistance to cooking with strange (but available) ingredients. Coch, French, and Marrow wanted to retool pajama production. In both cases, participation was a way of neutralizing unfavorable attitudes toward change. There was no concern with tapping creativity or ingenuity, though ideas of pajama workers were obtained and recorded; worker morale improved, but no one was concerned with cementing workers' loyalty or contributing to their personal development. The paradigm is to use participation to promote change; the impact of participatory change on participants was gravy in Lewin's dish. To explore this process, we must turn from postwar pajama problems to those of modern schools.

School Power

We have already implied that some managers institute participation because they are philosophically committed to it (see

Chapter 9). This means that they prize participation as an ethic or as a strategy that is congruent with their view of human nature. Such managers argue that formal and informal power are inversely related. They maintain (if pressed) that workers who are given autonomy are likely to work harder and/or better than those who are told what to do. They admit that autonomous workers determine the nature and direction of their activities. In the *aggregate,* however, the organization better serves the manager, whose job it is to generate quality work.

As an example, in a school system teachers design curricula, screen colleagues, prepare schedules and budgets, and negotiate with the board of education. According to an observer:

> Bruce [Caldwell, the superintendent of Mansfield, CT schools] has full faith in the principle he practices. The teaching staff, he feels, will do its best work as partners of the superintendent rather than as subordinates. With joint responsibility for the educational enterprise, teachers have a big stake in its success. In their classrooms, Mansfield teachers are testing the validity of their own judgments, not the decrees of a higher official. In these circumstances, Bruce believes, the creative resources of teachers can best be put to work [Weingust, 1980: 503].

In this type of participation (unlike that of Lewin, Coch, and French), change goals are not predetermined. In Mansfield, it is "obvious that teachers are making crucial decisions about the program of studies" (Weingust, 1980: 504). This is no abrogation of management (the Mansfield superintendent is consulted and viewed as a strong, charismatic leader), but there is an abrogation of classic top-down control. Weingust notes that "teacher power is a fact in Mansfield. Not the economic-political variety . . . but in terms of fundamental authority to shape and operate the program of studies" (1980: 506). "Power" means potency rather than control. It means that teachers face organizational problems and help to solve them. Such participation results in a merging of the organization's goals with those of individuals. Weingust reports that "again and again in talking with teachers I heard them refer to their 'ownership' in the schools' program. They [the teachers] are proud of their accomplishments" (1980: 506). The process generates group norms, but these are composites of individual acts of creativity and problem solving. Each worker knows that he or she has made—and can make—contributions that matter. (In the words of a Mansfield teacher, "I feel more respect as a person now" [Weingust, 1980: 506]). Such feelings encourage future contributions that develop the individual's problem-solving capacities and his or her organizations's capacity to change.

A more ambitious program of this kind is reported by Comer (1980) in an exciting book called *School Power*. The program covered an inner-city system in New Haven, Connecticut. Its main target was a school with long-standing and horrendous academic deficiencies and disciplinary and morale problems. Comer's assumption was that "the authoritarian management structure and style still present in many schools make it difficult for the school or school staff to address the problems which lead to poor student and staff performance" (1980: 39). Again, the issue of "power" arises not as formal control, but as a right people should have to help shape their environment and to design and influence change. In the words of Comer,

> You do not decrease distrust and alienation by simply moving the source of total power from one group . . . to another. This simply changes the location of power monopoly problems. It can best be done by enabling all persons and groups involved in a program to participate in decision-making; with the important stipulation that no person or group can be allowed to paralyze the person responsible for making the final decison, the person responsible for the program outcome—usually the school principal [1980: 69].

Each principal worked with a "representative management group" of teachers, parents, and (in more advanced schools) students. This group was charged with "a coordinated process of planning, identifying school problems and opportunities, establishing goals, mobilizing resources and developing problem-solving and skill development programs, evaluating these programs, and modifying them in response to evaluation findings on an ongoing basis" (Comer, 1980: 39). Other means of participation were available to parents and teachers, including regular summer workshops in which academic and extracurricular experiments were planned. Parents became individually involved—to the extent their time and skill level permitted—in work as roommothers and tutors, in activities in playrooms, lunchrooms, and libraries, and in outings, parties, and other special projects. Mixed membership committees planned and ran a variety of routine functions. Parent representatives were included on committees that screened and hired new staff.

"Teacher autonomy" was a component of program design. Comer writes:

> The notion of teacher autonomy was a shorthand prescription to remedy the fact that the classroom teacher is on the front line dealing with problems and opportunities on a day-to-day basis; nobody seems to pay too much attention to what he or she has to say about curriculum, school organization and procedures. Yet teachers are often blamed when students fail. . . .

> It appeared to me that this situation must stifle teacher interest in analyzing learning difficulties of particular children and developing creative ways to present material. I felt that this was part of the reason that some teachers become bored, lose their imagination and excitement, and become listless especially when the children, parents, and administrators all appear to be in a conspiracy, in one way or another, to promote teacher failure. I concluded that teacher powerlessness was more the problem than ineffective teaching methods or negative attitudes [1980: 149].

One gambit was to fund teacher proposals for classroom-based projects justified in terms of philosophy, practicality, and relevance and thoroughly reviewed by peer committees. Other teachers "developed innovative approaches on their own" (Comer, 1980: 156), sometimes as teams. More comprehensive programs were approved by advisory committees composed of teachers and parents. Expert consultants could be used if/when teachers felt they needed specialized help.

Outcome data showed increments in academic performance, attendance, and discipline. In 1969, the elementary school was 18 to 19 months behind the national average in reading and mathematics scores; this gap had closed to a two-month lag after program involvement. Attendance rose from abysmal to 94.5

percent; disciplinary problems became rare. Comer concludes that "in our program we demonstrated that when leaders share power wisely and appropriately, both parents and teachers can develop a sense of program ownership and pride" (1980: 234). "Ownership and pride" refer to programs that promote student-centered problem solving; it is assumed by Comer (1980) that the entire school community shared this goal. It is also assumed that community members shared (and prized) each other, as fellow developers of children and as partners in change.

Participation or Cooptation?

Some settings—such as those of Marxist self-managed or capitalist worker-owned industries—take terms such as "control," "power," and "ownership" very literally. In such organizations the workers work for themselves and managers are merely delegated to represent them. More psychological "ownership" or "power" is discounted; it would be argued that each manager giveth—and by implication, taketh—power that ultimately rests among employers and higher-level bureaucrats. In other organizations, "power" is no concern of consequence. Issues revolve around "consultation," "involvement," and "input from below." Participation follows planning as an appendage; it is designed to "sell," to ensure acceptability, and to reduce resistance.

Selecting a philosophy of participation presupposes that one has views about alienation (see Chapters 2 and 4) and about how it comes into existence and can be neutralized. Comer argued that

> a representative management group can reduce the distrust, alienation and acting-out behavior between home and school and among staff and students which plague the modern school. Parents and staff can again reinforce each other, enabling staff to serve as parent surrogates. The expectations and climate of a school functioning in this way can be changed from one of suspicion and conflict to one in which most people expect and work for the successful attainment of goals which they helped establish [1980: 40].

Alienation finds its targets inside and outside organizations. Such targets spell conflict. We know, for example, that in alienation-infested schools, the more

> alienated teacher is not only responding to the rituals of her supervisor—such as demands for lesson plans—but also to the behavioral problems of her dissatisfied students; the truant may not only be reacting to discontinuity between street and classroom, but also to the impatience, disinterest, and hostility of his disaffected teacher. This suggests that as part of the alienated premise, each group sees others as representatives of the alienating system; and they do this with consistent mutuality" [Toch, 1979: 5].

This implies that "it may not be far-fetched to suggest that alienation breeds counteralienation, though different components of an alienated system manifest qualitative differences. Thus, the absent worker and his pressured supervisor, the hippie son of the discontented middle-class parent, the unhappy student and teacher produce and recycle each other" (Toch, 1979: 6). If this view is accepted, "our hope for change may lie in the possibility of undermining the premise of each alienated group that *other* groups or segments of a particular institution are agents of total power, and that one's own group is powerless and suppressed" (Toch, 1979: 6). The means to achieve this end would include

> manageable segments, such as (1) highlighting areas of personal discretion and responsibility people do not realize they have; (2) inducing inquiry into restraining and facilitation properties of concrete situations that people face; (3) arranging preliminary proofs of competence in tied-down tasks; (4) staging problem-solving meetings with other groups or segments in the institution; (5) opening up opportunities for people to design and submit self-generated interventions; (6) encouraging individual participation in the implementation of group-generated policies [Toch, 1979: 6].

A program of this kind is described by Comer. It not only reduced alienation but affected *consequences* of alienation such as truancy and misbehavior, burnout, poor teaching and learning, and nonsupport of schools.

Marxists trace alienation to people's non-ownership of "means of production." Transposed, this means, "Who runs (owns) the schools?" It means that alienation survives until the community, students, or both control the school enterprise, set policy, and "run the show." Participation means votes, dominance, purse strings, decisions—in short, political and economic power. Short of revolutionary change, "power structures" are preserved, making some (students, teachers, parents) powerless, and others (the educational establishment) omnipotent and alienating.

A contrasting view is that undisguised exercises of power (driving forces) invite resentment (resisting forces) and bring alienation (tension). Persons who are thus managed (change targets) must be involved in change *only* so that their feelings (resisting forces) can be addressed. Groups in which change problems can be discussed and courses of action confirmed can create support for change.

Different emphasis and variations suggest that "participation" is a continuum within which one "takes one's pick," based on assumptions about the problem to be addressed and the goals to be achieved. Here, as elsewhere, one expert's meat is (but probably need not be) another's poison.

CHAPTER 11

RECEPTIVITY TO CHANGE

None of us is uniformly ready to become involved. If we truly participated in every facet of our existence we would (1) be spread exceedingly thin, (2) have to rehearse expertise or pretend interest when we have neither, and (3) act when we feel insecure or un-self-sufficient. The dictum "Thou shalt participate" applied across the board exposes those who care to the insecure posturing and wallowing of those who go through the motions because they feel obligated to get involved. The experience of participation would thus be diluted and the products of participation cheapened to the point at which discouragement is inevitable.

But each of us can easily play a role *somewhere*, in some area in which we feel competent. Each of us can thus affect policy in some setting that has meaning for us. It also matters that settings that affect people's lives have enough participants to ensure that they remain responsive. The absence of participation is corrosive. McGregor's point (see Chapter 3) matters. As he put it, Theory X management molds Theory X minds, and helplessness and insecurity deepen. This corrosion applies to nonwork settings (where we let elites arbitrate our tastes and arrange our affairs), but it is most consequential in organizations in which we work.

The premise behind McGregor's point is that the inability to participate is a conditioned response. A person may not be ready to play a participatory role because a life of continued dependence has not prepared him or her to play such a role. Nonreadiness for participation means that opportunities must be supplemented (or damage must be undone) before adult personal autonomy can be exercised.

We are also alerted to sequencing (see Chapter 3) in regard to work motivation. "Development" implies that a person's lower needs must be satisfied before his or her higher needs can develop and assert themselves. A worker who has faced starvation or is afraid to lose his or her job would be a poor candidate for experimentation. Risk taking is also unlikely if the worker *feels* insecure, though he or she has no "objective" basis for such feelings.

Is Job Enrichment "Ethnomorphism"?

Some students reject the argument (which no one makes) that workers are uniformly prime candidates for job enrichment. A variation of this charge is that middle-class professionals "project" enrichment needs into lower-class persons who, *if they are left alone*, prefer nonenriched jobs. Hulin writes that

> the ethnomorphising of the white middle class social scientists, executives, and managers may be as responsible for the job enrichment thesis as any set of data. That is, these influential individuals, starting with Adam Smith, with their years of education and their frame of reference developed by exposure to the academic environment and administrative jobs respond negatively to a routine job and make the assumption that all mature, healthy workers will do the same [1971: 165].

Such arguments invite the countercharge that pinpointed reforms would systematically let "the rich get richer" and condemn the most underprivileged workers to monotonous drudgery. The *Work in America* task force thus asserts:

> This problem of a fairly static occupation structure presents society with a formidable barrier to providing greater job satisfaction to *those below the pinnacle of the job pyramid*. Without a technological revolution there is little hope of flattening out this structure in order to give more workers higher-status jobs. It then becomes crucial to infuse *middle- and lower-level jobs* with professional characteristics, particularly if we plan to continue offering higher and higher degrees of education to young people on the assumption that their increased expectations can be met by the world of work [1973: 20, emphasis added].

Herzberg (1966) favors enrichment for most workers, but does not feel it "becomes crucial to infuse . . . jobs with professional characteristics." To Herzberg, professionalization is a reactionary (impoverishing) trend. In his own words (1966: 184):

> Paradoxically, the leaping trend toward professionalism, characteristic of more and more occupations, is acting as a force restricting the enhancement of the motivators of work. Professionalism, once a sign of true competence and dedication to excellence in performance, has now become a synonym for gathering the harvest of the hygiene factors of status and money. . . .
>
> The number of occupations that are seeking professionalization is equal to the number of organizations that hold meetings. . . . In the process, the motivator satisfaction, and in particular the pride of craftsmanship, is lost.

Hulin (1971) assumes that middle-class persons generally favor enrichment. They do so because they endorse the "protestant work ethic," which values *work* as opposed to the *money* work earns or the *avoidance* of work. Hulin refers to one study in which

> people were asked if they would continue to work if they suddenly inherited enough money so they no longer needed to. The majority, 80%, said they would. However, the percentage of people who said they would not continue to work increased steadily from the white collar workers, to the skilled workers, and finally to the unskilled workers, with only 50% of the unskilled workers expressing a desire to continue working. . . . .
>
> The study . . . provides evidence that work has different meanings within the different subcultures (defined by job levels) of the United States. Work is likely to be seen as a means to an economic end by the unskilled worker, while it has intrinsic meaning for the white collar worker [1971: 168].

A twist to this argument accuses *urban* lower-class persons of not only lacking "work ethic," but of goading each other to actively reject it. This inference derives from the finding that rural workers (who are preclassified as culturally "integrated") report themselves satisfied when their jobs improve, whereas workers who come from large cities seem dissatisfied with all jobs, and sometimes more dissatisfied with better jobs. Hulin (1971: 168) admits that this chain of cultural explanation takes "an unnecessarily indirect approach to the problem." His solution is to forget about explanations and to let the chips fall where they may. This means that "one should start with the viewpoint that different workers may well be motivated by strikingly different job characteristics and [that] we should design jobs accordingly" (Hulin, 1971: 188). If a worker (who just happens to be a white-collar professional) responds gratefully to enrichment, his or her job should be enriched; if a worker likes being a drone, or if he or she is alienated (and happens to be urban lower class), he or she had best be left alone.

Sorting Geese from Ganders

Hackman and Oldham's Job Diagnostic Inventory (which we described in Chapter 5) is commended by experts who favor dispassionate screening of job enrichment candidates. Wanaus (1976: 20), among others, asserts that the method "is aimed directly at the heart of the issue (that is, how closely job characteristics are associated with job enrichment)." The general contention is that if a worker prizes enriched aspects of work (if he or she scores high on Growth Need Strength on the JDI) he or she will bloom under job enrichment measured by the Motivating Potential Score (MPS) of the JDI. It helps if the worker is also satisfied (or not dissatisfied) with lower-order job features, because "when employees are not satisfied with their pay, job security, co-workers, and/or supervisors, their ability to respond positively to a job high in objective motivating potential may be severely diminished" (Oldham, Hackman, and Pearce, 1976: 396).

The case is usually not validated by enriching the jobs of workers and seeing how they respond. The procedure instead is to rate people's work situations and their responses to them. In such concurrent research the "results suggest that individuals are most likely to perform well on an enriched job when they are desirous of growth satisfactions and satisfied with the organization's internal environment" (Oldham et al., 1976: 400-401). The research also suggests that "if an individual has low growth need strength and is dissatisfied with work context, a complex job may have an *adverse* effect on that person's performance" (Oldham et al., 1976: 401, emphasis added).

One implication is that enrichment is *counter*indicated where workers grouse about their pay, their fringe benefits, and their job security. This inference is understandable in Maslowian terms. It can mean that workers who are obsessed with security or pay would be "simultaneously distracted from whatever richness exists in the work itself (because of their dissatisfaction with contextual factors) and oriented toward satisfactions other than those that come from effective performance on enriched tasks" (Oldham et al., 1976: 397).

The correlation between desire for job enrichment and responsiveness to job enrichment makes sense, but the desire for impoverishment does not. Why should some workers prefer uninteresting work? The question matters, because the way we answer it determines whether we listen to antienrichment workers and leave them alone, or persist in efforts to change their work and their attitudes toward work.

Is Nonenrichment Humane or Dangerous to Mental Health?

In the words of John Morse (1973: 72), the *facts* are that

members of organizations doing relatively certain tasks tended to be comfortable in relatively dependent authority relations, preferred structured and highly coordinated work patterns, had a lower ability to cope with rapidly changing and ambiguous situations and preferred to work on uncomplex cognitive problems. Members of organizations doing relatively uncertain tasks tended to prefer autonomy and independence in their authority relations, liked working on individualistic problems independently of others, preferred rapidly changing and ambiguous settings and thrived on tackling complex cognitive problems.

The *issue* these facts relate to is that "humanistic values recognize, respect and account for differences in individuals. Humanizing work is work that is motivating to the individual and suited to his behavioral preferences" (Morse, 1973: 74). But what are a person's "behavioral preferences"? If he or she compromises or gives up, must we take this reaction at face value? The NIMH task force (1973) quotes conclusions of a classic study (Kornhauser) to the effect that "the unsatisfactory mental health of working people consists in no small measure of their dwarfed desires and deadened initiative, reduction of their goals, and restriction of their efforts to a point where life is relatively empty and only half meaningful."[1] The NIMH task force characterizes this as a "Catch-22" in which "there are only two options: to maintain high expectations from work, and thereby suffer constant frustration, or limit . . . expectations, which produces a drab existence" (Special Task Force, 1973: 85). Though the task force admits that "the findings . . . show that workers in these low-level jobs adapt by limiting their expectations," it concludes that "the greatest mental health deficit suffered by these workers is lack of involvement in the job and, consequently, lack of self-fulfillment" (Special Task Force, 1973: 82).

This view—which is similar to McGregor's thesis—postulates a vicious cycle in which autocratic management and stultifying jobs produce self-limiting resignation or blind revolt. This is a *cycle* because both adaptations are inhospitable to reform. The "Humanistic" implication would *not* be to accept the situation, but to break the destructive cycle. This could be done (1) through disconfirmation, (2) by promoting new adaptive modes, and (3) by bridging from stressful contexts to opportunity structures. We know enough to expect (at least, initially) resistance to such effort, but would not see such resistance as the last word in "behavioral preferences."

Hulin and other differential enrichment students trace low-growth need strength to cultural values. They argue that humanism must respect such values because those who reject the importance of work have a right to their (nonwork ethic) views. Since workers must work, nonwork is not an option. What is an option is to see that workers are well compensated and fairly treated. Part of fairness means that no efforts may be made to force such workers into attachment to work.

Whence Alienation?

The cultural explanation poses new questions. If urban, unskilled, alienated workers have non-middle-class "subcultural" views, where do such views originate? Unless subcultural values (e.g., disinterest in work) are biologically produced, they must be products of experience that is shared by members of the subculture. Morse (1973: 73) provides a clue to what such experience could be when he defines enriched work as being responsive to persons who are "motivated to perform successfully to gain feelings of competence." Morse argues in more detail about motives that "if an individual values the reward he expects to receive for a higher level of performance and if he perceives that it is highly probable that his increased effort will result in that reward, then he will increase his effort—he will be more motivated" (1973: 70).

If groups in the community have life chances and opportunities that are so badly stacked against them that they could *not* perceive "that it is highly probable that increased effort will result in reward," then they would obviously come to see little point in effort; similarly, if such groups did not enjoy experiences of "successful performance" that yield "feelings of competence," then they would not pursue competent performance as a goal. If a group that feels this way about life generally rejects the "protestant work ethic," then theirs is an appropriate view of the life that they themselves have led. This life may be (and is) unfair, disadvantageous, and negatively skewed. But work settings need not be, and catering to the (alienated) inferences of disadvantageousness may make them so.

Neutralizing Alienation

The emphasis to which we are invited to attend by Hulin and other students of work shifts our attention from job enrichment to participatory job enrichment. This is so because the alienated state of mind that Hulin describes is an extreme Theory X state of mind, which is produced by Theory X life experiences or perceptions of experience. The dimensions of alienation we reviewed in Chapter 2 (powerlessness, meaninglessness, self-estrangement, and the like) are the antithesis of democracy. The NIMH task force points out that alienation at work "is inherent in pyramidal, bureaucratic management patterns and in advanced, Taylorized technology, which divides and subdivides work into minute, monotonous elements" (Special Task Force, 1973: 22).

Once this point is digested, it affects the distinction between societal explanations and those that stress work pressures. The two realms of experience (stultifying life experience and experience with autocratic work settings) can be congruent. The two can merge; they can confirm and supplement each other and reinforce alienation. The slum dwellers approach their places on the assembly line expecting to feel used and helpless, and they view paternalistic work reform as a variation on this theme. They prefer their impoverished jobs because they know they can do them. The jobs demand minimal surface effort (to be grudgingly expended for pay), but leave soul and integrity inviolate, carry no risk, and demand no investment. The alienated workers feel "set up" through enrichment; they see no point to challenge because they "know" themselves to be incompetent and unable to achieve. They expect impoverishment because they know that the world (including work) is meaningless and unrewarding.

It does not follow that the alienated workers' jobs cannot be enriched no matter what. It does follow that the jobs cannot be enriched without first dealing with the world view that defines enrichment as cooptation or as an invitation to defeat.

Involving the Alienated

The alienated respond to top-down enrichment by playing along with it, retreating, or circumventing their licensed mandate. In a pointed and touching vignette from an institution for the mentally retarded, attendants are depicted grousing to a reporter while a patient has been left locked in and abandoned—seemingly indefinitely—in a freezing shower. As the scene unfolds,

Another man joined the group. He was jaunty, both in dress and step. His bright clothing was topped off with a feathered wide-brimmed cap. His eyes appeared glazed.

He said he was in charge.

The first man kept talking, repeating that he and his peers had the knowledge and the concern to work with the retarded. The shower continued.

Isn't it time she came out? "Can't do that, man. She in a bad way. Need special handling," responded the second man.

A woman who appeared to be in her late thirties or early forties came down the corridor. She was older than the other employees. She was dressed in a white uniform. Her face was grim.

She told the second man to unlock the shower door. He was reluctant to do so, and mumbled something about it not being a good time. She repeated the order.

This time he unlocked the door and swung it open. She walked into the shower and ushered the young woman out, an arm around her shoulders.

The older woman led her away. The young woman's eyes, her demeanor reminded the reporter more of a frightened, helpless animal than a time bomb about to go off.

Why couldn't you do that? the attendants were asked.

"It take special knowledge," said the second man [Albany Times Union, May 5, 1975].

The attitude of these attendants stands in contrast to the response of psychiatric attendants to the enrichment experiments described in Chapter 6. The statement "it takes special knowledge" is insidiously self-confirming, because the workers act on this assumption rather than on the claim "we have the knowledge and the concern to work with the retarded," which is made for public consumption. The worker has no real concern for clients, and the mandate "thou shalt be concerned" is someone else's (top-down) definition calling for congruent verbal compliance, rather than for a value to be internalized and embodied in conduct.

One reason for this relates to the setting, and the other to the worker. The setting speaks with a forked tongue, accompanying an enrichment message with structural messages (professionals in white coats) that affirm hierarchical lines of authority. The worker sees the structure as an extension of a power-centered world. In such a world, success consists of exploiting loopholes for fringe benefits, working as little as one can, and asserting one's autonomy through posturing and pretense.

Surveillance and discipline intensify ingenuity, invite confrontation, and increase tension. Choosing congenial staff, i.e., selection, (1) presupposes a mythical pool of willing unalienated workers, and (2) creates a predestined underclass of persons whose feelings of powerlessness are confirmed.

The remaining formula is double-pronged. It builds security (reduces dissatisfaction with context) through material incentives and training, personal backing, and organizational support. As workers respond, it offers responsibility and self-directed enrichment where the worker has enough interest to explore the possibility of graduated experiences of success.

The Sequencing Issue

The task as we describe it is not all or none (a choice of enriching some and not enriching others), but involves decisions about whom to enrich when, how, and how much. The goal is that of maximizing the availability of enrichment opportunities that can be effectively pursued.

Part of the problem is one of sequencing. Sequencing means that opportunities must be orchestrated or arranged so that they respond to evolving interests and match each person's level of skill and self-confidence. It also means that one must start with workers who can better afford to take risks, but can also serve as models for those who feel hesitant, afraid, or vulnerable. Sequencing does *not* mean enriching the work of congenial workers and leaving "tough customers" (alienated workers) behind. Such sequencing creates a stratified society designed to cement alienated perspectives.

A second point is that enrichment for non-enrichment-oriented workers must mean "involvement in enrichment" rather than "benefiting workers through designed enrichment." This holds *particularly* for workers who already feel suspicious, powerless, and vulnerable, and who think themselves to be incompetent. It goes back to a basic change-related dictum—a truism established by John Dewey and Carl Rogers that *pre*definition of change implies "I (the change agent) am competent and you (the change target) are not." Predesign also implies that real power (which is a commodity that can be benevolently as well as destructively exercised) remains unrelinquished by those in charge.

Participating is particularly critical *because* workers are alienated. For one, disinterest in enrichment is a resistance to change. In this way, it is no different from disinterest in sweetbreads or in mechanized pajama production (see Chapter 10). Participation means bringing to the surface and exploring reasons for reluctance. It means sorting reasons into those reservations that can be addressed and those carryover fears that—given the right circumstances—can be laid aside. It means deciding—publicly, on one's own volition—to take risks, and it means having group support for one's decision and the risk-taking actions that may follow.

Participation means pacing one's change, provided one gets the support one needs to take each step along the way. In other words, participation calibrates sequencing. Participation serves as a barometer that tells the change agent what workers feel ready for, what they want, and what they feel capable of.

Participation does not mean *self*-enrichment. It is a play without a script, but it requires staging, props, and an audience. There is a need for structure to keep the show on the road and to ensure a defensible performance. There must be quality control in the form of research (see Chapter 12), incentives in the form of feedback, and bridging to the work setting. The formal organization and its technology must be accommodated, and it must learn to accommodate enrichment.

Participation must be formally initiated, and this means that there is a catalytic role to be played. Someone must legitimize the game, select the players, and throw in the first ball. In this connection, the initial resistance of workers (low growth needs, context dissatisfactions, reservations about the work ethic, and so on) may prove inconsequential compared to resistance by bureaucrats who see no need for enrichment and have no faith in the enrichment potential of workers—*especially* of workers who have no faith in their own potential.

In Chapter 13 we shall outline a strategy for involving alienated workers in work enrichment. We leave the problem of "How do we convince bureaucrats of little faith?" to those wiser (but less sad) than ourselves.

NOTE

1. Kornhauser (1965) suggested, as did Caplan et al. (1975), that structured, repetitive work had health and mental health repercussions, including psychological and psychosomatic disturbances. In more recent studies in England, Broadbent (1978) has shown that older persons working in fragmented, tightly managed jobs tend to age more rapidly than other workers, with more substantial deterioration of cognitive skills and capacities.

CHAPTER 12

RESEARCH, ACTION, AND ACTION RESEARCH

Frederick Taylor, whose ghost has cast a pall over the work humanization movement, nevertheless had refreshing things to say about job designing. One of his perspicacious observations was a casual self-effacing remark about his own performance on the golf course. Taylor wrote,

> I wish it were possible to convey to you an adequate impression of some of the beautiful movements that I have been working up during the past year. The only possible drawback to them is that the ball still refuses to settle down quietly into the cup, as it ought to, and also in most cases declines to go either in the direction that I wish or the required distance. Aside from these few drawbacks, the theories are perfect [cited in Kakar, 1970: 168-169].

Planned change may be plausible and elegant—or, in Taylor's terms, "beautiful"—but it may transfer imperfectly from the sandbox to the sandpit. Unless implementation of "beautiful" theory is followed by fact finding, change agents can overlook cues that tell them how to revise and/or supplement their plans to accommodate the complexities of life. Not only can they fail to discover that "the ball refuses to settle down quietly into the cup," but they may fail to give themselves credit for their successes. Since we learn both through failure and from success, our continued effectiveness as change agents, on the golf course and elsewhere, hinges on our ability to keep track of change results and on our willingness to revise our plans to accommodate our experiences.

This point may sound trite, but the fact that it *needs* to be stressed has been traditionally recognized in applied social science. One of the most painstaking sermons on the issue was delivered by Kurt Lewin, the most influential figure in our field. Lewin diagnosed the problem very similarly to Taylor, though he drew his illustration from experiences of community developers rather than of golfers:

> When the inter-group worker, coming home from the good-will meeting which he helped to instigate, thinks of the dignitaries he was able to line up, the stirring appeals he heard, the impressive setting of the stage, and the good quality of the food, he cannot help feeling elated by the general atmosphere and the words of praise from his friends all around. Still, a few days later, when the next case of discrimination becomes known, he often wonders whether all this was more than a white-wash and whether he is right in accepting the acknowledgement of his friends as a measuring stick for the progress of his work [Lewin, 1946: 202].

The question, said Lewin, is should the change agent feel encouraged or discouraged? Can he or she conclude anything from his or her experience? Lewin wrote,

> In a field that lacks objective standards of achievement, no learning can take place. If we cannot judge whether an action has led forward or backward, if we have no criteria for evaluating the reaction between effort and achievement, there is nothing to prevent us from making the wrong conclusions and to encourage the wrong work habits. Realistic fact-finding and evaluation [are] a prerequisite for any learning. Social research should be one of the top priorities for a practical job of improving inter-group relations [Lewin, 1946: 202].

What makes this reiterated point—this trusim—fundamental is that it has corollaries that define the relationship between parties involved in change. One corollary links the golfer or group worker with the researcher or fact finder through a chain of interdependent steps that improve the person's golf game or skill in community relations (contribute to learning) while they tell us more about golf or community change (contribute to knowledge). The intimacy of the link rests in a design in which research always answers change-relevant questions and always informs revisions of change theories or plans. Similarly, change technology always builds on research as it goes along. One way to think about this is to envisage "loops" in which research provides "feedback" to the change agent, who provides "input" to the researcher. At a minimum this requires that reformers and researchers work closely together; but it can also mean (as we shall see) that the roles of change agent and fact finder are combinable.

To describe the change/research relationship, Lewin coined the term "action research." More specifically, he said, "The research needed for social practice can best be characterized as research for social management or social engineering. It is a type of action, a comparative research on the conditions and effects of various forms of social action, and research leading to social action." Lewin added somewhat snidely, "Research that produces nothing but books will not suffice" (1947: 202-203).

Lewin outlined an action research *sequence* and described a *team structure* for getting the job done. In relation to the sequence, Lewin wrote

> Planning starts usually with something like a general idea. For one reason or another it seems desirable to reach a certain objective. Exactly how to circumscribe this objective, and how to reach it, is frequently not too clear. The first step then is to examine the idea carefully in the light of the means available. Frequently more fact-finding about the situation is required. If this first period of planning is successful, two items emerge: namely, an "overall plan" of how to reach the objective and secondly, a decision in regard to the first step of action. Usually this planning has also somewhat modified the original idea.

> The next period is devoted to executing the first step of the overall plan.

> In highly developed fields of social management, such as modern factory management or the execution of a war, this second step is followed by certain fact-findings. For example, in the bombing of Germany a certain factory may have been chosen as the first target after careful consideration of various priorities and of the best means and ways of dealing with this target. The attack is pressed home and immediately a reconnaissance plane follows with the one objective of determining as accurately and objectively as possible the new situation.

This reconnaissance or fact-finding has four functions. First it should evaluate the action. It shows whether what has been achieved is above or below expectation. Secondly, it gives the planners a chance to learn, that is, to gather new general insight, for instance, regarding the strength and weakness of certain weapons or techniques of action. Thirdly, this fact-finding should serve as a basis for correctly planning the next step. Finally, it serves as a basis for modifying the "over-all plan."

The next step again is composed of a circle of planning, executing, and reconnaissance or fact-finding for the purpose of evaluating the results of the second step, for preparing the rational basis for planning the third step, and for perhaps modifying again the overall plan.

Rational social management, therefore, proceeds in a spiral of steps each of which is composed of a circle of planning, action, and fact-finding about the result of the action [Lewin, 1947: 205-206]

Though Lewin insisted that action research must not "in any respect" be "less scientific or 'lower' " than "pure" social research (1947: 203), he did not conceive of independent research entities looking over the shoulders of change agents. "Socially," Lewin wrote, "it does not suffice that university organizations produce new scientific insight. It will be necessary to install fact-finding procedures, social eyes and ears, right into social action bodies" (1947: 206). Lewin's prescription called for two special ingredients; it presupposed (1) that organizational change agents could be oriented to see the value of knowledge and be receptive to it, and (2) that social scientists could respond to the needs and concerns of practitioners. Lewin's model ultimately called for "the training of large numbers of social scientists who can handle scientific problems but are also equipped for the delicate task of building productive, hard-hitting teams with practitioners" (1947: 211).

Variations on Lewin's action research formula envisage "in-house" researchers in organizations. Others provide substantial change roles to researchers and knowledge-building roles to agents and clients involved in change.

Research as Change Catalyst

Lewin saw knowledge as the honest broker of action, but also as a way of motivating people to act. In 1919, Lewin—whose father owned a farm—became concerned about ineffective farming. He wrote a paper in which he prescribed research to be done cooperatively by farmers and professional psychologists to improve the design of hoes and other farm equipment. One assumes that one aim of such cooperation is to motivate farmers to apply the lessons of research. In Lewinian parlance, self-generated knowledge would "unfreeze" knowledge seekers by undermining their prejudices.

The process is illustrated in a famous case study of social action research reported by Marrow and French (1945). Alfred Marrow—the president of the pajama factory we discussed in Chapter 10, and J.R.P. French, Jr.—a psychologist working for Marrow—were both students of Lewin. The issue of concern to them was the role of knowledge in resistance to change and the impotence of second-hand information compared to the unfreezing power of inquiry that is shaped and carried out by resisting persons themselves. Research used in this way does not operate to document or to guide change, but is a change strategy itself.

The problem Marrow consulted French about was the refusal of his supervisory employees to recognize the potential of some of their subordinates (in this case, older workers)—an obvious barrier to job enrichment. As a corporate president, Marrow could have confronted or bullied his resistant staff; instead, he and French suggested "a modest research project—to determine how much money the company was *losing* [!] through the employment of older women" (Marrow and French, 1945: 34; emphasis added). Not only were effectiveness indices advanced by managers used as criteria in this study, but "the group was fully questioned to make certain that no important criteria were omitted." Moreover, "all the methods of collecting data about these criteria came from the management." The research is a beautiful example of staff involvement through participation,

and it promoted commitment to the findings of the study. We are
told that the managers "were both excited and pleased at having
participated in this important discovery which had become their
own" (Marrow and French, 1945: 35).

So much for the good news. The bad news emerged (or
reemerged) subsequently, when *non*involved staff members were
presented with the data and resoundingly refused to accept them.
The implication is that the *process* of research is as important as its
product. It is in this sense that Lewin's "research in action"
translates into "*action* research," meaning changing through
participation in question asking, knowledge gathering, and
digestion of results. In Marrow and French's words, "facts are
useful only when the [resistant staff member] himself is reoriented
in his search for a new solution" (1947: 37).

The first Lewinian action research model we have described is
one in which the innovator uses research to monitor and guide the
process of change. A second model involved the target of change in
research, so as to secure his or her consent and partnership. This
process has been eloquently advocated by Chris Argyris (1970).
Argyris sees organic (participatory) research as a way of increasing
the competence of the people to be changed, of ensuring a
nondependent status for them, and as a way of guaranteeing that
the diagnosis on which change is based incorporates their
perception. These issues are particularly important when the goal
of change is to promote staff development and growth. A change
agent using a "canned" instrument risks insulting the intelligence
of workers, gaining limited trust, eliciting superficial responses,
and cementing feelings of powerlessness. If instead the
interventionist asks workers what should be researched, he or she
defines a researcher/subject relationship characterized by
mutuality and shared concern for problem solving.

Where participation is precluded, Argyris recommends
openness, disclosure, and feedback opportunities. The point is not
only to reduce suspicions, but to promote an understanding of the
purpose of inquiry and a feeling that one's concerns are attended
to. Argyris notes that reformers often see research as the tail that

aspires to wag the dog, while researchers see reformers as knowledge-resistant dinosaurs. Such problems cannot be solved unless they are faced.

A research executive, Howard Carlson, illustrates the dilemma by recalling the facetious accusation he sometimes encountered that "some researchers have never really accepted World War II because there was no control group!" More serious for Carlson (1977: 12) is the prevalent assumption that research furnishes "the technical ability perhaps to record change but certainly not to help bring it about." This accusation is self-fulfilling, because researchers who are seen as impotent are relegated to inventorying nonvital facts and to writing reports that no one in the "real" organization reads.

Carlson, research administrator of a large enterprise (General Motors), feels that he avoids the customary fate of the researcher (being typecast as inventory taker of esoterica) by making it clear that he rejects autonomy for researchers. "Researchers," he writes, "can ill afford to sit in their offices or next to their computers designing and carrying out projects without real involvement in the line organization" (1977: 14). The Carlson formula for "involving" researchers in the organization is to involve the organization in research: "This involvement," he writes, "should not merely be token in nature, but rather an implementation, analysis or interpretation of results, and development of recommended action steps" (1977: 14). The first order of business, argues Carlson, is to set out to solve problems that are seen by staff as problems. This means research *must* be introduced "where [the organization] is 'hurting,' and aware of this in some way" (1977: 15). A second stage invokes group process (task forces and the like) in which hypotheses about what is wrong can be formulated. Groups tease out parameters that plausibly make up the guts of the problem. The importance of such variables can be confirmed or disconfirmed only through data—hence, the advent of "diagnostic" research. When research enriches diagnosis, it performs a function that we have called "self-study" (Grant, 1980): It makes it possible for problem solvers to supplement their limited personal experience (unsystematic knowledge) by pooling their experiences in the group and by enriching them with externally gathered facts. This process translates staff hunches into research questions and defines arenas for experimentation; it also leads to expanded personal horizons, learning, and growth in the groups.

When a problem has been diagnosed and a solution to the problem has been framed, we enter Lewin's realm of research as feedback. In Carlson's (1977:16) words, "The basic intent of this strategy . . . is to provide the initiators or authors of a new program with some kind of feedback mechanism that will lead to real change and needed revision in the program." Research as feedback may have two separable functions. The first (discussed by Lewin) is to realign diagnoses and prescriptions as soon as disconfirmations accumulate to ensure that interventions remain effective. The second function (stressed by Argyris) is more subtle; it aspires to what Carlson calls "a progressive change" in organizational climate. The point is to create an organization that is "open"—one that responds to changing conditions with changed behavior. In this sense, feedback can lead to *anticipations* of change, because the point is not only to react to the last loop, but to proactively affect the next one.

The ultimate feedback involves concern with *process* as well as with product. An example of such research is an experiment reported by Carlson in which task forces of assembly-line workers were charged with reducing the absenteeism of fellow-workers. Two points are made: (1) *the task force members* "showed reduced rates of absenteeism during a scheduled work period of five months after their task force participation," and (2) "none of the recommendations made by the task forces were rejected by management." Beyond the impact of task force recommendations (reduced absenteeism of fellow workers), these *process* facts tell the organization about its progress toward "openness." Process data feedback facilitates participatory, democratizing, risk-taking enterprises. In the GM experiment we thus find that "with both management and employees enthusiastic about this approach, employee task forces were set up to deal with a wide range of other operating and employee relations problems in the car division" (Carlson, 1977: 19).

Experience, Research, and Human Development

Chris Argyris (1957, 1970) sees the goal of developing problem-solving capabilities as aimed at individuals in organizations and organizations as a whole, and sees the two as linked. The argument rests on old and new assumptions about the role of the worker in the organization. At one level, the concern is still Taylor's concern—the issue is one of scientific management—but the response—having the worker evolve the "science" in management—is sharply opposed to classic management philosophy.

The classic management perspective separated science from work. The new professions described by Taylor allocated to themselves the study of work (through time motion) the design of work (through industrial engineering), and the planning of work (through management). Workers were relegated the role of *doing* work. The workers not only had sharply limited discretion, but were forbidden to think about their jobs, to raise questions about the technical and human organization of those jobs, or to worry about the "meaning" of those jobs—the jobs' contributions to the organization's product or goals. This view of workers as robots underlies much worker discontent and is a major theme in extreme manifestations of discontent such as the Lordstown strike. The obvious disrespect implicit in the model is offensive to younger workers, and the disregard of worker intelligence grates on educated workers (see Chapter 1).

The problem is obscured in human service agencies, where bureaucratic *form* (e.g., quasi-military police and hierarchies, handmaiden roles in hospitals, lesson plans and scheduling of teachers) disguises informal exercises of discretion by workers. No ambiguity, however, extends to the "science" of the work, which is relegated to academia and management. No matter how many night courses the worker takes in "the philosophy of probation," "modern policing," or "social work policies," his or her perspective is assumed to be narrow gauged. The worker faces clients on a case-by-case basis, cannot inquire into their subsequent disposition, and has no data about the pattern of services rendered by his or her organization. The worker becomes a "practitioner." By consensus his or her expertise lies in his or her experience rather than in formal knowledge. The face-saving reaction to this view is often for workers to adopt it and to make virtue of their necessity. This creates a prototypic form of reverse snobbery in which "experience" is contrasted to ivory tower irrelevance and naiveté. This view is a legitimate definition of a situation in which experience is the only form of knowledge that is available.

Experience is often a superior approximation of reality, in ways that matter. The worker *knows* that prescribed nuts do not fit bolts, or that engineer-designed arrangements translate into logistical nightmares. Data compilers and knowledge builders who are far removed from front lines may deal in lifeless abstractions whose hollowness or caricaturelike quality becomes salient at the interface of science and practice. Police officers, teachers, or correction workers justifiably resent academic and managerial sermons whose translatability into practice is dubious. They are particularly apt to resent input from sources whose disinterest (and presumed helplessness) amid the complexities, stresses, and difficulties of situational realities is obvious from the way problems are defined—from the way they are simplified, idealized, or transmuted into abstraction. Human service workers tell us that they emerge from jungles and hear themselves enjoined to cultivate manicured gardens. Where those kinds of inputs are not rejected, they are heavily discounted.

The other side of the coin relates to the contamination of "experience" as a source of knowledge. Workers perceive the results of what they do. Unimaginative workers "experience" boring jobs, clumsy workers feel stressors, rebellious workers feel squelched, and alienated workers meet alienation above, below, and around themselves. Beyond such dangers lies the issue of representativeness. Experience may sometimes be "typical" and sometimes "atypical" but the experiencer has no way of telling one from the other. The sum of experience may be different from its parts: Maldistribution of work loads is the sum of underworked and overworked staff, each nurturing his or her skewed experience of "average" workloads.

Relevant science is attuned to personal experience, respects it, and corrects for its subjectivity while prizing its specificity, concreteness, and closeness to life. The core of a *real* science of work is the experience of work. The applied scientist's role must be that of assimilator and collator, and of supplementer rather than supplanter. This stance toward experience is one that combines scientific skills (data collection and analysis) with a proficiency in group dynamics and the clinical artistry of sympathetically eliciting, verifying, and recording personal experience. The classics in the science of work, such as the Western Electric studies and the contributions of Lewin, McGregor, Herzberg, and Argyris lie in the borderland in which traditional research is combined with clinical science and group dynamics. This has been particularly emphasized by Argyris, who highlights the reconstruction of work incidents and the in-depth interviewing of individuals and groups as the methodology of choice in organizational research.

Where science reflects experience it has the power to "unfreeze" the mind (as in the Marrow and French study) because it dramatizes the limitations of experience without denying the integrity of experience. Experientially based research widens the experiencer's horizons by adding the experiences of others (and more formal sources of data where they are available) to his or her personal experience, without challenging or denying the legitimacy of experience, which injures self-esteem and promotes defensiveness. Potent feedback—feedback that leads to change—is the sort of feedback that is assimilable, is enriching rather than confronting, and is experience relevant rather than "artificial." Such feedback develops individuals who are exposed to it by enlarging their behavior repertoire, and it develops organizations by enhancing the validity and reliability of their data base.

Mind Enrichment and Job Enrichment

In most organizations, data are used by managers to assist them in "planning," which Taylor described as a chess game for managers in which workers serve as rooks and pawns. Taylor, who did not play chess, assumed that rules are built in, so that the manager with more data could prevail. Unlike modern experts, Taylor was not concerned with the manager's "openness," his or her flexibility and imaginativeness; he assumed the planner's college-trained capacity as data consumer and inference drawer. Taylor also did not worry about nonchess attributes of the game, such as the interpersonal skills deployed within management "teams."

The improvement of managerial competence and the building of management teams has become an obsessive concern of modern organizations over the last several decades; the development of managers' data utilization skills (including the interpersonal skills that go into listening to data providers and selling to data consumers) has been the key feature of the organization development (OD) landscape. The movement is really a drive for the job enrichment of managers, and the thrust has been premised on the non-Tayloristic assumption that it is *people* who manage, not the facts about work extrapolated into projections by disembodied minds. In its extreme form, the OD movement rejects scientific management—it throws out the baby (systematic knowledge) with the bathwater (static planning) and denigrates facts about work at the expense of interpersonal facts.

The OD goal is to improve the problem-solving capacity of organizations—meaning the problem-solving capacity of managers. The notion of humanizing the workplace is congenial to the OD thrust, but this does not include seeing the worker as fellow planner or problem solver. At best, OD rejects Taylor's image of the worker as pawn and prefers to think of him or her as a rook with a congenial social climate and chances of advancement.

The more we move to strategies of worker participation, to job enrichment and QWL, the more democratized our conception of science becomes. The arena of science becomes more circumscribed as we move from strategic panoramas of organizational chessboards to the concern of participatory rooks, but the mechanics of inquiry and the dynamics of experimentation are no less complex on the assembly line than in managerial boardrooms. The quality of scientific expertise that is made available to the front-line workers must thus be commensurate with the research and consulting resources that are available to managers.

The quality of work life movement is explicit about its concern for disseminating problem-solving activity. The prescription provides for groups in which workers must consider problems related to their jobs with a view to effecting improvements in working conditions. QWL groups are furnished with data—including data about the organization as a whole—to inform their deliberations. The products of QWL groups are change proposals that are evaluated by *higher* echelons; any of the projects that are implemented are conscientiously monitored. (The "independence" of this research is a limitation of QWL; there is concern with selling QWL to the world at large rather than with developing group members through participation in research design and data feedback). QWL groups use consultants whose expertise lies in promoting and facilitating problem solving, which for only some consultants includes research.

Job enrichment fosters autonomy, variety and "ownership"; it deals in esteem needs, in work products that fill producers with pride; it promotes actualization through learning. An enriched job is not "just" a job: It is a job that provides a vehicle for personal growth and development.

Knowledge building enters variously into the job enrichment model. It enters with surveys used to select program participants. It enters in the enrichment phase, where new knowledge must be obtained by workers and where they need data to make decisions and exercise options. Learning and discovery imply content; they presuppose increments of knowledge. Such increments must be work derived, so the presumption is that the knowledge must be nonclassroom learned, though academic components (such as inservice training) are not excluded. What is crucial is that *by definition* provision must be made for mind enrichment in job enrichment.

The goal of participation strategies is to circumvent chains of command in the organization, giving workers input into determining how work is to be done. The key inputs have to do with change, because participatory approaches stem from the discovery that innovations are resisted when they are imposed from above. Participation implies a data base in the shape of knowledge about change technology and about options for doing the job better. Such knowledge involves diagnosis, prescription, monitoring of outcome and feedback; it is experience based and it builds commitment to change. To the extent to which knowledge is systematically used, such strategies engage researchers with men and women at the lowest echelons of organization.

The models are variously combinable. QWL prescribes collaboration; it involves participation and, though not limited to job enrichment, concerns itself with job enrichment issues. Neither QWL nor participation are *requisites* for job enrichment (which can be management sponsored), but the enriched worker is *participation prone*, not only because he or she has more autonomy, but because he or she cares. Various research approaches are also combinable. Worker attitude surveys, for example, can (1) "diagnose" a change problem by highlighting alienation, (2) pinpoint program participants by tapping interest levels in job enrichment, (3) serve as a baseline for a pre/post evaluation, (4) "unfreeze" managers in data feedback sessions, and (5) help groups of workers to think about their jobs. Few substantive proposals that are considered by workers are devoid of research questions, and these can be either (1) buried, (2) informally broached, or (3) systematically pursued. All that is needed to systematize knowledge is to pounce on any hypothesis that emerges and to provide technical assistance to permit its exploration. Similar formalization permits a group to track its development and to pursue the fate of its product through implementation/nonimplementation, success/failure, and diffusion.

The introduction of research in participatory change is not (as Argyris, 1970, has noted) contaminating. It is especially not contaminating when the genesis, implementation, and consumption of research is participatory and when working and thinking about work (action and research) are linked. In such ventures (1) participation gains credibility through documentation, (2) continuity is achieved between management planning and indigenous planning, (3) information becomes more available and consumable, and (4) the worker's intelligence is manifestly respected.

What we sometimes miss in translating Maslow's hierarchy is his listing of "cognitive needs" among those that are liberated as lower needs are satisfied. The transcending of extrinsic rewards does waken, in Herzberg's terms, a slumbering Jacob Principle; but but a Job Principle—a doubting, searching, questing-to-know principle—similarly emerges. Civilization is ultimately a product of achievement needs, but doubt renews, and knowledge cements, progress.

PART IV

The Demonstration

CHAPTER 13

GRASS-ROOTS MANAGEMENT

We have noted in the preface to this book that our enduring concern has been with improving the delivery of human services. Our initial interest lay in participatory strategies for the recipients of human service. Our argument was that clients (the product of human service assembly lines) have useful experiences and information to offer to those who try to help, control, or change them. We felt that the sharing of client experience would benefit both the clients (by turning their passivity into activity) and those who deliver services to them. We later extended the notion to the benefit to be derived from staff participation. Like Argyris (1970) we envisaged a merging of the development of organizations with the development of their staffs (Grant, 1966; Grant and Grant, 1966). Such merger implies that persons who learn from their experiences can help the organizations to which they belong cope with the demands of a continually changing world.

Our attempts to implement this model date back over 25 years. The initial structure we explored was that of a total self-study community involving the administrators, staff, and clients of a correctional facility (Grant, 1957). We have tried out variations on this idea in a number of settings. It is from these experiences, and from reflections on our mistakes, that we arrive at the concept of grass-roots management that we discuss in this book.

The reader will note that we have a latent overriding concern— with research. Our notion of research has been "hands on" and we have believed, with Lewin (1948), that there is no good theory without action and no good action without theory. We have not only wanted to bring experiential wisdom—the wisdom of those experiencing a problem—to bear on developing solutions to the problem, but we have also wanted to apply this rudimentary wisdom to help develop general knowledge about problems. In the days of expanding job markets, we saw room for experienced nonprofessionals, as well as for professional social scientists, in the business of evolving knowledge.

The Oakland Experiment

We will not subject our readers to the vagaries of our separate and joint intellectual histories. We must, however, review a five-year relationship with the Oakland, California, Police Department, because it forms an immediate background to the correctional officer work reported below and to the development of our current thinking (Toch, Grant, and Calvin, 1975)

The intervention began inadvertently, with an off-hand remark that we decided to take seriously. At the time we were studying the nature of institutional violence, using confined offenders with a history of violent behavior as our coinvestigators. We reported on this work at a meeting held by the School of Criminal Justice at the University of California at Berkeley. In the audience was the chief of police from Oakland, Berkeley's adjoining city. He interrupted the presentation to remark that if we were really interested in the problem of violence we should take a look at his department. We took the chief at his word. We soon discovered that the chief was concerned with a high incidence of citizen/officer conflict and community complaints of police harassment and brutality. Our discussion of how we might study this problem led to a formal proposal and to its funding (see Acknowledgments in this volume). Soon, the chief retired but the problem did not, and we began a five-year relationship with the police department and its new chief.

Since our strategy was to work with those who were participants in the problem, our colleagues were largely officers who had been involved in violent confrontations with citizens. We proposed to start small, developing first a nucleus group of officers who were opinion leaders within the department, counting on "contagion" (Redl, 1966) to spread our work with this group to larger numbers of officers. We obtained a list of the 60 officers who had had the largest number of incidents of conflict with citizens over the previous two years. The average in the (800-man) department was less than one incident per year. In the group of 60, the range was 8 to 32 incidents. We met with the officers in groups of five to discuss the nature of the proposed project, and we made independent ratings of the amount of influence each man seemed to have on the group he was in. The seven men who were finally selected were those we judged most potent in peer influence.

We met with the men two full days a week. (The chief's parting comment was, "You want them for only *two* days?") The group's discussion of the citizen/officer conflict problem began with complaints about the courts and the city administration, the education system, and the nature of citizens in general and some black citizens in particular. These early discussions with the men were interspersed with "war stories"—descriptions of incidents they knew of or incidents in which they had participated. In time the discussion moved to current image problems, and we began to get more even-handed definitions of the problem.

A breakthrough came when we suggested that the officers were hypothesizing more variance in what citizens do than in what officers do. Their point seemed to be that since officer behavior is defined by law and administrative mandate, what happens when an officer deals with a citizen is determined primarily by the citizen's behavior. The implication of this point being that if we really wanted to understand the violence problem we should be talking to citizens rather than to officers. If this was the assumption, we argued, it could be tested. If other officers were presented with examples of potential conflict situations drawn from war stories and asked to indicate how they would handle such situations, they would respond in the same way as the officer had responded in the actual situation. We had been handed a subject for use of the scientific method, we supplied a critical incident methodology, and the group developed its first questionnaire.

The results of this questionnaire, given to a group of some 40 officers and supervisors, were a surprise to the men—and to us. There was extensive variation in what the respondents said they would do. This variation presented both an intellectual and an emotional challenge to the men. It was also a challenge to the chief. His responses to the critical incidents were the most deviant of the group, which included a deputy chief. The chief realized, he said, that the men were not necessarily doing on the streets what he thought ought to be done; but he did think that there was enough understanding of his position that, when subordinates were asked to commit themselves in writing, they would at least *say* they were following policies. The result was a full-scale administration of the questionnaire, under the chief's order, to the uniformed force of the department. The variation in response persisted, and our group came to the recognition of officer behavior variation as a contribution to the problem of citizen/officer conflict.

The group's next idea was to wear miniature recorders and to make live tapes of incidents as they occurred. This provided more material for study, but did not get at the issue of addressing the violence problem. The men struggled with the question of their own competence to do anything, which gave them trouble at times, but they struggled even more with the question of whether the chief would take their efforts seriously. By this time the men had selected three additional groups of officers to work under their leadership. The second set of groups proceeded to study specific kinds of violent confrontations: landlord/tenant disputes, family quarrels, disturbances involving youths. The groups were able to test the chief's commitment by developing formal proposals for action. They submitted these proposals for staff review, and received encouragement to proceed with proposed innovations (see Chapter 17).

The groups' most powerful innovation began with the concept of peer review of officer behavior. This represented a 180-degree shift from the premise with which the original group of seven had started. The officers had begun by saying that they did their own time (like offenders) and could not criticize each other's work. One of the group's members now said, "We know who the men are who are having all the trouble out on the street. Why don't we get them in here? We'll have them talk with us like we're talking with each other." They tried this formula with a few officers. The experience led to the establishment of a Peer Review Panel, which was staffed and run by officers. Men whose incident count exceeded a given level were invited to meet with panel members to review their contributions to specific incidents, and to try to understand their dynamics. (Subsequently, the subjects of panels became eligible to be peer review panelists with other officers.) The review panel became the hub of a Conflict Management Unit established by the chief for ongoing study of police violence.

A second group innovation involved setting up a Landlord/ Tenant Unit that led to changes in the way officers generally responded to this type of conflict. The stance had been that such disputes were civil matters and that there was no contribution that could be made by the police. The new unit encouraged officers to work with tenants to obtain legal assistance. It involved the officers for the first time in directly using the resources of the department's legal counsel, and it brought them into contact with law students. A third innovation was the implementation of a Family Crisis Intervention Unit (FCIU) that encouraged mediation efforts on the part of officers. FCIU programs—starting with the first FCIU in New York City—have involved clinical psychologists or social workers or students who train FCIU members and/or consult with them. In Oakland, the officers relied on the peer-nominated selection of unit members and on continuing self-training through pooled on-the-job experiences.

The products that emerged from the Oakland groups converted our experiment from a research-centered QWL (bottom-up OD) project into a more obviously composite enterprise. The reason for this fact rests in the officers' own concern with job enrichment, which they expressed through "built-in" features of innovations such as the indigenous (officer-centered) Oakland version of the FCIU. The officer peer review panel may well be "pure" QWL because its aim is self-governance, but most other proposed responses to the Oakland violence problem (which the officers defined very generously) featured specialized assignments and expanded service functions for patrolmen or new roles (e.g., training involvement) for the group members themselves.

In the sequel that we evolved from this experience—which we describe in detail in the next chapters—we enhanced the job enrichment component of employee proposals by (1) sharing job-enrichment-related survey data with groups of union officials and managers and (2) expounding the premises of job enrichment early to group members. Given such inputs, it is no accident that the correction officer proposals we shall describe (Chapter 16) called for job enrichment experiments.

Throughout the Oakland project we made efforts to keep the responsibility and initiative in the hands of the men themselves. Our position was that *they* were experts on the phenomenon they were studying while *we* were experts on how to do action research. We reserved the right to bring in content related to our expertise—how to write a proposal, how to design a questionnaire, how to summarize data—but the definition of the problem and the strategies for addressing the problem were in the officers' hands. We could raise issues through questions, but we avoided imposing our frame of reference insofar as our capacity for objectivity would allow. This approach is perhaps more art than science—as anyone who has worked with groups will recognize—and personal "styles" of working with groups do not depend upon a particular consultant style.

Participation and Organization Change

We were impressed with the changes experienced by the officers in the Oakland groups, including their views of themselves and their ways of looking at police problems. We were equally impressed with the innovations introduced as a result of the officers' work, not the least of which was the establishment of the ongoing problem study (conflict management) unit. We had been convinced of the value of participation in self-study for improving human services and simultaneously contributing to the personal and professional growth of self-study participants. We congratulated ourselves on demonstrating this result to others and on showing that "products of a problem" could help illuminate our understanding of a problem and contribute to its solution. The Oakland Police Department, we felt, might become a model for other departments. Some cross-department visits were actually made around this project, but our problem study model did not spread. Nor did Oakland continue with the self-study thrust.

In retrospect, we were naive in expecting a snowballing or perpetuation of organization change. We had successfully established an "innovation ghetto" (see Chapter 9), but it could not withstand cumulating resistance outside the ghetto or withdrawal of support.

We owe much to Chief Gain, who supported our initial entree into the department and implemented the efforts of our study group members. The chief was concerned with building relations with the community, particularly the minority community, but was at odds with much of the rank and file within his own department. The results of the critical incident survey made the problem very real to him, and he was quick to grasp that there was limited payoff in issuing directives on how officers should behave. However, our association probably proved a mixed blessing. Though officers generally had respect for what the study group officers were doing, the project was also seen as an example of the chief's authoritarianism—of innovations being rammed down the departmental throat. While the group members received considerable support from the chief, they ran into trouble when the chief ran into trouble. After six years in the department, the officers' fraternal association gave the chief a vote of no confidence, and a few months later he resigned. A new information system run through the Conflict Management Unit was maintained, but the self-study thrust was not. A new administration felt that it could not afford the time for a selected group of officers to study departmental operations.

Participation may be a necessary condition for developing grass-roots management within an organization, but it is not sufficient. We had assumed that study group officers could successfully negotiate the formal and informal power structure within their department. Though the officers spent a great deal of time gossiping about who was running what, we could not help them make a concerted effort to analyze and work out ways to get along with this new set of forces—the division chiefs, the training unit, the existing information system. Support at the top is essential, but it is clearly necessary to build a base that is not solely dependent on the top.

Instituting Grass-Roots Management

The model we are proposing is based on three concepts: participation, opportunities for the development of ideas, and contagion.

Participation means having a role in developing approaches to organizational problems that lead to decisions about the policy and operation of the organization. To have such a role clearly means something more than casting a vote or dropping an idea into a suggestion box, both of which are very marginal forms of participation. Employee ideas or suggestions must derive from responsible study of a problem, take account of the context in which the problem is embedded, and be made with some plan for plausible strategies of implementation. This kind of participation should increase the knowledge base of participants. If it succeeds, it should foster their sense of coping competence and their belief that they can make a difference.

Opportunities for the development of ideas means that the organization must foster a climate of trust. Employees must feel free to engage in problem solving without fear that their ideas will be held against them. Employees must also feel that their ideas will be taken seriously. This means that time must not only be made available for participatory efforts, but that the organizational structure must allow ideas to have an impact on the organization.

Contagion means a spread of effect from a small group to a larger group, the chance to show that one can "start me with ten who are stout-hearted men and I'll soon give you ten thousand more," that the same kind of growth that goes on within the person can go on across people. You can start small, with a problem with which people are familiar and with which they are able to cope. This experience builds skills, knowledge, and an incipient sense of competence (Hammerstein, 1927).

Transmitting skills and knowledge to others is part of what we mean by contagion, but not all of it. There must also be a way of transmitting a feeling of strength—a feeling that this is a group worth joining, a problem worth studying, a cause worth fighting for, a team to take pride in, in which one can play well enough to help (Grant and Grant, 1971).

Setting the Process in Motion

An organization using grass-roots management involves itself in the generation of ideas. It is willing to consider ideas in making decisions about its operation. It makes decisions on rational (knowledge-based) grounds, rather than letting them emerge as a resolution of competing sources of power.

To set up grass-roots management, four things are necessary:

(1) access to decision making within the organization,
(2) access to information about the organization,
(3) provision for staff involvement in the ongoing study of the organization and its operation, and
(4) sharing of problem-solving efforts across subgroups within the organization and across organizations.

As we talk about strategies for putting this model into operation, let us keep these four objectives in mind. They are basically parallel rather than sequential thrusts, and the strategies should aid movement toward more than one goal at a time.

THE INITIAL APPROACH

Without a problem, without some pressure from within or without to "do something," no administrator is likely to take on the game of grass-roots management, unless he or she is the type of enlightened administrator who has an intellectual or emotional commitment to democratization of the workplace. The more typical administrator does not have to be convinced that organizational self-study will necessarily solve *all* his or her problems, but he or she must feel that it is at least worth a try. It may take considerable time to develop even an initial understanding and commitment to a grass-roots approach. To avoid isolating the administrator (as may have occurred in Oakland), key members of the administrative staff should be involved in early discussions as soon as possible. This should lead to the formation of a management planning group.

There must obviously be understanding at the top. It is an error to assume such understanding and to crowd administrators too much, or commit them too much, or engage them in too much detail. Administrators must be clear about the full extent of what they undertake and must be helped to develop strategies to make it work. The task is to work with management groups to analyze forces—both within and outside of their organization—that affect the operation of the organization and are affected by innovation and experimentation.

Diagrams help. Any organization has formal and informal links in which key persons can be identified who are potential resources and obstacles to the implementation of grass-roots management. For example, a state agency may have to contend with the department of finance, the legislative analyst's office, the personnel department, legislators, lobbyists, the press, and the employees' union. Contacts should be made with each of these groups to promote some initial understanding and support for the new approach, and these contacts should be continued throughout implementation.

The alert reader will note our use of the conditional voice in the preceding paragraphs. We assume the presence of an outside person, team, or group able to work with the organization in these initial stages and to continue in a (diminishing) consultant capacity in the implementation of the grass-roots approach. (An initial investment of two days, or even half-days, a week might be sufficient). The necessary skills might also be found within the agency and, if not, they can be developed through the activities of management self-study groups. Ultimately, we would hope for transfer of skills across agencies with similar problems, so that the need for consultants drops sharply or ceases altogether.

THE INITIAL INFORMATION BASE

We have argued in these pages for the value of surveys. This implies that one must create management interest and participation in developing an organization-wide survey that covers staff and, where appropriate, client perceptions of the organization and its way of operation. One object of the survey would be to identify subgroups that have specific patterns of attitudes toward, and perceptions of, the organization.

In contrast to Emery and Emery (1976) and others who use survey information to pinpoint specific organizational problems, we see the survey primarily as a way to assess organizational climate, to gauge the quality of organizational work life. But the initial survey serves several functions. It can help us mobilize administrative concern and interest in proceeding with organizational self-study (objective 1). It can represent a tangible administrative commitment to feeding back information about the organization (objective 2). And it can serve as a source of data for initial problem solving by the study groups (objective 3).

FORMATION OF THE NUCLEUS GROUP

We have said that we would start small, but suggest starting small in several places at once. The best strategy would be to develop a number of study groups—each of which is reasonably homogeneous in membership. The homogeneity could be based on job classification, employee characteristics (e.g., age, time with the organization), employee attitudes toward the organization, or some combination of these. One goal would be to facilitate initial trust and communication among group members and groups.

The survey provides the group members with some information on organizational problems. Their own experiences give meaning to this information. Starting from this base, the group can arrive at a definition of organizational problems and of possible solutions to them. It is not important what problem a group decides to address first (all problems lead ultimately to other problems), as long as it is a problem the group members have actually experienced and with which they are able to cope. Initial challenge is important, but so is initial success. Commitment (and by this we mean ownership) is fostered by a sense of competence and by a sense that one can make a difference (Argyris, 1970). Having one's proposals for problem solving taken seriously builds a climate of trust, which in turn facilitates the maintenance of a group. To be taken seriously, proposals must be based on knowledge of the force field within which the proposed change is to take place, and they must include strategies for reaching specified objectives within this field. Consultants can help develop group skills in proposal development and provide access to side sources of information, thus building a sense of competence. If proposals are approved, group members should ideally become involved in the implementation of specific projects. This experience, particularly including feedback on the extent to which the proposed projects are having their desired effects, builds additional skills and knowledge.

It should be clear from what we have written that we do not expect a smooth flow of proposals from study groups to management, with a rubber stamp of approval, and orders to put the proposals into operation. There will be many ideas that die in transit because they are impractical, costly, or compete with needs of other groups within or outside of the organization. Feedback on *why* proposals are not viable can also be a source of learning.

What matters is that proposals for change are considered seriously and that a dialogue begins between employees and management. This process should serve to widen the awareness of the group members (including those of the management group) and lead to greater sophistication about the field within which the organization is embedded. We should expect that interest would grow in sharing information and experiences and that the sharing of different perspectives would increase the awareness and sophistication of all group members.

SECOND-STAGE GROUPS

The problem of elitism is one reason for proceeding very quickly to the formation of a large number of study groups to be led by members of the nucleus groups. One by-product of this strategy is to consolidate the self-study skills of members of the nucleus groups—learning by teaching others—and thus to strengthen ownership of a participatory approach to organizational management. A larger number of groups expands the participatory base, makes possible a greater number of potential change projects, and increases the chance of making visible critical differences in the operation of the organization.

The second-stage groups might or might not be homogeneous in membership. When such groups are formed, we are entitled to expect increased interest in sharing experience and perhaps project activities across groups. We could also encourage the building of linkages between groups and outside persons who can offer relevant knowledge and skills. Graduate students would be one example of such persons, though we should by no means limit the role to members of the academic world.

Knowledge development is an important issue in our model; it is one of the features that distinguishes our participatory approach from others that have many of the same features. We want self-study experiences not only to increase the knowledge base of participants in such experiences, but also to contribute to knowledge. Theory—the explanations that academics advance for why things occur in the real world—helps build a rationale for attacking a given problem in a particular way. Knowledge development comes out of what happens as a result of this action: It helps us to know to what extent outcomes of a given action support the rationale on which this action was based and, in turn, lend support to (or suggest modifications in) larger theories. We envision an ongoing interplay between efforts to attack specific problems with specific interventions—interventions that participants have reason to believe will be effective (rationales or quasi-theoretical statements)—and the development of theories concerned with larger classes of problems.[1]

THE GRASS-ROOTS MANAGEMENT UNIT

We have noted that commitment from the top is necessary for change, but that it is not enough. It is also true that employee participation in self-study groups is necessary, but is also not enough by itself. Ideally, a permanent structure must be created that facilitates the developmental process within the organization beyond the commitment of top management to it. We see change as a legitimate and permanent organization concern, on a par with operations, personnel management, and fiscal accounting. The exact form for institutionalizing this function remains unclear—and might in any case vary from one organizational setting to another. For purposes of the model we are calling one version of a "change unit" a grass-roots management unit.

What would such an entity do? The initial survey represents the beginning of efforts to provide management and employees with systematic information on their organization. The grass-roots management unit would provide such information on an ongoing basis. It could do this through repeated surveys. It could also make use of participant observers, key people within the organization (and possibly outside of it as well) in the form of a panel of observers. Periodic interviews with this group, focused on their perceptions of grass-roots management efforts, the obstacles they foresee for them, and expectations about development over the short run, would provide first-hand information for planning by both management and study group participants. Discrepancies between perceptions of any current effort and what had been expected to occur at an earlier interview would also provide important feedback.

Besides supplying ongoing information, a prime function of such a unit would be to promote participation in study group activities throughout the organization. It could develop strategies for extending participatory activities through staff groups (and clients, where appropriate), keep track of the effectiveness of these strategies, and feed back information on successes and failures. The unit could have an open-door policy, and serve as a place to which staff could bring ideas or concerns about the organization's participatory management thrust. It could even take an ombudsman role around problems and conflicts arising out of efforts to make participation in change a way of organizational life. Finally, the unit could serve as a hub of knowledge dissemination and utilization. It could be a resource to study groups in the development and implementation of proposals. It could foster linkages across study groups. It could promote networking with other agencies and organizations and serve as a liaison with the academic community.

The entity we have described should not be imposed by fiat, nor should it necessarily be turned over to an existing research and development unit for implementation (particularly considering the adversary status these enterprises have in many organizations). The establishment of this and of any other component should be a matter for organization-wide planning. One form of planning could consist of a task force, with members drawn from opinion leaders within study groups as well as from management planning groups. A task force mandate could be to develop a strategy for instituting self-study throughout the organization and for creating a mechanism (such as the unit we have described) for coordinating ongoing self-study activities. Plans could be reviewed by study group members and top management, and feedback from and across these groups should be incorporated into the organization's final plan.

In practice, our composite model might take many forms. There are some features, however, that we consider crucial to its success. First of all, we assume the goal is permanent change (not a quick fix or one-time effort) in the way an organization manages itself. We start with a commitment from top management and the development of a climate of trust that allows the free expression of ideas and permits the creation of structural opportunities for employees to meet and carry out study efforts. We begin with one or more small groups, working on problems of immediate concern to participants. We strive to develop a higher level of commitment, and to this end, we expand opportunities that build a sense of competence and the experience of success in carrying out change efforts. We move as rapidly as possible to the development of a network of study groups, relying on peer teaching and learning and a process of cross-fertilization (contagion) for spreading commitment to participation and its products. Our aim is to avoid the creating of innovation ghettos. To this end, our notion of organizational self-study places emphasis on understanding force fields within which change efforts take place and on ongoing assessment of the effectiveness of these efforts. We are concerned with building linkages, expanding existing bodies of knowledge, and adding to these. Finally, our model includes some vehicle for institutionalizing the process of learning and change as a legitimate organizational function.

Will It Work?

After many years of trying to get the ideas we have outlined in this book understood, let alone implemented, it is both encouraging and chastening to find that these ideas are widely shared. The charges that we are impractical dreamers or that our modest successes have been due to ephemeral, charismatic qualities and can thus not be duplicated, are measurably weakened by the experiences of others working in a similar vein and by their successes, which go well beyond our own.

In this country, efforts to transform schools into self-study communities have illustrated the usefulness of a participatory approach and its viability over time, even under conditions of crisis (Comer, 1980). In the criminal justice field, Stotland (1982) has proposed building ongoing information into police decision making and using feedback about decision outcomes to improve policing operations. Stotland's "police feedback cycle" is a self-study process that involves grass-roots participation.

The most impressive reported work we have seen (aside from reports about participatory management in China, by Walder [1981] and others) comes out of Scandinavia, where groups of social scientists have been working for the past 15 years with employers, unions, and governments groups to democratize work.[2]

The Norway *Balao* project (Johansen, 1979) began in 1973 as an effort to develop vertical integration of work on board merchant ships. (Earlier projects had dealt with the somewhat easier task of horizontal integration). The project emphasizes strategies such as

- the need for participation in planning, implementing, and evaluating work changes;
- the linkage of work planning and training (in our model, learning) as a way to develop new and more diverse competencies among workers;
- a process of continuous learning through involvement in cycles of planning, implementation, and evaluation; and

- contacts with other experimental programs and with trade and research groups (networking).

The learning-related changes resulting from the *Balao* project occurred on three levels (individual, organizational, and social interactions) simultaneously: On the individual level, worker competencies were increased and the work force became more stable, with less time lost because of illness or injuries. There were also self-reports of increased satisfaction with both work and free time on board. On the organizational level, the program developed a process of continuous surveying of problems by ship members, a systematic search for alternative ways of handling problems, and built-in evaluations of effectiveness of new approaches to problems. Work planning, training, and personnel policy were increasingly integrated. On the social interaction level, there was more observed mutual help and tolerance among individuals and groups. There was also, interestingly, an improvement in relationships with families off the ship.

The *Balao* experience is one of many items of documentation that suggests that the grass-roots management model is indeed viable. The theme of this model, as summarized by Johansen (1979: 127) is that "when you are participating in developing your own organization, . . . you are also creating your own relationship to other people and your view of yourself and others. *You become a product of your organizing.*"

We now turn to a *partial* demonstration of our own model. It is not partial by design, but because we have disconfirmed our hope that the first steps we have outlined (those promoting grass-roots participation) would lead to the subsequent steps (those involving grass-roots management). Chapter 17 deals with problems in the transition from participation to its assimilation by participation-relevant management.

Chapter 14 describes the research component that we regard as essential to participatory knowledge building. The reader will recognize the content of the research from discussion of parameters in earlier chapters. Chapter 15 provides the details and some of the flavor of the technology we deploy to generate grass-roots participation. Chapter 16 illustrates the results we obtain from efforts such as these. We hope the reader will be impressed (as we have been) with the quality and soundness, and with the creativity, of ideas that are fleshed out when informed participation is unleashed.

NOTES

1. Herbst (1976) describes this interplay and diagrams its operation.

2. In a book that has come out of this experience, Thorsrud, (1981: 323) describes the involvement of workers, managers, students, and others in "new roles as researchers in a participatory learning process which I would call 'policy-making to democratize work.'" The democratization of research is also an aim of the Center for Action Research and Training in Small Communities and Organizations set up by Ben-Gurion University of the Negev to develop collaborative project work by community members and social scientists. Among their current projects are efforts to democratize work, to improve the quality of work life, and to diffuse the results of these self-initiated projects. Although we have seen only a brief description of this program (QWL Focus, 1981: 23), the work of the center appears to follow much of the reasoning we have outlined here on participation in project learning.

CHAPTER 14

THE NEW YORK PRISON SURVEY

In late 1980 and early 1981, we were able to translate the prescription we have outlined into action, an adventure that involved three of us[1] with 36 experienced correction officers at four New York prisons.

Our experiment was sponsored by the National Institute of Corrections (NIC), an agency in the Federal Bureau of Prisons that is respected in the field for its interest in correctional innovation.[2] We approached NIC after we first discussed the project with top prison executives and officers of the correction officers' union. Following each step of our work, we relayed our experiences to managers and union leaders, and secured their authorization to proceed to the next phase. The first of these meetings were joint meetings (thanks to collaborative links created in New York corrections in the wake of a correction officers' strike); subsequent encounters were sometimes separate encounters with officers and managers or involved members of a newly created Quality of Working Life Committee (see Chapter 17).

It will soon become clear that we enjoyed considerable support from management officials and union leaders. All our efforts—beginning with the survey we shall describe in this chapter—demanded allocations of money, time, and manpower. The fact that such allocations were made during a "budget crunch" is a testimonial to the model—at least, to its timeliness and interest to "consumers."

Our Four Prisons

The places where we worked were selected by a planning group that included correctional managers and union leaders. The choice was limited to seven maximum security prisons that had a large enough manpower pool. One institution was picked for logistical reasons; a second (Ossining) yielded access to a group of minority officers. The three prisons that were not included in the study were seen as similar in officer attitudes (and problems) to the institutions we covered.

The Clinton Facility is a walled prison with a medium-security annex that is located in the village of Dannemora near the Canadian border. The inmate population of the prison complex (over 2500) is the largest in the state, and it is extremely heterogeneous. Clinton formerly served older and long-term offenders; the annex (at one time a psychiatric prison) has specialized in mental health programs. The Dannemora area is predominantly rural, with few sources of employment. Being a prison guard can be a family business. Officers often look back on three or four generations of prison workers; car pools often contain members of the same family. Clinton is noted for the esprit de corps of its officers, which in other prisons is sometimes referred to as "clannishness."

A different situation is that of Ossining (Sing Sing) prison, once known as "the big house" or "up the river." Ossining is small, though it has prospects of being enlarged. The population totals 700 inmates, with a medium-security facility (Tappan) containing another 450. Ossining is in Westchester County, thirty miles north of New York City, and it is easily accessible by train and by bus. Logistics and location have largely determined Ossining's fate. Most recently the prison has been deployed for the shortterm storage of men nearing discharge or parole, who prize Sing Sing's closeness to the metropolitan area. As a prerelease facility, the prison has had few programs or job assignments available, but has hosted community volunteer activities. The program vacuum is slated to be filled in the near future. The expansion is essential: Ossining's inmates are now long-term residents in the facility, and idleness is a problem.

Ossining's staff—including most officers—are commuters from "the city." Commuting decreases solidarity and makes logistical problems (the inconvenience of getting to and from work) important. Competing jobs, such as municipal corrections and police, are located in New York City, and they gain attractiveness from proximity. Other state prisons are mostly upstate and appeal to less urbanized staff. Not surprisingly, most (85 percent) of Ossining's personnel—including supervisory staff—are black or Hispanic and originate in the greater metropolitan area.

Auburn Correctional Facility stands within the city of Auburn, an industrialized community of 35,000. A larger urban area—Syracuse—is 25 miles away, and another—Rochester—is within 60 miles. Since the inception of Auburn as New York's first prison, it has been a program-rich institution. In addition to vocational and industrial training, it offers educational programs and caters to inmates "motivated for academic and vocational training." The institution is noted for its "progressive" programming of large numbers (1500-1600), though staff shortages have created idleness, and programs have been closed down. Officers live mostly in Auburn, and many have worked in blue-collar settings before joining the department. The Auburn officers see themselves classified elsewhere in the system as flaming radicals because of the "Auburn tradition" for innovation.

A contrasting stereotype is applied to Great Meadow (Comstock) prison, located north of Albany near Glens Falls. Great Meadow houses younger inmates (16 to 30 years of age) and has a reputation for being "hard nosed." The prison is large (1400 to 1500 inmates) and once had a sizable farm annex. Comstock has much formal programming (including college courses) and many inmate groups. Though the prison is "tough" (all officers wear batons), the atmosphere is relaxed; staff are informal and inmate/staff relations friendly. The prison currently has high inmate turnover and a stable staff. Most officers are "locals" and come from farms or small towns. Some officers commute, however, from cities such as Glens Falls, twenty to thirty miles from the prison.

The Correction Officer Survey

We initiated the program with a survey of correction officers' attitudes in the prisons that had been selected for our use. The main purpose of the survey was to explore the need for a program such as ours and to gauge the readiness of officers to participate in it. Other goals of the study included

(1) helping managers and union officials to obtain a more reliable (less impressionistic) picture of officer attitudes than might be available through other sources;

(2) providing superintendents and local unions information about the climates of their institutions;

(3a) exploring the accuracy of the correction officers' perceptions of other officers' responses, and

(3b) showing that survey data could be used as a corrective to "pluralistic ignorance" among officers (see Chapter 4).

As a measure of *need* for employee participation we relied on the extent of officer alienation; we translated potential as the officers' desire for job enrichment. In toto, 75 questions (exclusive of background information) made up the form that we finally administered. The 75 items can be subcategorized as follows:

ALIENATION[3]

The first third of our questionnaire comprised 25 statements that were designed to determine whether the officers were alienated. Most of these items were inspired by the three dimensions of Seeman's (1959) taxonomy we described in Chapter 2. These dimensions are powerlessness, meaninglessness, and self-estrangement. We may recall from Chapter 2 that powerlessness denotes a sense of impotence or the feeling that one cannot affect outside forces. Deescalated from society to prison, powerlessness refers to items such as

No one ever asks a CO [Corrections Officer] for suggestions related to his job.

If it's an officer's word against an inmate, they'll believe the inmate.

We're damned if we do, and damned if we don't.

Meaninglessness summarizes the view that one does not know what is expected. It covers such items as

You don't know from one day to the next how the department expects you to act.

The inmate rule book means nothing in prisons these days.

A CO is told what his job is only when he does something wrong.

Self-estrangement is (among other things) "the loss of intrinsic meaning or pride in work," or "an inability to find self-rewarding... activities." This has to do with job impoverishment or concerns such as

The only thing the CO's job has going for it is job security.

The CO's job is a treadmill.

No matter how hard one tries, one feels no sense of accomplishment.

We included a fourth dimension that describes bureaucratic indifference, a concern that emerged frequently in surveys we have reviewed. The dimension refers to a feeling of not being appreciated or esteemed, a sense of being cavalierly treated, of being insufficiently supported—particularly by persons in authority. Relevant items included

Supervisors care more about the inmates than about the COs.

If a CO does good work, he gets recognition.

Most sergeants and lieutenants are concerned about their COs' morale.

JOB ENRICHMENT (PROFESSIONAL ORIENTATION)

The second set of 25 statements in the questionnaire dealt with inmate contact or rehabilitation-related activity. Most items in this section measured (1) interest in (or sympathy for) noncustodial work and (2) preference for low (or high) social distance from inmates. The interest in high-contact jobs was defined through items such as

The most satisfying jobs involve inmate contact.

The CO's only concern is with prison security.

Counseling is a job for counselors, not correctional officers.

Sometimes a guard should be an advocate for an inmate.

Social distance items included such statements as

The best way to deal with inmates is to be firm and distant.

A CO should work hard to earn trust from inmates.

A good principle is not to get "close" to convicts.

A personal relationship with an inmate invites corruption.

There were also a few items (e.g., "There would be much less crime if prisons were more uncomfortable") that tapped a generic hard-nosed or soft-nosed stance in penological matters. More broadly worded job enrichment items were included in pretest, but the unpopularity of the *non*enriched responses made such items useless.

OFFICER OPINION ESTIMATES

In the third section of the questionnaire, half of our 50 items were repeated, and the officers were asked to "guess how other officers in your institution will answer each question." The response choices were

almost all agree ("over 80% of officers would agree with the statement");

most agree ("more than half but less than 80% would agree");

most disagree ("fewer than 80%"); and

almost all disagree ("80% or more").

The purpose of the exercise was to document for the officers' benefit the prevalence of pluralistic ignorance relating to interest in job enrichment (seventeen items) and to alienation (eight items). The point of having such data available, as we discuss them elsewhere, is to explode the myth that "suggests that the brave feel lonely because they *are* lonely, [which] implies that officers who admit that they want to help inmates and/or improve prisons must swim against the tide, that they must run an embarrassing gauntlet of irate fellow-guards who vociforously demand conformity to a cynical, dinosaur view of the world." If pluralistic ignorance emerges in a correction officer survey, it means that "the officer subculture becomes *imaginary*. In other words, the brave can afford to be braver than they suspect, because consensus on such premises as 'never talk to a con' or 'never rat to a sergeant' is *falsely* assumed, and no guard group really cares whether Officer Jones lets a depressed inmate show him pictures of his unfaithful wife, or runs a counseling group in the protective segregation gallery" (Toch, 1980: 29).

Pretests and Administration

Our instrument evolved through several pretests that employed the expertise of an Officer Advisory Group including two union representatives. The first pretest was conducted using 69 officer candidates for positions in therapeutic communities. The second pretest group comprised 64 officers who had been appointed as inservice training officers in major New York prisons. The second group was more representative than the first because it covered New York geographically, but it was no more a random sample than the first pretest group. Results from our first survey were submitted to the Officer Advisory Group, which expanded the item pool for the second pretest. The data from each pretest cycle were subjected to item analysis. Responses on the alienation and job enrichment scales were analyzed separately. Items for which there was little variability in the responses, or which did not discriminate between high and low scorers on each summed scale, were rejected. Item-to-scale correlations on the retained variables ranged between .31 and .72. The product-moment correlation between the final job enrichment scale and the alienation scale was zero (.09). Items in the estimate section ("guess how other officers . . . will answer") were selected when officers' estimates on the pretest varied substantially from the distribution of their own responses on the items. The final questionnaire also contained some indicators of the respondents' demographic characteristics.

At each institution the survey was jointly sponsored by local management and union representatives. Plans for the survey were announced during lineup, and survey forms were distributed to all available officers, to be returned to training staff or union representatives. In all, a total of 1739 survey forms were distributed, and 832 completed questionnaires, or 47.8 percent, were returned. (These samples proved representative of their populations.) Officers were given the option of signing their names to their questionnaire, and most (77 percent) of the officers provided their names.

Survey Results

Overall, it seemed clear that correction officers are disaffected. Table 14.1 illustrates their discontent and points up its magnitude. Seven out of ten officers agree with statements such as "we're damned if we do, and damned if we don't." One out of four hold such alienated views strongly. Three out of four officers feel that the average correction officer would change jobs if he could.

Fortunately, some responses point to remediable conditions. One can remedy the fact that "no one ever asks a CO for suggestions"; one can induce sergeants to be "concerned about their COs' morale"; one can foster a "sense of accomplishment" and assure officers some recognition.

Moreover, officers are not equally alienated. The average scores in our four prisons ranged from 17.2 (Ossining) to 10.1 (Clinton). As a group, the more urbanized the officers, the higher their level of discontent.[4] The extent of differences one uncovers can be gleaned from Table 14.2. Urban officers have strong feelings about bureaucratic indifference—the way officers are treated by supervisors. A majority at Ossining (as opposed to a minority at Clinton), feel "officers are really treated worse than inmates" and "supervisors care more about the inmates than about the COs." Such statements reflect strong views.

Alienation among officers *also* varies with seniority (time on the job). The relationship follows a "U" curve; officers of five to nineteen years of experience are more alienated than those with less than five years or more than twenty years on the force. Only

TABLE 14.1   Items Yielding Extreme (high-intensity)
Alienation Responses (N = 834)

	Response			
Item	Strongly Agree	Agree	Disagree	Strongly Disagree
The average CO would change professions if he had a chance.	27.2%	47.7%	24.0%	1.1%
No one ever asks a CO for suggestions relating to his job.	25.3	46.0	27.2	1.4
You don't know from one day to the next how the department expects you to act.	29.4	40.6	27.8	2.2
A CO is told what his job is only when he does something wrong.	21.9	38.0	37.7	2.4
Most sergeants and lieutenants are concerned about their COs' morale.	3.1	30.2	43.4	23.3
We're damned if we do, and damned if we don't.	26.6	49.7	21.5	2.2
No matter how hard one tries, one feels no sense of accomplishment.	23.4	43.9	30.1	2.4
If a CO does good work, he gets recognition	1.3	23.1	54.4	22.1

SOURCE: From Hans Toch and John Klofas, "Alienation and Desire for Job Enrichment Among Correction Officers," *Federal Probation*, 1982, 46, 35-44. Reprinted by permission.

one out of four midrange officers feels that supervisors are concerned about officer morale; four out of ten less experienced and more experienced officers share the sentiment. Half the COs in the midseniority range think they are "treated worse than inmates"; the statement is endorsed by one-third of both the senior and junior groups.

CO professional orientation (desire for job enrichment) tends to be high, and averages are comparable for the four prisons. Where differences exist, however, the rural prison (Clinton) yields the most enrichment-oriented (and inmate-oriented) responses; the most urban prison (Ossining) shows more custody orientation. Some may be surprised by this fact, given the

TABLE 14.2   Responses of Correctional Officers
to Select Alienation Items

	Percentage of Officers Who Agreed with Statement at			
	Ossining Prison	Auburn Prison	Comstock Prison	Clinton Prison
To work as a CO means to have no chance of advancement.	55.8	39.7	42.5	23.7*
You don't know from one day to the next how the department expects you to act.	85.5	75.1	78.4	55.6
The inmate rule book means nothing in prisons these days.	76.6	52.0	42.8	30.1
A CO is told what his job is only when he does something wrong.	83.1	57.1	69.0	46.9
Most sergeants and lieutenants are concerned about their COs' morale.	10.2	25.2	31.0	49.1
When a CO takes action, he generally gets backing from superiors.	35.6	57.0	55.7	79.8
If it's an officer's word against an inmate's, they'll believe the inmate.	54.4	29.6	30.4	18.7
Officers are really treated worse than inmates.	71.2	46.0	41.6	28.3
Most supervisors treat their COs fairly.	55.1	76.7	77.7	92.8
Supervisors care more about the inmates than about the COs.	64.2	32.8	36.2	18.2
Management expects too much work from correctional officers.	51.1	44.9	31.1	19.6
100% totals approximately	139	205	168	320

SOURCE: From Hans Toch and John Klofas, "Alienation and Desire for Job Enrichment Among Correction Officers," *Federal Probation*, 1982, 46, 35-44. Reprinted by permission.
*Chi-square significant beyond .001 level for all variables in this table.

assumption that rural guards are custodially oriented and that urban minority officers tend to constitute a "new breed" of liberal COs.[5] Equally surprising is the finding that officers tend to mellow with age. Very young officers (who are underrepresented in our prisons) are custody oriented; "human service" orientation increases steadily (monotonically) with age. Similar results appear (less dramatically) with seniority. Of officers with fewer than five years on the job, for example, 46 percent feel that "rehabilitative programs should be left to mental health professionals"; the view is held by only 30 percent of the 5- to 10-year group, 28 percent of officers with 11 to 19 years on the job, and 25 percent of those with 20 years or more experience. Similarly, 85 percent of the over-twenty-years-experience group feels that "it's important for a CO to have compassion." This proposition is endorsed by 66 percent of the officers with fewer than five years experience.

We uncovered high pluralistic ignorance among correction officers. Table 14.3 displays the officers' responses and their estimates at Great Meadow Prison (Comstock). We see that the officers tend to overestimate their peers' alienation and consistently assume that the majority is more "custody" oriented (less job enrichment oriented) than they are. The most dramatic finding relates to those officers (one out of five) who assume that COs agree *completely* on a cynical, custody-oriented stand—a stand that is rejected by the officers. Closer analysis reveals that "high pluralistic ignorance" (high PI) officers *repeatedly* assume (over many different items) that there is imaginary consensus of fellow officers taking an alienated, custody-oriented stand.

Extreme "high PI" officers are alienated, and they are very custody-oriented officers. They are also young and (relatively) inexperienced. *Less* extreme "high PI" officers are often liberal, *very* job enrichment oriented, older, and more experienced. We called the high PI, alienated, custody-oriented officers "smug hacks" or "subculture custodians." We refer to to more liberal, professional officers who imagine themselves outnumbered, as the "lonely braves."

**TABLE 14.3   Actual Officer Responses and Officers' Estimates
of Officer Responses at Comstock Prison (N = 168)**

Statement	Actual Responses (in percentages)		Percentage of Officers Who Estimated That			
	Agree	Disagree	Almost All Will Agree	Most Will Agree	Most Will Disagree	Almost All Will Disagree
I'm proud of being a correctional officer.	61.8	38.2	3.7	31.9	45.4	19.0
The inmate rule book means nothing in prison these days.	42.8	57.4	25.0	36.6	32.9	5.5
Officers are really treated worse than inmates.	41.6	58.4	19.5	42.1	33.5	4.5
Management expects too much work from correctional workers.	31.1	68.9	13.5	43.6	38.0	4.9
The CO's only concern is with prison security.	17.4	82.6	14.7	38.0	40.5	6.7
The best way to deal with inmates is to be firm and distant.	36.7	63.3	19.6	49.7	28.8	1.8
Rehabilitative programs should be left to mental health professionals.	30.6	69.4	19.6	37.4	35.6	7.4
It's important for a CO to have compassion.	73.8	26.2	5.5	41.7	41.7	11.0
Any infraction of the rules by an inmate should result in disciplinary action.	34.5	65.5	19.3	44.1	32.3	4.3
Counseling is a job for counselors, not correctional officers.	26.8	73.2	21.7	34.8	32.8	10.6
Improving prisons for inmates makes prisons worse for officers.	40.4	59.6	28.0	34.8	32.3	5.0
Sometimes a guard should be an advocate for an inmate.	56.4	43.6	3.1	23.7	61.9	11.2
If a CO wants to do counseling, he should change jobs.	29.5	70.5	19.6	38.7	34.4	7.4
Rehabilitation programs are a waste of time and money	43.7	56.3	36.2	42.9	17.8	3.1

SOURCE: From Hans Toch and John Klofas, "Alienation and Desire for Job Enrichment Among Correction Officers," *Federal Probation*, 1982, 46, 35-44. Reprinted by permission.

To be sure, there are also many *low* PI officers; they are *invariably* professionally oriented, and they tend to be older and more experienced officers. Such men are professional but are not held back by imagined opposition. The term "liberated professionals" aptly describes them. In our sample, the largest "type" (30 percent of officers) fell in this (LP) category; the nextlargest type (25 percent) were "lonely braves"; 15 to 20 percent of the officers were "subculture custodians." The latter (as expected) were overrepresented at Ossining; "lonely braves" were overrepresented at Auburn, and "liberated pros" were overrepresented at Clinton.

Feedback of Survey Results

We prepared five packages of tables based on results of the survey. There was one set highlighting data from each prison and one "overview" set, which covered the four prisons. In making up packages we tried to set up tables for easy reading, and we arranged them in what we hoped was a logical order.

The overview package was presented to top management and to union (Council 82) leaders. The other four packages were taken to the prisons. Feedback sessions all involved "walking through" tables in turn, reviewing highlights and discussing their implications. The sessions were animated, and there was much speculation; the groups saw findings as plausible and often as compatible with other available data and impressions.

In two prisons (Clinton and Auburn) we met with large groups comprising union, middle management, and management representatives. In the other prisons we reviewed the data with the warden and his staff. Albany meetings (with the commissioner and commissioner's staff and with the union) preceded prison meetings.

Among the implications that were explored in the groups were those related to our proposed program. Groups agreed that the problem (officer alienation) and the potential (officer interest) were confirmed by the data. We were therefore authorized to proceed with the "training groups," including the selection of officers with whom we would work.

Selection and Composition of the Officer Groups

With the exception of the president of the correction officers' union at one institution and the union vice president at another, the members for our groups were chosen based on their questionnaire responses. The first criterion we used was a high job enrichment (professional orientation) score; the second was high alienation for half the officers and low alienation for the others. The preliminary list was longer than our final roster, in order to allow other criteria (such as problems involved in assigning officers) to enter.

The names of the officer candidates were submitted to wardens at the four institutions. This was done during the survey feedback sessions in which the relationship between the data and the groups was discussed. The wardens selected group members in consultation with union officers and managers. Assigning the officers to our groups entailed use of overtime, juggling of officers' days off, and other inconveniences. Six officers (at least one per group) had to change their shifts (others normally worked days).

Two of the prisons (Clinton and Comstock) provided us groups of ten officers; other groups (at Ossining and Auburn) contained eight men each. The seniority of officers varied, though none of the officers had fewer than four years of experience. Our greatest reservoir of experience was in the Clinton group, which contained four men with 26 years on the job and two with 25. The average seniority level at Clinton was 19.6 years.

The next most experienced group was the Comstock officers, who averaged 16.8 years on the job. One of the Comstock officers had 31 years of experience, six of which (the last six) had been spent on tower duty. At Auburn and Ossining the groups had moderate experience levels: at Auburn the mean seniority level was 9 years (the range, 4 to 18); at Ossining, the mean was 10 and the range, 6 to 20. Ossining officers tended to be older: five men were over 40; one, over 50. At Auburn, six officers fell into the 30- to 40-year-old age group.

Of the 8 Ossining officers, 6 were black, 1 was Hispanic, and the other was of Jewish extraction. The 28 officers in the other three groups included 3 Spanish-American officers; the rest were white.

The officers were all professionally oriented. At three institutions (Auburn, Comstock, and Clinton), the range in job enrichment scores was from 18 to 24, except for one union official who had a score of 15 (the other's score was unknown). At Ossining, six of the eight officers fell into the high (17-23) range. Alienation scores of group members at Auburn and Ossining ranged from a low of 1 to a high of 24; at Comstock and Clinton, high alienation was harder to find: three Clinton men, each with 26 years on the job, had alienation scores of 0 to 1, but high alienation scores at Clinton ranged from 15 to 18. At Comstock, two midrange alienation scores (9 and 12) had to be accepted.

Many officers in the four groups had high inmate-contact positions, though at Auburn half the officers worked in housing blocks. Assignments ranged from the gymnasium, the hospital, the mess hall, orientation (training), and the program committee, to the superintendent's office. In addition to our tower guard, two officers had spent years in the tower. One had left the post when he finished school and "didn't need to study"; the other told us he had seen himself "turning into a vegetable" and decided to change his assignment.

NOTES

1. Project staff consisted of Hans Toch, J. Douglas Grant, and John Klofas.

2. NIC grant No. CD6, "Research/Training/Development Program for Correctional Officers." Our project monitor was Phyllis Modley; Larry Solomon was program manager.

3. The text of the next sections and the material following, which detail the survey results, are here reproduced with permission from "Alienation and Desire for Job Enrichment Among Correction Officers," by Hans Toch and John Klofas, *Federal Probation*, 1982, 46, 35-44.

4. As noted in Chapter 1, national surveys of worker attitudes have consistently found urban/rural differences in alienation among blue-collar workers.

5. The finding did not really surprise us. It parallels the conclusions from a survey in Illinois (reported in Jacobs, 1978) conducted in 1974-1975.

CHAPTER 15

THE CORRECTION OFFICER TEAMS

The aim of the project was to involve officers in prison reform. The proof of this sort of pudding consists of enacted reforms— reforms designed by officers after study of prison problems and exploration of their solutions. It was the task of our groups to produce detailed blueprints for reform (change proposals); it was to be the correctional manager's subsequent task to review and implement these ideas. This chapter describes the process whereby the officers (with our help) originated change proposals; the next chapters deal with results of the officers' efforts.

As planned change, our model for *originating* proposals had evolved in enough detail to permit a blow-by-blow description (below). Our model for *implementing* proposals (see Chapter 13) was at the time inchoate and largely developed in light of events we experienced later and in response to the proposals originated by our officers.

As noted (Chapter 14), we formed our groups armed with promises we had secured that the officers' ideas would be studied and probably be implemented. We passed this promise on to the officers when we convoked them. We further told them that we would do our very best to present and "sell" any ideas that they evolved.

We could not tell then, nor can we tell in retrospect, whether the officer took our commitment seriously and assumed a response from management. The inference is that they must have done both, because it is hard to imagine that they would radiate enthusiasm, agony, concern, involvement, and toil for the sake of an "academic" exercise or as an end in itself. It is also hard to assume—though immensely touching to infer—that there was no cynicism and no memory of past disappointments and past failures. If the officers *did* suspend judgment—as they must have—the prize (of managers adopting officer proposals for reforms that included opportunities for job enrichment and continued participation) must surely have seemed worth the risk of being again rejected or ignored.

The resources at our disposal in the prisons included: (a) five 8-hour work sessions, (b) groups of eight to ten officer trainees, and (c) two group leaders, with staff support. These resources permitted us to divide our trainees into two subgroups of convenient size (four or five per subgroup), and to divide our training period into two comfortable (two-day) cycles culminating in two sets of products. There was also time for a lead-in session and a climactic final period for a report to the prison warden.

A more stripped-down program is undoubtedly feasible, but some advantages would be lost:

(1) Dividing a group is a source of novelty and variety for its members; changing composition furnishes new audiences, reliability checks, and feedback; subgroups develop loyalty to their products; a spirit of friendly rivalry and competitiveness ensues.

(2) Having two or more cycles increases the variety of products, gives group members more chances for having their interests represented, and mobilizes different dynamics as subgroup composition changes.

(3) If staff load is spread, groups get the benefit of varying leadership styles and perspectives; postsession process review becomes possible; the editing of group products can be done promptly.

The Training Module

Our work weeks ran Monday through Friday, with Monday mornings serving the function of introducing ourselves and the program, providing relevant background information, and defining the group's mission. The officers had all nominally assented to their involvement; out of 36 men, none had rejected the invitation. The presumption—judging by comments—is that the trainees were motivated by curiosity and by the spice of anticipated variety. We know that the officers did not know what to expect (there was talk of interviews related to the survey) and that they expected very little.[1] We were an unknown quantity, except for our provenance (Albany is the prison system's headquarters) and our connection with the survey. Since the survey had enjoyed management and union sponsorship, we were presumably acceptable figures.

The morning agenda was variegated (to prevent boredom), it was information loaded, and it was fortuitously more academic than is desirable. The latter feature was due to a desire of officers to "lay back" until they were certain of what they were up against.

Staff introductions were followed by the project introduction. This involved a history of the project, including its NIC sponsorship, the union interest, the commissioner's commitment, the survey, and the planned role of officer groups. The description of the groups permitted us to talk about quality of work life strategies, which helped the officers to understand the type of enterprise into which they had been recruited.

The introduction was followed with a preview of the agenda, which led to the question "What's in it for us?" (the staff's role). This discussion centered on staff's commitment to participatory strategies. The presentation included a review of our prior involvement with the Oakland Police Department, with emphasis on patrolman participation in study and planning.

Next was a "statement of the problem." This dealt with questions relating to the CO's job in the prison and with the interest of members of the group in defining and expanding this role, as manifested in their responses to the survey. The discussion included a review of job enrichment concepts and the suggestion that our products would further CO job enrichment.[2]

The rest of the morning was spent in a review of survey results. Each group discussed the questionnaire responses of officers at its own institution and compared them with those in the other prisons. The procedure varied somewhat with the group, because some groups showed greater affinity for tables and numbers than other groups. In the feedback sessions, the officers tended to focus on CO problems and on the more discouraging implications of the survey. The level of interest was high and the discussions were lively.[3] In subsequent group sessions, survey highlights tended to be raised as documentation; this made it obvious that the men had assimilated the survey results and were impressed by them.

Monday afternoon the group was asked to list work-related problems of COs and to think of solutions to these problems. Two areas were selected by the end of the day for workups over the next two days. The format was one of brainstorming. Index cards were distributed, and the men were invited to characterize problems (white cards) and solutions (green cards) in succinct phrases. Problem cards and solution cards were pasted on walls, with staff grouping problems into categories and matching solutions with problems. This process of instant content analysis yielded walls covered with cards, with problem-cards arranged in columns (under headings such as "morale problems," "supervision problems," "communications," "inmate assignments," "mental health," and so forth.) Each column of white problem-cards had accompanying columns of colored solution-cards, though the latter were in shorter supply than the former. The session ended with officers selecting two problem/solution packages to work on, after which the day's experience was summarized and reaction forms were filled out. Summaries were round-robin statements addressed to a cassette tape recorder. During the first day, staff started the process; on subsequent days, summarizing was initiated by a group member acting as secretary.

Tuesday began with a minilecture outlining the components of the proposal. These were specified as including (a) a statement of the problem to be addressed, (b) a description of the program proposed, (c) a list of the activities required for implementation, and (d) a specification of resources or budget required. Following this introduction, the officers were divided into subgroups to begin work on their first proposals. Their assignment was to flesh out the "description of the program" section, with emphasis on the "what, how, who, and when" of the proposed program. The task involved hard work and took up most of the morning. A half hour before lunch, the subgroups reconvened to report to each other and to engage in discussion. A short lunch break ensued.

The afternoon brought a sharp change of pace. To highlight implementation concerns, subgroups completed force-field analyses listing "anticipated resistances" (obstacles) and forces favoring their programs. The results of this exercise were recorded on large sheets, pasted end to end.[4] After reviewing the force fields, subgroups drafted implementation sections for their proposals. The group then reconvened, reported to each other, summarized, completed reaction forms, and adjourned.

The next morning each task force drafted its resources and budget section and wrote the problem statement for its proposal. Sometimes the first day's brainstorming procedure (grouped index cards on the wall) proved helpful. At other times, individual officers (or drafting teams of two officers) wrote sections of preamble draft; the separate drafts yielded redundancy, but produced nice turns of phrase.

The task of writing a budget came easy to some groups, and the men broke down anticipated costs in exquisite detail. Other groups discussed program needs in more general terms, noting program components that were free or cheap or expensive (mostly highlighting the former).

By Wednesday afternoon, a complete set of two draft proposals was available for review. Some minor details were added by the group, but the officers were generally amazed at what they had accomplished. The importance of selecting a convincing third and fourth proposal was now clear. By the end of the day (late Wednesday), two more proposal topics had been spelled out and the subgroup composition for Thursday and Friday had been settled.

The next two days paralleled the previous ones, except for the last afternoon session. In three groups, the Friday session was taken up with a report to the superintendent; the fourth group discussed officer problems in seminar fashion. All of the final sessions ended with staff and officers exchanging words of appreciation and personal regard.

Officer Reactions to the Experience

Our session evaluation forms (Figure 15.1) provide cues about how the officers reacted to the program. At first glance, the

<table>
<tr><td>Name</td><td>Date</td></tr>
</table>

SESSION RATING FORM

Check (√) the appropriate box

	Very High	High	Average	Low	Very Low
Productivity					
Interest					
Group Participation					
My Own Participation					
Group Morale					
My Own Morale					

CIRCLE THE ADJECTIVES THAT DESCRIBE TODAY'S SESSION:

Academic	Fun	Promising	Instructive
Enjoyable	Torture	Thought Provoking	Bland
Sick	Monotonous	Critical	Silly
Sensible	Relevant	Creative	Helpful
Beautiful	Wasteful	Phoney	Informative
Constructive	Pleasant	Puzzling	Frustrating
Challenging	Painful	Aimless	
Inconclusive	Unfair	Enlightening	Damaging
Slow	Immoral	Great	Confusing
Purposeful	Subversive	Nonsense	Encouraging
Uninformative	Strange	Weakening	Pointless
Valuable	Practical	Sane	
Hopeless	Sad	Weird	
Rambling	Honest		
Annoying	Exasperating		
Inspiring	Tense		
Irritating	Dry	_____	

USE BACK OF PAGE FOR ANY ADDED COMMENTS:

FIGURE 15.1   Session Rating Form

TABLE 15.1 Composite Ratings of Five Sessions by the Officer
in the Four Groups[a]

Dimensions	Session				
	1	2	3	4	5
Productivity	1.4	5	4.4	6.7	7.2
Interest	4.7	5.8	5.3	6.4	7.5
Group Participation	3.3	5.6	4.7	7.2	7.5
Group Morale	1.7	4.2	4.4	6.7	7.5
All Six Categories on the form:	2.3	4.3	4.1	5.9	6.4

a. "Very high" ratings only (number of officers out of ten).

information looked nondiscriminating and indecently flattering.
The average rating of the sessions was "very high." Below, a
profusion of laudatory terms was circled to describe the group
experience. (The exception is Ossining, where the adjective
checklist was used very sparsely).[5]

A closer look (Table 15.1) reveals a profile of the officers'
reactions. The first session does relatively poorly, particularly in
ratings of "productivity" and "group morale." The officers felt
their "interest" held; "participation" is rated fairly highly. This
picture makes sense if we recall the time we spent in introducing
our program and the nonparticipatory format of the morning
session. Product-oriented work began seriously the second day,
where "productivity" ratings jump from 1.4 to 5. Sessions 2 and
3—during which the first proposals are crafted—show
comparable patterns, though a slight slump (particularly in task-
related ratings) occurs in Session 3. Work on the second set of
proposals shows a cumulative effect. The last session—in which
all tasks are complete—is climactic. This cumulation occurs
across the board, but "participation" and "interest" show curves
that are somewhat flatter. A sense of accomplishment builds as
the products emerge; the officers are intrigued early (half of them
rate "interest" very high in the first session); they sense themselves
participating fully in the fourth session (seven out of ten).

The adjectives the officers circle are also revealing. By far the
top choice is the adjective "constructive." Excluding the Ossining
group, we find "constructive" circled 118 times out of 136 officer

sessions. This statistic is dramatic if we notice the large number of adjectives on the list. It suggests that the experience was *not* classed as a training exercise, but as useful and goal related. The most popular adjectives following "constructive" make a similar point. They include "promising," "encouraging," "challenging," and "informative." With one exception ("informative"), these terms denote an enterprise in which energies are harnessed toward constructive ends. The next group ("creative," "purposeful," "valuable," and "enjoyable") is more of a mixed bag; it credits the intrinsic experience as well as the means/end connotations.

Group Process

The officers seemed convinced early of the "constructiveness" of the program. The task-oriented process is no doubt responsible for this fact. There is also the backdrop of the program (evidence of commitment and backing and the survey), which may have accentuated the importance and seriousness of the enterprise.

The term "training" was tone setting, because "training" can mean talk and/or work. An early talk/work exercise was our use of cards. Grouped cards (as opposed to free association) discourage catharsis. Some wallowing in alienated complaints occurs in every group, and it is expected. It comes in waves, and such waves break over a group. But *if there are tasks to which the group must return*, the waves can be broken up. Problem-solving exercises act as "reality checks": If a group becomes excited and forgets its mission, any member can invoke group tasks and redress the situation.

Differences in leadership are accommodated in a replicable process; we have mentioned leadership style variations.[6] The word "variation" is important because it implies a theme that remains the same. Group problem solving requires that content come from the group. The leader must "hear" content (with prison staff, correctional expertise matters), encourage the appearance of ideas, and arrange and shape them. This implies some competence in working with ideas (to help promote rational problem solving) and with people in groups (to mobilize their interest, participation, and creativity).

The leaders' contribution is important, but is ultimately catalytic. Group process and product hinge on the quality of the group. Our officer proposals were rich in *detail*—the sort of detail that no manager or planner or any or us could know about and supply. The proposals reflect a closeness to prison problems that makes diagnoses and proposed solutions consequential. In different prisons, different problems emerged because different men were differently attuned to them. Clinton—through its annex—had a unique history involving disturbed inmates. This made it possible for our officers to point out to managers that

> officers feel the need for more information and training to help
> them deal with emotionally disturbed inmates. They need
> information about program options available for such inmates,
> and many COs want opportunities to work in programs that are
> designed to deal with emotionally disturbed inmates. On the other
> side of the ledger, DOCS has many officers who, because of special
> training or involvement in programs in Dannemora, Mattawan,
> and elsewhere, have expertise in the area of inmate mental health,
> that is related to the management of emotionally disturbed
> individuals.

The officers' experience spelled out the problem and solution, as did another Clinton proposal in which the problem ("the routine process of program asssignment for inmates is of necessity an assembly line . . . some inmates require more personal attention because they have serious adjustment problems") was familiar to the officers, a few of whom had also experienced the solution, ("which could be explored, and frequently remedied, through individualized classification"). At other times the problem is experienced, but the solution is *not* available. Such was the case with Ossining problems (How can one build some esprit de corps in a disaffected staff? How can one restore lagging confidence in dubious leaders? How can one "shape up" unmotivated workers?) that seemed to defy anyone to solve them. Such problems invite despair, and they often require choices between feasible solutions that fall short and utopian options. Such choices are agonizing, and—in a group—can be divisive along risk-taking lines. Our group faced the temptation to abandon core issues and turn attention to lower-order concerns, but the officers persevered and trod the difficult path of balanced compromise.

Some group members have "hobby horses"—concerns that matter to them. In our groups several proposals originated with *personal* concerns. Some were lofty or dramatic, others less so. One officer who had considered suicide felt kinship for other men in crisis; another (an exmember of the wartime Marine Corps) felt offended by sloppiness and casual dress and by his peers' "lack of pride." A third officer was concerned about his perceived "loss of control" in disciplinary matters.

Groups transmute and temper hobby horses, and convert them (if the idea has potential) into germs of realistic proposals. Where a concerned individual gains subgroup support and secures group endorsement of his premises, his involvement is substantial. The price he pays (seeing his hobby horse become part of a package and/or deescalated in totalistic scope) is worth the price of the hearing and constituency that is gained. The process can also be educational, as with our "inmate control" officer who had to absorb and accommodate "abuse of authority" concerns of fellow officers in shaping a consensus product. Force-field analyses are "educational" because they force advocates of ideas to take the views of opponents into serious account.

A more important "reality check" evolved in our groups. Time after time in considering potential opposition, someone suggested that the question was empirical and that an interview might be instructive. In response to such suggestions, group members approached (1) inmates to be affected by a proposal, (2) psychologists whose "turf" might be invaded, (3) supervisors who were to be involved in projects, (4) counselors to be "served," (5) training personnel being "written in," and (6) members of staff committees and others. The interviews were enriching as well as reassuring. The experience was stimulating, the activity invigorating, the officers enlightened, and the products (their proposals) improved.

NOTES

1. During the last session of the first group, the men told us that they had arrived Monday expecting to waste their time with aimless and unproductive talk. When we suggested this frame of mind to another group, a member objected to being "stereotyped," but added that the characterization was accurate. The hilarious reaction loosened tension and proved to be a groundbreaker.

2. Inspired by this prospect, our first group called itself the "Job Enrichment Team" and the members referred to themselves as "JET officers."

3. We explained how group members had been selected (based on high job enrichment scores and on high or low alienation level), but the officers were less concerned about which officer might have met which criterion than we anticipated.

4. It is hardly surprising that the groups soon competed in terms of which subgroup could produce the longest chain of sheets listing relevant forces.

5. In the first session an officer loudly pointed out that completing the checklist was a good way to miss one's carpool. Other officers seemed to view the argument as persuasive.

6. One of us is probably a taskmaster; the other, a "tough" Rogerian; the combination embodies features of Mutt and Jeff. Our third team member (John Klofas) played the role of Sorcerer's Apprentice.

CHAPTER 16

TEAM PROPOSALS

Each team of correction officers faithfully produced four proposals, in the sense that it specified the problems, originated the solutions, worked out the details, worked through the ramifications, supplied most of the language, and reviewed what it had done.

Sixteen very different reform ideas originated with the 36 officers (see Figure 16.1). In each of the groups, however:

(1) Some proposals were "inmate oriented" and some "officer oriented," in that some proposals *primarily* advanced the goals of inmates, others, and those of officers.

(2) Some proposals envisaged further participation (QWL), and others prescribed ways of "enriching" the job.

(3) As noted (Chapter 15), the problems of each prison were represented in its proposals.

(4) Problems highlighted by the survey were also represented in the proposals.

(5) In each group, at least one member held strongly felt concerns that were endorsed by other members and represented in proposals.

(6) Problems discussed in each group *invariably* surfaced as concerns in other groups, but not necessarily with the same priority.
priority.

The proposal titles included acronyms, and programs were often named with one eye on the catchiness of abbreviations. Great Meadow (Comstock) prison, for instance, produced FIND (Facility Inmate-Need Deployment) and FACE (Facility Assistance to Correctional Employees). Auburn came up with COOP (Correction Officer Orientation Program), and Clinton, with CCC (Case Conference Committee). Other acronyms were discarded because they yielded (if one carefully strained the ear) off-color or pejorative connotations.

**FIGURE 16.1   Descriptions of the Sixteen Proposals
                 Drafted by the Four Officer Groups**

A. Proposals by the Auburn CO Group

  (1) *ACT (Area Coordinating Team):* The concern is with procedural inconsistency in the running of housing units; the proposed solution involves First Officers of housing units reviewing and coordinating procedures. They would function as a team to work out consistent procedures and to conduct periodic reviews.

  (2) *COOP (Correction Officer Orientation Program):* The program responds to the problem of unsystematic on-site indoctrination of new officers. The group suggests an on-the-job training schedule and procedure, and includes provision for systematic input of CO judgments into the rating of probationers.

  (3) *CCO (Counseling Correction Officer Program):* What is proposed is a job enrichment effort through which officers in high-inmate-contact posts can request special training to upgrade their counseling functions. The program includes liaison arrangements with prison counselors (service unit staff) and a special record system.

  (4) *OPD (Officer Professional Development Program):* The concern is with low self-estem and with the need for a vehicle to instill pride in the job and raise the level of CO aspirations. A workshop is suggested in which officers can discuss the morale problem and suggest inexpensive ways of boosting morale. Several preliminary suggestions (including an Officer of the Month program) are included in the proposal.

B. Proposals by the Clinton CO Group

  (1) *CCC (Case Conference Committee) Program:* Program Committees as a vehicle for making inmate assignments are unequipped to pay individual attention to the adjustment problems of those inmates who require scrutiny because of their inability to adapt to their assignments. The supplementary mechanism suggested for such inmates is the Case Conference Committee, whose convocation would be the task of an officer serving as coordinator.

  (2) *REACT Program:* A procedure is designed that would give front-line staff the opportunity to have input into noncontractual policy issues that impinge on their jobs. A form is proposed in which staff could "react" to problems created by, or to advantages of, new policies and procedures for their own work. There would also be provision for suggested remedies and for suggestions of new policies and/or procedures. The logistics for processing the new input are spelled out in the proposal.

  (3) *HDI (Help for Disturbed Inmates) Program:* The proposal addresses a concern about increasing numbers of emotionally disturbed inmates in prison population. Two surveys, a training program, and a planning process are spelled out. The last two components capitalize on the expertise of COs who have worked in programs for disturbed inmates and/or received special training in mental health matters. Close teaming of COs with mental health experts is envisioned for various phases of the program.

(continued)

FIGURE 16.1 (Continued)

(4) *Legal Conflict Performance and Prevention Program:* The concern is with the vulnerability of COs to legal problems and their insufficient preparation and resources in the area. A training program is suggested that involves the creation of CO paralegal aides, who would function in cooperation with facility and departmental attorneys. There is provision for a cumulatively updated handbook designed not only to help officers cope with legal problems, but primarily to prevent such problems by ensuring law-abiding and due-process-related behavior.

C. Proposals by the Ossining CO Group

(1) *OSH (Officer Self-Help) Program:* The concern is with the need for a resource for officers who have personal problems on the assumption that such problems can impinge on the institution. There is also provision for intervening with officers whose performance (e.g., time abuse) is already affected. The program relies on peer assistance through panels of COs (including COs with special skills) who can do counseling and referring to community agencies. COs are expected to volunteer for the program, but training and release time are provided for to make the program work.

(2) *OCR (Officer Control and Responsibility) Program:* Two review groups are suggested—each comprising a cross-section of institution staff—to clarify and expand the officer's role as inmate supervisor. The first group is discipline oriented and is concerned with expanding the officer's role in dispensing disciplinary sanctions, with controls for possible abuse of discretion; the second group would clarify the officer's role as inmate work supervisor, who needs civilian resources to do his job. Both groups would ensure against dilution of the CO's authority by supervisors who bypass the CO in the chain of command.

(3) *Supervisory Study and Training Proposal:* This proposal responds to a concern with quality of supervision (middle management). The suggestion is for teams of middle managers and COs to conduct staff surveys and design middle management training responsive to supervision problems that surface in the surveys. There is also a system for continuing meetings of COs and their immediate supervisors to resolve problems arising in their immediate work areas.

(4) *WPR (Work Problem Review) Program:* The program is based on the assumption that neither system reforms nor officer "shaping up" can independently solve quality-of-performance problems. The program calls for an inventory of efficiency-related problems and for the creation of problem-solving "study groups" that can call for performance increments and supportive steps from the administration.

FIGURE 16.1 (Continued)

D. Proposals by the Great Meadow CO Group

   (1) *Facility Assistance to Correctional Employees (FACE):* The program seeks to reduce employee turnover by addressing local quality-of-life issues. Each facility would have a FACE Coordinator who would help new employees get settled by serving as an information source and by preempting problems that surface in exit surveys. The coordinator would also be concerned with recruitment–particularly of minority candidates from nearby communities. A sample FACE project (involving staff housing) is delineated.

   (2) *FIND (Facility Inmate-Need Deployment):* This program addresses aspects of the classification problem, including (1) idle inmates, (2) needs for labor that are unmet and could be addressed with the help of inmates, and (3) high inmate turnover. One program component involves familiarization experiences for civilian classification analysts, requiring one-week visits at each facility, including a "reality tour." The other components set up FIND Teams to inventory human resources and work possibilities at each prison and to design short-term and long-term projects.

   (3) *Employee Public Relations (EPR) Program:* An EPR Committee is proposed to locate, publicize, and reward meritorious staff contributions and community involvements. There is provision for staff/inmate cooperation including a special project of CO-coached intramural inmate teams, and a chance for inmates to record their appreciation for officer assistance. The EPR Committee would prepare news releases, coordinate speakers, assist with prison/community day arrangements, and otherwise improve the prison's public image. Issues related to uniforms and appearance are also addressed, particularly as they impact on the public.

   (4) *Supervisor Quality Control and OJT:* The proposal sets up an inservice training and testing program for current supervisors and new supervisors to ensure their familiarization with principal work areas in the prison. Diagnostic tests would be constructed by pooling items submitted by area COs and sergeants, and supervisors would undergo familiarization training selectively where testing indicates relative unfamiliarity.

The Proposal Preamble

The format or shape of the proposals differed in some respects. The first section, the statement of the problem, ranged from succinct to elaborate and from factual to melodramatic. The Auburn group described the need for an officer-run policy-coordinating mechanism (ACT) in one terse paragraph:

The problem addressed in this proposal is that of serious inconsistency in institutional procedures at Auburn. Our prime concern is with housing blocks, because we see housing as the hub of the wheel that makes up the prison for officers and inmates. Variations in procedures are a problem at Auburn that depresses officer morale and causes confusion, frustration and apathy among inmates. The problem has other effects as well, including reducing the efficiency of supervision, inmate orientation, discipline and counseling.

In this case the problem was seen as self-explanatory and deemed sufficiently concrete not to require exegesis. A similar type of proposal from Ossining kept its preamble brief by relying on survey data for documentation. The introduction reads:

> Officers at the Ossining correctional facility voice widespread complaints about COs being unrecognized, unsupported and underused. One area of CO concern is the officers' feeling that they are not permitted to exercise their professional judgement and to make necessary decisions in day-to-day supervision of inmates.
>
> There is special concern about the officer's inability to discipline inmates without prior involvement from supervisors, and about direct transactions between inmates and supervisors that bypass or ignore the officer. Another concern relates to restrictions on officers that make them unable to respond to the emergency needs of inmates, so that the inmate learns to view the officer as superfluous or as impotent.
>
> There are additional complaints about lack of recognition of officer contributions to the institution, lack of trust in officers' abilities, unresponsiveness to officer suggestions, and disregard of officers' expertise.
>
> There is a need to define the CO's area of authority and responsibility vis-à-vis inmates and supervisors or other staff. There is additional need to support the officer who responsibly exercises his authority, and to deal with occasional abuses of discretion without penalizing or handcuffing the officer who does his job honestly, fairly and humanely.

Other statements were longer, either because (1) the program was multidimensional, (2) the problem was complex, (3) justifications took a variety of forms, or (4) there were strong feelings that demanded explication.

An example of multidimensionality is a package (Employee Public Relations) from Comstock prison. The following are preamble excerpts. They anticipate program aspects through problem aspects:

> Prison employees must deal with the public's lack of information—or misinformation—about prisons. Employees who are the most seriously affected are the correctional officers whose public image ranges from unflattering (turnkey) to degrading (brutal turnkey). The CO's knowledge of how he is seen contributes to his low morale and deflates his pride and self-esteem.
>
> Outstanding work is ignored, and it goes unrepeated. At minimum, extra effort yields no sense of accomplishment, but it can also bring trouble. The CO feels disapproving peer pressure; his supervisors rate him negatively; others hog credit for his actions. In the absence of incentives, the CO gives up, and drops back to the bare bones of his job description. The result is boredom and unused potential. The problem is aggravated by the consequences of lowered pride among a few officers, who become rotten apples (and get away with being rotten apples), set bad examples, and increase the burden and the risk that other officers must carry.
>
> It is ironic that self-rehabilitating inmates are in the same boat with officers where bad press is concerned. No one expects prison inmates to make constructive contributions, and there is no incentive for them to do so. Peer pressure against officer-inmate involvements is experienced by inmates as well as officers. What is silliest about this peer pressure is that in the name of security it undermines security. Where discipline problems arise, it is not the officer who "keeps his distance" but the one who enjoys inmates' confidence who has the edge. Good inmate relations is good public relations and good security practice.

The Comstock FIND program exemplifies *problem* complexity. The concern of the program is to match inmate resources with prison needs. The preamble deals with underutilized resources and deployment possibilities. For instance,

> There is inmate idleness. This includes inmates who are not idle by choice—inmates who want to work. Other inmates have at one

time wanted to work, but have lost motivation as they have lost hope of finding work, or have discovered the length of waiting lists. Idle inmates are inmates who cannot develop or grow or learn. They are inmates who don't look rehabilitated to parole boards. Concern about looking rehabilitated makes inmates choose the wrong jobs for the wrong reasons. There is no pattern to their program involvements, because such inmates are intent on building resumes rather than careers. Inmates who are more motivated (and would be ideally placed in certain assignments) get lost in the crowd.

Idleness is a destructive influence. Idle inmates become emotionally disturbed, tense, frustrated. Idleness means idle hands available for trouble. On both counts, idleness breeds prison incidents. It leads to inmate conflicts, which cause some inmates to arm themselves. It leads to exploitation and victimization.

There are programs on the books with no staff; there are staff who do nothing or next-to-nothing, and staff with jobs that do not seriously engage them. COs are under-utilized in running inmate programs and no one (including the CO) ever asks why.

Tangible needs are visible elsewhere: Knee-high grass in summer, and no flowers; unwashed windows, dirty blocks, unpainted walls, unhygienic conditions. When an area deteriorates, it stays deteriorated. There is no renovation, repair or construction. Prison maintenance beg for help to get their jobs done, and the farm—which could yield vegetables and rehabilitative training— lies fallow. Beyond this are other needs, such as those of the community. There is no sense in children having broken toys when inmates lie idle.

A Clinton proposal for training officers to deal with emotionally disturbed inmates (HDI) is more formally introduced through separate sections. Section titles read, "How Many Disturbed Inmates?" "The Impact of Disturbed Inmates," "Mental Health (professionals) and Custody," and "Officer Needs and Resources."

Programs were justified by pointing up their advantages to (1) officers, (2) other staff, (3) inmates, and (4) the agency. Others were defended by stressing (1) custody concerns and (2) rehabilitative goals. An example of the former is an Auburn proposal for a Counselor Correction Officer (CCO) program, which points out,

> Due to the work load placed on Service Unit counselors (150 inmates per CC at Auburn, with commensurate case loads elsewhere), the SU counseling system has become weighted down to the point where response time, personalized service, time spent with inmates, and comprehensiveness of answers are impaired.

> Counselor morale is seriously affected, and there is evidence (according to an SU representative) of burnout among counselors.

> Most of the problem, however, is experienced by inmates, who feel frustrated, neglected and cynical, and are anxious to find solutions elsewhere.

> Preliminary inquiries about inmate attitudes suggest inmates (1) value a reduction in response time (2) feel comfortable about approaching select officers, (3) have confidentiality concerns, and (4) feel a need for more and better information. Response time is particularly critical.

> At one time, the correctional officer was a recognized prime counseling resource, and today COs engage in counseling continuously in the course of their work. The results of a CO survey suggest that officers are open to increased counseling involvement. At Auburn, 81% of officers disagreed with "The CO's only concern is with prison security"; two thirds (66%) disagreed with "Rehabilitative programs should be left to mental health professionals," and 69% with "If a CO wants to do counseling, he should change jobs."

Other long preambles dealt with issues that concerned the officers personally—issues invested with strong feelings. Many passages combined logical arguments with emotional appeals. The most eloquent example of such a statement precedes the Ossining Officer Self Help (OSH) proposal. It is well worth quoting *in toto*:

> There is no easy way of distinguishing purely personal problems of officers from problems that are job-related, or that are problems both for the institution and the officer. Three recent officer suicides have been a serious loss for Ossining just as in a trival way they have diminished its manpower pool. Human tragedies invite Ossining to examine itself, and to ask how such losses could have been prevented.

An officer with emotional problems may bring these problems to the job, or may stay away from the job because he is disturbed and unmotivated to work. Personal problems may lead to drinking, which may lead to absenteeism, tardiness, or the physical presence on the job of a man who is in no condition to perform responsible, professional work. Unhappiness may lead to alienation, which may contribute to an officer resigning his job.

The other side of the coin is the fact that poor work performance and time abuse need not reflect poor motivation and incompetence, but may result from legitimate or serious reasons, which must be separated out of the disciplinary ball game through closer scrutiny. Management has a stake in making sure that the officer with a history of loyalty and dedication who reacts to a personal emergency is not treated the same way as the officer who engages in negligent behavior because he is lazy, disinterested or incompetent.

A prison may not have the *obligation* to help an officer who is depressed or is struggling with a family problem, but it may be wise for it to try to help the officer before his problems escalate to a point where they affect his work, keep him from his job, or deprive the institution of his services. An officer may not have a *right* to expect his employers, supervisors and fellow-officers to help him when he is in trouble, but he has a right to react to his employers, supervisors and fellow officers in terms of the decency and concern, or indifference and lack of concern they show him when he makes it obvious that he needs help and has nowhere to turn.

Another aspect of the problem is *precisely* the fact that Ossining is an indifferent place—that is, the type work setting to which men commute, in which they work in isolation, and from which they leave to go their separate ways. Extending human assistance (as we shall propose should be done) builds bonds that tie people to the institution and each other. It can foster a spirit of brotherhood at Ossining.

The last point to be mentioned is that extending help to officers with problems performs important functions for those who do the helping. Such activities call for skills, and exercising these skills can raise self-esteem and provide a sense of accomplishment. If a helping program is carefully designed, it can benefit officers with problems (those who need help), it can satisfy those who help the officers with problems, and ultimately it can improve the facility as a whole.

"Carefully" designed means that help is extended in confidence and constructively by persons a man can trust. It means that help is extended by persons who want to help rather than being paid to help; and it means that the type and the level of help matches the nature of the officer's problem. The program described below is designed with these objectives in mind.

Program Narratives

The activity in which our officers uniformly excelled was the drafting of the "Description of the Program" section, in which the exactness of the information they supplied was awesome, and their work precise, taxing, and meticulous. The narrative following the OSH preamble illustrates the complexity of the details the officers had to anticipate and plan for. The complexity included such issues as selection, training, supervision and coordination, scheduling and resources, and the anticipation of junctures at which contingencies involved in operating the program had to be specified. The OSH implementation sequence is laid out as follows:

(1) The program (if approved) would be initiated through announcements in lineups and through posters on locker room bulletin boards which describe the project and ask officers wishing to volunteer for the program to contact local 1413 of the union. The invitation would stress the need for officers who have special qualification, experiences, education or training in areas such as counseling and social work or social service work.

When a roster of initial volunteers is drawn up, organizational meetings of volunteers will be held in the training area. In these meetings, a steering committee of three OSH volunteers will be designated to meet with the training lieutenant to set up a brief training program for the volunteers. This training program would minimally involve,

(a) the chaplain
(b) psychologists, counselors and other mental health professionals from the institution

    (c) representatives of select community agencies
    (d) some of the specially qualified OSH officers as trainers of
        the other officers.

The training would include a survey of community and
institutional resources available for referrals; it would also cover
techniques of listening, problem diagnosis and counseling.

At the termination of training, a final roster of OSH members will
be prepared. Such a roster might exclude officers who leave the
program by common consent, but the principal screening issue
will be the officers' commitment to serve in the program to the full
extent required of its participants. This entails serving as program
coordinator and as OSH panel member whenever called upon to
do so.

(2) The OSH membership roster will be subdivided into three lists,
one for each shift. Each of the three rosters will be further
subdivided into (a) specially qualified OSH members and (b)
others. Rosters will be arranged in alphabetical order.

(3) The officers with the first two names on each of the three rosters
will serve as coordinator and backup coordinator of their shift.
They will serve in this capacity for three (3) months, after which
the assignment rotates to the next two names on the roster. The
backup coordinator serves as coordinator on the coordinator's
days off, or whenever the coordinator is otherwise unavailable.

The work of OSH takes place through OSH panels. Each panel
comprises three OSH members, at least *one* of whom must be
drawn from the "specially qualified" section of the roster. Panels
are constituted from names selected in alphabetical order
(modified to ensure panel membership of qualified officers), and
are convoked when they are needed, as soon as they are needed.
The convocation of the panel is the job of the OSH coordinator. A
panel only serves to deal with one officer and his problems, with
another panel drawn for the next officer.

(4) A CO may request a meeting with a panel. The panel also
accepts referrals from supervisors, fellow-COs and other staff,
provided the CO to be interviewed consents to referral. Requests
or referrals for panel interviews are phoned to the Duty Officer.
The Duty Officer has the names of the coordinator and backup
coordinator, and contacts one or the other, furnishing him with
the name of the CO to be interviewed, and the source of the
referral. The coordinator

    (a) selects three names for the panel,

    (b) contracts the source of referral for a brief description of the CO's problem,

    (c) contacts panel members to make sure they are willing and available; (panel appointees may refuse to serve; however, two refusals without substantial reasons will result in removal of the CO's name from the OSH roster),

    (d) contacts the CO to be interviewed, confirms the CO's willingness to meet with the panel for a substantial and appropriate reason, and asks the CO if he has reservations about any of the three panel candidates. (In case of such reservations, the coordinator appoints a substitute or serves on the panel himself.)

    (e) The coordinator contacts the watch commander with the names of the panel members and the CO to be interviewed. The watch commander arranges for relief officers, and instructs the panel and interviewee on time and place for the panel. Given the possible emergency nature of some problems, such arrangements would be made as promptly as possible.

A Clinton proposal (REACT) set out a feedback procedure to acquaint administrators with unanticipated problems produced by policy changes, directives, memoranda and orders. The proposal contained a draft of the form to be used (including size and design, number of copies, and type of paper), a specification of the timetable and routing procedure, and a flow chart. Much thought went into every detail, including the following instructions for the back of the form:

The Purpose of the REACT Form

The REACT form was devised by a representative group of correctional officers as a means of opening up lines of communication between front-line staff and administrators at each institution and in Albany. It is designed to allow you to examine policies which relate to your job and to make suggestions for improving these policies. Include on the form your reaction and/or suggestion relating to a particular policy, memorandum or order. Use the lower part of the form for suggesting new policies or procedures relating to your job.

Guidelines

(1) The REACT form must deal with non-contractual issues. If you think the contract has been violated, use normal grievance procedures.

(2) To be processed, the REACT form must include the name, item number, badge number (if appropriate) and signature of the person submitting the form.

(3) Only constructive, well thought out comments should be made on a REACT form.

(4) Do not abuse the use of this form. It is a chance for *serious* input into policy which affects you.

(5) Keep one copy of the form for your own records. Send two copies to your superintendent and send one to your local union for its records.

You will receive a response from your superintendent or from central office in Albany within a reasonable period of time.

Another Clinton proposal set out a program (Legal Conflict Performance and Prevention) to provide law-related training and resources to COs. In prescribing legal training, the officers did not merely advance a generic prescription ("let there be training") but included curriculum details such as the following:

Twenty-eight hours of incident-focused training (4 hours charged against the current training commitment plus an additional 24 hours of one-time special training) would be offered at the local facility to existing personnel, including officers, supervisors, counselors, teachers, shop foremen, and stenographers. The same updated, incident-based training would be given recruits at the academy.

The curriculum would not be limited to the following or necessarily so arranged, but should cover *at least* the following areas of officer concern:

(1) on-the-job incident-prevention law training,

(2) updated commentary (on regulations) concerning the use of force,

(3) report writing,

(4) prisoner rights and responsibilities,

(5) officer rights and responsibilities,

(6) legal issues likely to arise in decisions the officer n make,

(7) legal issues in visitor processing, search and seizure,

(8) legal issues when working outside the facility,

(9) the handling and presenting of evidence,

(10) inmate and officer rights and responsibilities, and prison procedures,

(11) inmate and officer rights and responsibilities in processing of inmate correspondence,

(12) general search and seizure issues,

(13) legal knowledge needed to participate in inspector general interviews, contacts with the Attorney General's Office and Bureau of Criminal Investigation, as well as Prisoner Legal Services' obtaining of depositions,

(14) problems that come up when testifying in court,

(15) removal of inmates from cells,

(16) legal issues and Departmental policy concerning riots and the use of gas,

(17) rights and responsibilities officers must keep in mind in incidents that involve a danger of officers getting hurt.

In addition, the training should cover how and when to use the proposed legal handbook and the procedures for its updating. The training should conclude with procedures, examples and discussions of the role of paralegal aides, including how and when to use them.

In the case of every prescription the questions "how," "when," and "what" are minutely addressed. A post-academy-training package comes with a "Block Training Check List" covering more than fifty topics, and contains a rating form for peer evaluation. A proposal for refreshing the training of middle managers includes "Sample Quality Control Questions" arranged by prison work areas. The Correction Counseling Officer (CCO) program includes a Daily Work Sheet and a referral form.

Where research is proposed, procedures are spelled out. The following are the sample questions proposed for a Work Problems Survey (at Sing Sing):

What problem(s) (difficulties) have you recently experienced in performing your work (job)?

What ideas do you have for solving the problem(s) and/or improving the work you can do?

What problem(s) (difficulties) have you experienced with administrative or personnel procedures?

What ideas do you have for solving and/or improving institutional procedure(s)?

If not sufficient space attach extra page(s).

The Comstock FACE (Facility Assistance to Correctional Employees) proposal includes a draft of an exit questionnaire for employees who are about to leave—or are proposing to leave:

Survey of Staff Members Resigning or Transferring

From _____ Correctional Facility

The survey will help identify the reasons for staff turnover at this institution. We are particularly interested in your feelings about the living conditions and quality of life in this area. With your assistance we may be able to identify and address some of the problems that officers and their families have living and working in this area. Thank you for your help.

F.A.C.E. Coordinator

Name _____ How long have you been a C.O.?_____

How long have you worked at this facility? _____

Are you transferring? _____ Resigning? _____

Does your family live with you in this area? _____

Did you encounter any problems at this facility that are related to your transferring or quitting? If so, what problems?

Were you satisfied with the living conditions in this area?

Did you locate adequate housing?

If not, what difficulties did you run into?

Were you informed of local facilities, including educational, recreational, medical facilities, etc.?

If yes, by whom?

Did you find these facilities adequate for your needs?

If not, what other facilities would you have needed?

Do you have any suggestions that might help improve the local community and living conditions?

Do you have any other suggestions that might help us to retain staff members and their families in this area?

Descriptive detail marks the difference between top-of-the-head brainstorming and backbreaking work. Detail also is a measure of involvement. The following, for instance, shows evidence of loving attention related to content (sports) and to clients (officers and inmates) of the projected service:

The institution should immediately initiate a program of intramural sports, involving competing inmate teams coached by correction officers. The EPR Committee should compile a list of officers with interest and competence in sports. This list would be limited to COs who volunteer (firmly committing their time) to try to coach inmate teams in the sport of their choice. Where two correction officers are available for any given sport, a two-team league can be formed by circulating signup sheets among inmates through the good offices of the Inmate Liaison Committee. Sports that should be included would be softball, soccer and basketball. There is also interest in competitive boxing. Secondary sports would be ping pong and volley ball.

The teams would function under the auspices of staff now assigned to the gymnasium and the school; they would be managed by inmate-managers appointed by CO-coaches. Each team would have its color and uniform (which the coach could wear as blazer), and a name reflecting sponsorship by a staff or inmate organization (see budget). If security considerations can be satisfied, the teams could compete against extra-mural visiting teams, as well as each other.

Detail shows the sort of familiarity with workaday realities that no manager can claim. In this sense participation not only substitutes for management planning, but improves on it.

Program Force Fields

Officers were at a disadvantage in anticipating "big picture" resistances to proposals (see Chapter 17). Force fields dealt with psychological rather than organizational forces. Some force fields were long, and even one of the most succinct ones (the force field of the Officer Self Help program) is a strikingly successful attempt at empathy with groups affected by the program that ignored competing thrusts the agency had under way:

Resources	Obstacles
1. Administrators might be relieved by COs taking over a function that is needed but not performed.	1. Administration might object to the expense and trouble OSH involves, particularly to the load placed on watch commanders.
2. Self help takes away stigma.	2. Competing commitments for training time.
3. Officers might feel that they have peer support for their problems.	3. COs might not trust COs with confidentiality.
4. Resource experts might be pleased to feel that their skills can be used by COs who don't usually come to them.	4. Resource persons might feel they are already overloaded.
5. The system might be happy to have some means of addressing problems that lead to absenteeism and other time abuse.	5. Some COs might make fun of OSH participants (peer pressure).
6. This is an unprecedented opportunity for COs to feel that they are doing something worthwhile.	6. Some officers may have less dedication over the long haul than other officers.
	7. Officers may feel that OSH are Finks working for the Administration.

7. Officers will feel that their special skills are used to a full extent.

8. OSH beats being brought up on charges (gives you a fighting chance).

9. OSH would give COs who feel boxed in an outlet for frustrations.

10. COs headed for trouble might feel that it can be headed off in time.

11. Assurance of confidentiality helps.

8. Officers who perform below standards might feel that their shortcomings could be exposed.

The Battle of the Budget

Variations among proposals occurred in the budget sections which—as previously noted—sometimes were concrete (and exquisitely detailed) and sometimes were not. The Great Meadows public relations package, for instance, confined its budget to one of its elements, that of the staff-run inmate intramural sports program. The brief but ingenious statement read:

Budget and Resources:

The cost of the program suggested in this proposal is modest and flexible, because much of it can be absorbed or contributed. The intramural program is a case in point: The education and gymnasium budget can be drawn on for equipment. Additional expenses can be born by team sponsors, such as inmate civic groups (JCs, Friends of Fortune, NAACP, AA) and the employees' unions. Commissary funds are an option. Cost of uniforms can be modest if one enlists the cooperation of a tailoring class. Manpower costs include gymnasium staff (CO and recreation instructors), whose role would be expanded.

Coaches would require only limited relief, to cover events or preevent training dates that are fixed. Where such situations occur, the coaches must provide the chart sergeant with appropriate (48-hour) notice.

As the example shows, (1) money might help, but (2) funding is not an issue in the implementation of this proposal.[1]

[1]The exception to this rule is the idea of reinstating competitive boxing, which requires some equipment.

The Clinton proposal for expanded legal training envisaged an expensive paralegal aides program. The budget section mentions this fact in passing, but goes on to argue:

> Although the initial investment is substantial, the cost over time should be markedly reduced. The Department's personnel will have been upgraded through training; they can rely on a relatively inexpensive ongoing legal support system with annual updating. Further, this proposal should be viewed as an alternative to the expanding costs of lawsuits and of performance inefficiencies, as well as the costs resulting from court decisions. The preventive nature of this proposal must be considered in relation to the rapidly expanding costs of legal conflicts.

The tendency to minimize cost accounting may be understandable on at least two counts: (1) officers lacked necessary budget information and found it difficult to predict the expenses of hypothetical contingencies, and (2) there was fear that to admit that a program cost money might invite its rejection. The extreme of the second concern was the type of budget that discussed savings much more prominently than expenses, as did the budget of an Auburn proposal for an inservice addendum to CO recruit training. This program, the Correction Officer Orientation Program, or COOP, prescribed that new officers be rotated through prison assignments under the auspices of more experienced officers. The budget section read:

> As an alternative to the 13-week academy recruit training, this proposed integration of 40 days at the Academy and 54 days of institution-based OJT has appreciable cost advantages:
>
> (a) extensively reduced Academy residence costs:
> (b) staffing costs—Training COs incorporate the training function into their existing functions.

As an alternative to the existing insufficient 8-week Academy training, additional budget allocation is required for the 54 days the recruit is in OJT at the local institution rather than being budgeted as CO manpower while not qualified to perform as a CO.

The point is that budgets evoked anxiety. The officers tried to make up in persuasiveness what they lacked in data, or stressed minor details of estimates ("5 members at 5 man hours × 12 months = 60 man hours per year"; "office equipment: two desks, three chairs, typewriter, telephone, two filing cabinets, and office supplies"; "one permanent position, G14 at $1,745"; and the like).

Budgets are dreams framed by hope. In the absence of contextual data about priorities and prospects, resources, and competing claims there is no way of knowing what a budget must look like. The suspicion arises (justifiably, as it happens) that a budget can kill the juiciest fruits of planning. Most managers live with this fact, but groups such as ours blame themselves for failing.

CHAPTER 17

FROM CUP TO LIP:
IMPLEMENTATION OF PROPOSALS

Administrators as planners have a virtue: being administrators, they can implement what they plan. Workers, on the other hand, must convince administrators to enact the reforms they have proposed or to let them carry the ball from bench to field.

Grass-roots management presupposes top-level receptivity to grass-roots participation. It assumes a promise to at least *try* to enact proposals, as opposed to viewing them as training exercises or learning experiences for workers, or as charming (but unsophisticated) expressions of front-line opinion. The size of organizations matters. Most managers can seriously listen, but not all can easily act.

In the Oakland Police Department (see Chapter 13), the chief (who had clear, unobstructed authority over 800 officers) could not only act, but his ability to translate new ideas into action was surpassed by his search for new ideas. When the chief's receptivity was discovered by our troops, they were awed and pleasantly shocked. A first-phase subgroup delegation reported to the group:

Jack and I met with the Chief on the field training officer study. He had a copy of the study beforehand and as he indicated later, he read it in some detail. I don't know about Jack, but I was totally surprised at his first reaction. He indicated to us that he thought we had a heck of a good thing here and that we'd researched it and we'd come up with some real good ideas, which right off the bat gave us the impression that he'd bought the program in totality—and in effect, at this point he has [Toch, Grant, and Galvin, 1975: 58].

The men discovered (with mixed feelings) that implementation meant being drafted to follow through—the obligation to play a new role as implementation-facilitators:

> He threw the ball right back to us: "You guys have got it started, now . . . you can follow it through by doing the staff study routine." . . . I think what he's saying to us in effect, you know, "You've come up with a good thing here, and you're familiar with what you want, and if we just hand this paper to somebody else and have them working on it, that a lot of your ideas are going to be lost. Since you are familiar with it, it's more or less your responsibility to go into the staff studies and to learn that these things are feasible or not feasible and keep as many of the points in your original proposal as possible, in the end product." Although he's thrown the ball to us to get this thing going, I think . . . we've impressed him with this thing to the point that he's willing to give us the responsibility of carrying this thing on through [Toch et al., 1975: 58-59].

Another discovery was that there was reciprocity in the transaction—that top administrators, too, have ideas. The chief suggested plausible extensions of group projects and possible variations to them. The shoe changed feet, with the administrator as coplanner and workers as managers:

> Another ball he kind of threw to us just in passing, which I don't really think I got the impact of until later, although I think I turned to Jack and thought "Oh my God, now what are we getting into," was the fact that he was talking about what the course content should be for this field training officer training class. There were some little words passed there to give me the impression that we may be involved in writing the program, what's going to be taught the field training officers [Toch et al., 1975: 59].

The chief in the project also sometimes acted as a co-researcher. He studied results of our pilot study using the critical incident questionnaire and issued instructions (drafted by the group) over his signature:

Special Order No. 1400

To: All Members
Subject: Critical Incident Questionnaire

Recently a Critical Incident Questionnaire was completed by a limited number of members of various ranks, including the Chief, at the request of the Violence Prevention Unit.

The results of the Questionnaire suggest that a great degree of confusion exists as regards Departmental policy and, in some cases, interpretation of the law itself. In order to determine how extensive the confusion is, why it exists, and how to correct it, more information is needed from various members of the Department. Therefore, each sergeant and each patrolman in the following organizational units will complete a copy of the Questionnaire and submit it through channels to the Chief's office: Patrol Division, Preventive Services Division, Youth Section of Community Relations and Youth Division.

Each sergeant and patrolman who completes the Questionnaire shall enter his name, rank, serial number and present assignment in the space provided on the form.

The commanding officers of the above named organizational units shall use an alphabetical roster to ensure that each designated member receives and completes a copy of the Questionnaire. A date entry shall be placed after the member's name when he is given the Questionnaire and a date entry shall be placed after his name when the Questionnaire is returned by the member. The alphabetical listing and the Questionnaires (compiled in alphabetical order) shall be forwarded to the Chief's office by the date designated [Toch et al., 1975: 369].

The group experimented with innovations to test their feasibility. When the chief was satisfied that an idea might work, he authorized a full-scale trial. For example,

As a result of a 16-month experimental Landlord-Tenant Dispute Settlement Program, a new Landlord-Tenant Intervention Unit is now being established in the Conflict Management Section. It is believed to be the first of its kind in the nation.

Rather than dismiss landlord-tenant calls as "civil matters," the Unit will attempt to achieve a settlement of the dispute, often by referring the parties to other agencies, such as the Small Claims Court. By early settlement of the dispute, the Unit is expected to deter violence that otherwise might occur.

The Unit will operate for an experimental period, after which time its operations will be evaluated and its methodology, if found to be effective, utilized throughout the Department.

The Unit is presently operating Monday through Friday, 1000 to 1800 hours, and can be reached . . . [Toch et al., 1975: 359].

The chief ultimately institutionalized our group (as per its own proposal) and it entered the agency's table of organization, as follows:

The Violence Prevention Unit is directly responsible to the Chief of Police. The Unit is organizationally assigned to the Office of the Chief of Police.

The Unit consists of three sections. These are the Action Review Section, the Training Research Section, and the Experimental Projects Section.

The Action Review Section will analyze in a nonpunitive manner the activities of individuals who seem to be having difficulties during inter-personal contacts. Its activities will include the identification of such individuals, the review of their handling of interpersonal contacts, the convening of Action Review Panels, the discussion of cases, and the recommendations of remedial actions.

The Training Research Section will engage in a variety of developmental activities. It will plan, execute, and evaluate training programs dealing with violence reduction for clientele both inside and outside the Department. Of particular importance will be the Section's involvement in exploring new training approaches and applying them in the program of violence reduction.

The Experimental Projects Section will design, execute, and evaluate new organizational approaches to the problem of violence. Operational activities in areas where there is a high potential for violence will receive considerable attention [Toch et al., 1975: 375].

The Oakland experiment—through the 1979 budget crunch that terminated all city support functions—was solidly institutionalized. The reasons why it was implemented are only rarely attainable. They included an ideal administrator and an outside climate favorable to reform. The organization was small enough, yet large enough. Such combinations are rare. More usual is a mixed picture. A picture of this kind is illustrated by the New York corrections scene, to which we turn next.

We Shot Ideas into the Air . . .

New York corrections belongs in a category in which (1) the setting is a central bureaucracy that loosely runs plants (prisons) where the work is done, (2) there is an active and concerned union, and (3) the external climate is unstable. The project was cleared with a top agency administrator and with union leaders. Both promised to review group proposals and to back their implementation. We submitted all sixteen proposals as they emerged from the groups. Prisons and local unions received subsets (four proposals) for their institutions. We waited for reactions. For a good many months, however, nothing happened.

This delay ultimately proved instructive. We discovered, among other things, that

(1) Unstable climates often become crises. In a crisis (such as drastic prison overcrowding) survival issues must take precedence for top administrators, who ignore precrisis concerns or relegate them to subordinates.

(2) Short, written documents (such as six- to eight-page proposals) in aggregate (multiples of sixteen) become intimidating and defy reading. Such documents end up in desk drawers. Inquiries elicit expressions of goodwill or promises to "read the stuff as I can get to it."

(3) Further pressure displaces material to desk tops of lower-ranking officials, with instructions to "look these over." Recipients of this delegation chain may ignore their mandate. Others write memoranda in which they take exception to minor details (usually financial). Some counter with ideas of their own. Such memoranda are filed.

Developments of this sort represent victories of bureaucratic roots over grass roots. More substantial victories entail setting up a group of junior officials to "staff" a project, i.e., to emphasize obvious difficulties in implementation. Another gambit allocates single proposals to scattered officials (who never heard of the program) or merges proposals into a composite (training, morale boosting, and so on) that fits an innocuous preexisting thrust.

There are many reasons for bureaucratic inertia. One is *assimilation*. New ideas are compared to ideas and to programs that are already on the books. Ideas can thus be rejected as (1) redundant or as (2) competing, depending on whether the proposed reforms are similar to, or different from, programs that are already under way or contemplated.

Another reason for inertia is *blindness to process*. New ideas are familiar grist for bureaucratic mills; they are neutrally processed in terms of criteria such as programmatic coherence and feasibility. The question "How did the idea come into being in the first place?" is put aside or ignored. A more serious process-blindness relates to program *content*. A proposal that envisages democratic process looks strange and unfamiliar. This means that it is likely to be rejected. If it is not, democratic components become the nearest bureaucratic equivalents, which destroys the value of proposals as vehicles for disseminating participation.

Meanwhile, Back at the Target Sites . . .

At our four prisons, officials had been supplied with proposals, had read them, and discussed them. In three of the four prisons, two or more circumscribed proposals were available for implementation by the prison.

One superintendent convened a "proposal presentation" meeting, in the course of which such a proposal was presented and adopted. During discussion of this project, it became obvious that it had already generated underground discontent and resistance. Middle managers (sergeants and lieutenants) felt excluded from the concept. They also felt offended because they had not been represented in the groups. We accommodated the first concern by modifying the proposal to provide for a sergeant in the program.

This also defused the more general concern, in the sense that it did not surface in subsequent meetings.

The role of the warden was supremely important. The warden was conciliatory and task oriented. He did not allow quibbles over details to pass as arguments against programs. (He also did not let our group insist that their draft was sacrosanct). The warden closed off what became a popular avenue of filibuster, the tendency to ignore programs and to embark on a seminar (preferably free floating) about the problems that the program addressed.

No action (beyond inhouse communications) was taken elsewhere. This did not reflect disapproval, but simply meant that proposals *of themselves* were not incentives to action. They were not a force sufficiently powerful to break through daily routine and cause departures from it. Nothing seemed likely to happen in the absence of (1) a mandate from "headquarters" (administration or union), (2) a commitment to a "presentation" meeting as part of the program, (3) a consultant's continuing physical presence, or (4) some other force. The latter (residual) category became crucial to us later.

The Joint Committee on Quality of Working Life

As we have seen (Chapter 7), quality of work life (QWL) efforts are ways to achieve worker/management collaboration toward common QWL goals. The *typical* program involves shop-floor groups seeking to improve their work climate; the suggestions of such groups are reviewed by a top-level group (a QWL Committee) composed of union and management leaders.

QWL is separable, in that it can emphasize process (shop-floor committees) or goals (QWL Committee). Agreements between public employees' unions and their employers generally have created a *goal*-oriented QWL process consisting of Joint (union/state) Committees on Quality of Working Life. Such a linkage joins N.Y. State with its corrections officers (Council 82, AFSCME). The Committee comprises an "executive committee" of top officials and a "project identification committee" of union and management representatives; these committees are supported by a staff headed by a staff director.[1]

The QWL Committee is empowered to fund proposals that "can lead to improvements in employee morale, productivity, and labor management relations." Requisite is that a "proposal must represent joint labor-management agreement—particularly at the facility and department level" (State of New York, 1981). Ways of attaining agreement are not specified, except that "it is advised that labor-management agreement be attained at the earliest stages possible in developing a Quality of Working Life project" (State of New York, 1981).

The impasse relating to our proposals was broken when a decision was made (somewhere in the corrections agency) to transmit the documents to the QWL Committee.

The QWL Committee is *inter*bureaucratic in the sense that two bureaucracies (union and management) are responsible for seeking neutral ground. Suggestions emanating from each side are scrutinized to ensure that they are not abrogations of responsibility and do not yield unilateral benefits. Ideas must demonstrate that they are entitled to reasonable bilateral consensus. If a proposal is thus acceptable, the committee can support it financially through subsidies, but it cannot set up or direct implementation of programs.

Acceptability of our proposals to union and management representatives thus was the first issue. QWL staff contacted superintendents and union officials to ascertain their reactions. After the proposals had passed this test, they were distributed to members of the QWL project identification committee. This group read the proposals, and it urged their implementation.

Back to Square One, On to Square Two

The next step was for QWL staff to visit the four prisons. On these prison visits, QWL staff were accompanied by an agency representative and by ourselves. The meetings at the prisons varied from discursive to pointed and systematic. The *outcomes* of the meetings were as follows:

(1) In two institutions, problems developed around the fact that the proposals envisaged setting up democratic, group-based procedures. Groups were referred to as "committees," as in the phrase, "the last thing we need are more . . . " The argument was

raised that (a) it is impossible to get groups convened while manpower shortages last, and (b) experience shows that "talk" (groups being equated with seminars) is a waste. More charitably, goals were relegated to bureaucratic units (such as personnel clerks) who could "do them just as well."

(2) Several times, proposals were integrated into existing or projected programs. In Ossining our "self-help" coordinator became Employee Assistance Coordinator. In this capacity, a member of our group now shares responsibility for ameliorating problems of employees, which was the goal of the officers' proposal.

In some cases, proposal goals were scaled down. At Auburn, the prison's summary of our meeting records that

> We doubt that staff will be available to allow [the proposal to train and involve correction officers to assist inmates through counseling]. We will make changes that will provide interfacing by Counselors in the program areas. Superintendent plans to meet with counselors on this.
>
> We also want to arrange a meeting between counselors, correction officers and supervisors to exchange ideas and perceptions.

The agency representative became a crucial figure. He carried several proposals back to the agency and arranged for key elements to be incorporated into ongoing programs. A sample letter from this representative to the QWL committee reads

> I have forwarded the Auburn Task Force proposal for a Correction Officer Orientation Program to Mr. C., with the suggestion that Mr. H. develop an orientation program along these lines. Since that time, I have been informed that Mr. C. has requested from Mr. V. that Mr. H. make an effort to implement on a statewide basis those suggestions put forth by the Auburn Task Force.
>
> I have also discussed with Mr. C. the possibility of Honor Guards in each of our facilities who are dressed and trained in a uniform manner. He has again requested that Mr. V. meet with Capt. R., to begin discussions of a uniformed Honor Guard.
>
> I am in hopes that before the end of the year both proposals will be in place.

(3) Wardens and union officials often strongly endorsed a proposal. One superintendent prefaced his reaction to our law-related proposal with the words, "From where I sit as the superintendent of the largest prison in the state I can say without qualification that [this is] the most urgent problem we face . . ." At another juncture the same superintendent noted that "if I had two million dollars, I would put it in this area alone." Such reactions closed off the question of nonimplementation and shifted the ground to the question, "How do we go about doing this?" Conversely, reservations by a warden (e.g., "I don't know whether we need all this") left proposal ideas swinging in the wind.

(4) Resistance at the prison level proved insurmountable. Where QWL staff tried to counter such resistance with a request to "send a bill we can submit to our committee," no proposal or budget arrived. A last-minute offer (from us) to help shape a proposal was not taken up. The QWL process could *unfreeze* staff members (get them to discuss proposals), but could not *move* them (get them to take action) where resistance was substantial. This contingency faced us in two prisons, and it lowered our implementation "score."

The Scoreboard

Out of four settings we could claim two as providing success stories. One of these settings was headed by an administrator of the kind beloved by Socrates. This scholar-administrator started as a correction officer and rose from the ranks. As a scholar he was not only familiar with organizational literature, but committed to participation (e.g., team management) as a goal. As an administrator he internalized our model, reconvoked the group, and took their thinking seriously. He also explored (with a view toward implementation) ways of generalizing grass-roots participation as a process.

A second administrator also proved supportive, but his support rested on different grounds. This executive had acquired notoriety as a "strong" manager, famous for his effective, enlightened, firm-but-fair style of management. Our endorsement by this "strong" administrator was grounded on (1) his appreciation of the content or goal of the proposals, and (2) his commitment to job enrichment opportunities for correctional officers. The same orientation describes an agency representative who proved our strongest ally. This ally (again, a former officer) combined an appreciation of work reform with the most exquisite skill for negotiating bureaucratic complexities.

The settings in which we worked served as gracious hosts to our sessions, but two of them did so (in retrospect) to promote inservice "training." In one of these settings, the proposals were seen as academic exercises. The second setting viewed our proposals as complaints about an imperfect but irremediable world. In the first setting, endorsement took the form of a vague approval. The second setting reacted to any raising of implementation issues as pressure to be—at any price—ignored.

A tally of "implemented proposals" cannot be arrived at. This is so because (1) the process of implementation seems never-ending, (2) ideas can be abstracted for separate adoption, and (3) ideas can be merged with preexisting ideas, at which point relative contributions become hard to assess.

Every proposal that is to be implemented in an organization is screened for the acceptability of proposed changes to the organization. What is screened *in* are reforms that are compatible with directions that have usually been previously considered. Proposals that have the best chance are those that end up with managers who are partisans or proponents of their goals, but who have failed—usually for lack of resources— to advance their cause.

Proposals furnish rank-and-file backing, they help with planning (through proposal content), and they supply whatever commitment the organization makes to the project. They do *not* supply money, and it is the manager's task to shift budget items to proposal-related efforts or—a much-favored option—to find new resources using the proposals as ammunition. The latter enterprise (which in our case centered on QWL funds) is a symbiotic one. The manager gets resources he needs to achieve desired ends. In return, he shapes goals *partly* based on proposals, and credits (to proposal writers) the authorship of change.

Problems arise if cooptation occurs. The danger is that proposals can become means to managers' ends, with resemblance between program goals and proposal goals becoming coincidental. What can happen in such instances is that the spirit of proposals is violated as goals are ostensibly adapted for implementation.[2]

In our case, an amusing minor example was provided by QWL staff. It involved the officer "react" form designed for pinpointing work-related difficulties created by policies and procedures. The proposal was discussed and procedural details were somewhat modified. At this point, QWL staff offered (unsolicitedly) to "help" revise the form. When the prospective draft arrived, it was headed "Quality of work life ... make it your business!" The form then called (in single space) for QWL ideas and suggestions.

In several instances, cooptation transferred responsibilities from a democratic, enrichment-oriented group to a clerk in someone's office. Program goals were often stressed, ignoring participatory mechanisms laid down for achieving these goals. The QWL strategy of supplying resources for programs encourages acquisitions of goods and services. Our groups were seen as a "plus" because they enhanced the acceptability of CO proposals, not because group planning dovetailed with a QWL (staff participation) philosophy.

Not surprisingly, we won battles without advancing our campaign. We "sold" proposals, but not the concept of participation as a vehicle for promoting change in the organization.

Terminal Implementation: Is It Curable?

Several "wish-we-had-known" principles come to mind in relation to implementation problems:

(1) Top-level backing can mean "we'll use ideas that fit into the planning we'll be doing" rather than "we'll give precedence to front-line staff proposals." The former must *never* be confused with the latter.

(2) Precedence must be given to working with any manager who values the process (participation) and sees the program as a means to initiating this process.

(3) The managers' problems and their force fields cannot be fully visualized by front-line workers. This limitation must be approached by supplementary "staffing" rather than by shooting down ideas because they have not accommodated unforeseeable complexities.

(4) Implementation mechanisms must be spelled out in advance. This not only includes provision for reviewing anticipated ideas, but it means being ready to make the necessary accommodations on issues involving resources and changes toward increased democratization and job enrichment.

(5) What are the winds of change that blow in the organization? What has been proposed without success, but is still secretly cherished? Who are prospective partners in change available for given areas of reform? Such facts must be known at least to consultants, and possibly to groups.

(6) Plants can be chosen in terms of the way local managers feel about change. In addition, one needs high-level liaison and support contacts at central administration and union headquarters—"friends in court" with clout.

(7) Groups can be heterogeneous. They can include middle managers (potential sources of resistance) as well as union officials. If time permits, persons affected by proposed reforms should be invited as honored guests, because such persons subsequently act as lobbyists and friends.

(8) Workers may test the wind—ask managers about their interest in congenial topics. This must be done before serious work (and involvement) on (in) proposals begins.

Such prescriptions reflect general themes. One principle is that implementation must be faced in detail at the program's inception, rather than being unearthed (with risks of disillusionment) as the final program component. A second theme is that grass-roots participants are invariably un-self-sufficient. To succeed, they must have allies, and these allies must gain something (but not too much) from their alliance. The best allies are like-minded ones rather than participants in quid pro quo (I-scratch-your-back-if-you-scratch-mine) arrangements. In the latter sort of alliances, cooptation is prevalent.

The most crucial theme is indivisibility of the grass-roots medium and its message. Worker-participants must feel they have impact, which means their products must sell. But if products sell and the process does not, the message of the medium (participation) has not been received. Participants feel used, just as they are used at work. In such transactions, the point that workers can plan and that they can significantly change their environment—has been lost. Workers' ideas may be adopted, but the minds that shaped these ideas have been disrespected, and their ability to shape the ideas has been ignored. Such reactions are alienating, because they imply the familiar premise that bureaucrats own places of work and shape them at will.

NOTES

1. If QWL strategies are designed to (a) democratize organizations through (b) worker participation, *ideally* with (c) union/management sponsorship, the goal (dog) must be participation, and the means (tail), cosponsorship. In the "joint committee" process, the latter (tail) wags the former (dog), and if there are no core groups involved, the model is that of a dogless tail. In this sort of model, the *form* of QWL is emphasized at the expense of *content*, and the rationale is hopelessly violated. QWL "proposals" originate with bureaucrats and officials, and resources are distributed to satisfy lower-order needs (for the construction of club houses, beautification of cafeterias, expansion of parking lots, and the like) rather than to help employees to grow, learn, and become involved.

2. Cooptation is self-destructively short sighted. As Silvan Tomkins (1981: 314) has pointed out, "It makes a great deal of difference whether one regards the automobile as a new invention or as a horseless carriage that must be fed gasoline rather than hay." Group products differ from ideas evolved by managers (see Chapter 16). To ignore the uniqueness of grass-roots inputs means (among other things) that one does not use them to advantage.

CHAPTER 18

EPILOGUE:
WHERE DO WE GO FROM HERE?

Rightly or wrongly, concerns about the allegedly low productivity of American workers compared to their Japanese counterparts (Ouchi, 1981) have spawned a variety of participatory training programs and a profitable new management consultant industry. Worker participation is probably not the cure for American industry's ills, but it is clear that the concept will get a real play in the next decade or two.

On the assembly line, productivity can be measured by the number and quality of cars or cartridges or cornflakes. The worker boredom, alienation, and hostility that lead to low output can also be measured, but they are usually seen as a problem by management primarily through their links to output. Low productivity is expensive. In the public sector, output is not so readily assessed, but there are similar measurable worker problems. They go by the name of "burnout." This phenomenon is also getting a real play (as we have seen in Chapter 2) and some systematic study. Efforts to deal with the problem tend to focus on self-awareness and human relations training, which in turn are expected to translate into improved coping skills. Participatory approaches can focus on the causes and consequences of burnout. Direct participation in organization reform, as in the correctional officer study reported here, is analogous to the quality circles and other work-related approaches used in private industry.

Human service clients are not immune from the alienation and hostility that plague both industrial workers and human service providers. Clients are probably the most vulnerable and the most damaged (in terms of loss of human potential) of the three groups. They are caught with a vengeance in service provider/recipient games that serve only to intensify feelings of helplessness, exacerbate dependency, and increase symptoms of both mental and physical ill health: And poor health, the country is learning, has the highest price tag of all.

If human service workers are getting less attention than industry management/worker groups in participatory approaches to problem solving, client groups are getting the least of all. Yet there is evidence that moving people from passivity to activity, from recipient to participant roles, can improve both health and the ability to cope with life problems. In a pioneering set of studies, Rodin and her associates (Rodin, 1980; Rodin and Janis, 1979; Rodin, Janis, and Langer, 1977; Lefcourt, 1973; Schulz and Hanusa, 1980) explored the relationships between control over the environment and subjective feelings of wellbeing, physiological measures of health status, and morbidity, in an aging population. Using random assignment designs with nursing home residents, these students examined effects of the availability of environmental choices, resident control of time available from nurses, feedback on the exercise of control, new experiences through shifts from negative to positive attributions, and training in the exercise of coping skills. Such interventions yielded improved measures of health, activity, and sociability and decreases in perceived stress and pituitary-adrenal measures of stress. While this work suggests that almost any approach that allows a person to become an active participant in determining his or her fate may have an immediate impact on both psychological and physiological functioning, it particularly suggests that long-term effects can be maintained with systematic training in skills that allow people to actively cope with the stresses in their environment. In an era in which the exploding costs of services are running headlong into demands for balanced budgets, the implications of this discovery are staggering.

This book has argued the case for grass-roots participation. We have suggested that participatory strategies may have applicability to a broader set of problems than worker *ennui* and to a greater range of outcomes than improved productivity. We can now turn to some of the ways in which the participatory thrust can be extended. The human service field, as well as industrial settings, can probably benefit by

(1) using participation in program planning and development as a way of introducing new knowledge to staff or client groups, and then building this knowledge into further planning/development decisions;

(2) making evaluation an integral part of the way one operates, and extending participation into the ongoing evaluation of service delivery;

(3) building participation across groups (agencies, organizations), as well as within groups, to aid in solving common problems;

(4) extending the content of participatory decision making from solving concrete problems in the present to developing ways of coping with ongoing change; and

(5) developing the capacity to envision and implement new integrations (paradigms) of present knowledge and experience that will allow increased planning for and control over the future.

We will look at each of these plausible extensions and consider their implications for an illustrative example (corrections).

Experience is Not Enough

Creating opportunities for participation in decision making invites a learning-through-doing approach to the development of staff and/or clients. Paulo Freire (1970), a priest who worked as an educator with peasants in a rural area of Brazil, took the position that every human being, no matter how "ignorant" or "submerged in the culture of silence," is capable of looking critically at his or her world in a dialogical encounter with others and that, when provided with proper tools for such an encounter, he or she can gradually perceive more of his or her personal and social reality and deal critically with it. A current Social Science Research Council study committee on Life-Course Perspectives on Middle and Old Age states that

in order to have a sense of self, one must have a sense of the world; in order to have a sense of personal control, one must have a sense of what or who controls world events. Thus, the individual must develop a theory of social and physical causality, including his or her own role in it [1980: 63-65].

The concepts outlined in this book are an approach to problem solving that uses the experiences of persons who are part of a problem in efforts to solve the problem. However, experiences (and goodwill) only provide a base for effective problem solving. With Freire, we would suspect that virtually anyone can contribute to problem solutions. But we would argue that problems can be solved effectively only when they are put into the larger framework within which they are embedded. *Informed* participation in problem solving allows and invites knowledge input beyond the wisdom derived from the experience of participants. Problem solving allows for education, for learning how to use knowledge. Merging education with problem solving contributes to the development of the person and enhances the effective development of new programming.

The grass-roots approach to planning forces participants to be clear about their goals and objectives, the strategies they will use to reach them, and the rationales (theories, hypotheses, hunches) that underlie their choice of strategies. Participants must also be clear about the "force field" within which their strategies will be carried out. The force field concept (see Chapter 10) refers, not to interstellar events or cosmic energies, but to the organizations and persons, the behaviors, attitudes, constellations of powers, the resources, and the obstacles that constitute the environment in which one must act. The force field for beginning a new training program for correctional officers, for example, includes not only the size and physical layout of the prison and the number of officers and their work schedules, but the age and educational background of the officers, their attitudes toward themselves and their role, the values and management style of the warden, the level of unrest among inmates, the likelihood of budget increases or decreases in the near future, the attitudes of the public toward crime, and so on. Failure to take account of some potential obstacles may doom a program to oblivion; failure to take account of some potential resources may increase the difficulty of putting it into effect.

The notion of a force field provides a conceptual base for introducing formal knowledge. As a problem-solving group begins to consider the forces in its immediate setting, its members begin to organize experiences around such parameters as organizational structure, formal and informal power networks, and the interface of the organization with the surrounding community. This opens the way for considering forces in the wider environment, such as state and federal policies about the allocation of resources, and issues of human rights. The force-field concept can also be applied to constructs concerning the future, a point to which we shall return.

Knowledge is not only introduced in our participatory model; it is also created. If one is to learn from experience, one needs to observe and reflect upon it. Good program planning requires knowing not only where one wants to go and how one plans to get there, but when one has arrived. If a group decides to slay dragons, its dragon-slaying participants, having decided on poison as the optimal strategy (considering the relative size of dragons and available weapons), need to know whether or not the poison was administered and whether or not it incapacitated the dragon. Feedback on the outcome of program efforts becomes further knowledge that may lead to modification of objectives or strategies, or to rethinking of the rationales that link them. It also becomes knowledge that can be shared with others and contributes to the expanding body of knowledge that will be used by other groups of problem solvers.

Evaluation and Change

Reforms in evaluation and grass-roots management are not merely coincidental developments. Both are efforts to cope with problems of elitism. Cronbach and an interdisciplinary group studying program evaluation reform argue that:

An open society becomes a closed society when only the officials know what is going on. Insofar as information is a source of power, evaluations carried out to inform a policy maker have a disenfranchising effect [1980: 4].

The model of informed participation we have outlined places evaluation squarely in the lap of grass-roots participants. Evaluation, in this sense, becomes an ongoing process of learning from one's program efforts, building knowledge, sharing it with others, and using it in further problem-solving efforts. (A relatively new evaluation journal— *Knowledge: Creation, Diffusion, Utilization*—is dedicated to a recognition of these blurred and overlapping functions.)

We are arguing for "understanding" in the use of data that respond to questions asked by participants in problem-solving strategies. Our own guard survey (see Chapter 14) is a case in point. Given the expense and trouble of running a survey, it is not evident that we should have bothered. It is also not obvious why we insist (as we do) that surveys and other information-gathering tools must be part and parcel of grass-roots management strategies.

Most managers use data, but the data they use tend to be tangible sorts of data, usually having to do with inflow and outflow, with counts of resources and demands, such as inmates and cell spaces. Such data show the managers how well or badly off they are, both across the board and in detail, so they can "adjust" populations, e.g., by moving inmates around. *Staff* management uses similar data, related to skills of staff and slots that are available (or not available) to accommodate qualifications.

The key management concern is that of ensuring survival, and often (when managers face strikes, riots, or grievances) they see themselves subverted in achieving this goal. It rarely occurs to most managers that one reason for "subversion" is that their use of data transmutes people (inmates, staff) into objects of management, a fact that makes disaffected or unhappy people unhappier. We assume that this risk of creating resentment is not neutralized by *not* collecting data. We propose, rather, the collecting of *different* data, the sort of data that suggest to people that managers care how they feel and are willing to take their interests, needs, preferences, and ambitions into account.

The point (which is hardly original, since it was noted by Hawthorne researchers fifty years ago) is that surveys have a humanizing influence, because they bring people's feelings to the surface and make such feelings hard to ignore. Survey impact of this kind gets lost in survey contexts. Surveys are usually part of "liberal" programs. Prison climate measures, for instance, are *invariably* collected in therapeutic, or unit-managed, settings. The presumption of programs is that we care, and surveys are for checking to see whether we have succeeded. But surveys can be *preludes* to reform, and they are used in this sense in participatory programs. Surveys are climate setting, alerting staff that its views are now a management concern. Subsequent personal involvement (like in QWL groups) "makes sense." Programs become follow-up efforts, putting face-to-face meat on the bones of questionnaire responses. A second benefit—except in total participation—is that those who become involved in "pilot" groups gain a sense of representativeness. Unless the first participants are idiosyncratic, their views gain reliability from survey responses of their fellows. Such reliability can be increased (as in our prison program) when data are presented to participants. It can be further increased by mandating activities *based* on data, or by requiring more surveys to check the acceptability of group products to fellow employees.

Surveys can be used to select systematically staff participants. In our case, we "stacked the deck" by requiring that officers show interest in job enrichment; we picked highly alienated men to maximize program relevance and less alienated men to prevent cynical, pessimistic wallowing.[1] Groups can be formed around special concerns revealed through surveys; staff can be "mixed" or "matched"; employee groups that are identified through survey responses can be shaped by including nonsurvey criteria, such as work assignments and experience levels. More problematic is the use of surveys to tell an agency where to start intervening and with whom. It is human to prefer congenial clients; yet the need—as at Ossining and Auburn—may be most acute where morale is lowest. Where alienation is extreme—where men and women have "given up" and where they "do time" on the job—the work may be cut out for us. Being forewarned, however, helps us to be forearmed. Where we are fortunate, staff believe (or many do) that they are worse off than they are. The direction of pluralistic ignorance exaggerates such variables as cynicism and antiprofessionalism. This being so, employees can be reassured through feedback. The minority supported by pluralistic ignorance (such as "smug hacks" among officers) can—maybe—be disabused of their cynical smugness.

Surveys help assess needs and define problems. They are also a means of learning about force fields within which planned change is to take place, and they therefore aid in planning appropriate strategies. Repetitions of surveys after a program is in operation offer one means of assessing change, though they are far from being the only tool available, and it is probably better to rely on a variety of indices of change (self-reports, observations, records, interviews, and so on) to get a feeling for change. The point to be made is that the use of data—their collection and interpretation— is inextricably bound up with good program planning, development, and assessment. The evaluation process begins with planning and is a proper concern of program participants.

But in addition to creating and using knowledge in planning programs (defining input) and in assessing their outcomes, attention needs to be paid to what goes on in between, inside the "black box" between stimulus and response. There is growing concern in the evaluation field with what is called "process" evaluation, and this concern is fueled by the concerns (and the funding) of people responsible for making policy. Evaluation was sold to the policymaking community on the grounds that it could help in the decisions they make, but definitive outcome studies are few and usually arrive when the time for decisions is past. What we need to make informed decisions about a program is the best information currently available relating to the *workings* of the program. As Cronbach and his associates state (1980: 2), evaluation should be used "to understand events and processes for the sake of guiding future activities."

Evaluation of this kind is a self-perception of program—an integral part of program operation. Participatory management calls for participation in evaluation by those being evaluated to facilitate shared decision making based on available approximations of the truth. There is a role for *systematically* obtained information as a corrective or as quality control of the approximations to be used, but the need for accurate information must be integrated with the need for shared immediate decisions. Fortunately, participatory evaluation provides informational vigor, even though sometimes at the cost of rigor (Kelman, 1968).

Participation Across Groups

A problem-solving group is likely to find at some point that its new program efforts require interfacing with other groups, either within the same organization or across organizations. Within organizations, the efforts to solve problems perceived by line staff may quickly run up against roadblocks created by the problems with which middle management or top administration are trying to cope, or by the problems faced by the client population. They are all, of course, a part of the immediate force field.

Any intraorganizational change effort is probably better carried out with the involvement of all levels of participants, but the notion of problem-solving groups in which clients, staff, middle managers, and administrators sit down in a position of equality or parity offends enough to quell most change efforts. A few years ago, Hammond and his associates (Hammond, Wilkins, and Todd, 1966; Miller, 1973; Miller and Davies, 1972) at the University of Colorado dealt with this problem in a very innovative manner. Working with secondary schools, probation offices, and police, inimical groups of probationers and police each taped their problem-discussing meetings. The tapes were exchanged between groups and, after a small number of such exchanges, the groups voluntarily requested to work together on their common problems.

This approach to the interfacing of initially incompatible groups encourages a spread of effect of the participation strategy. All problems lead ultimately to other problems. When groups share efforts to solve what may seem to be disparate problems, the local problems merge quickly into larger or more general ones.

In a similar way, one can think of a spread of participatory efforts across organizations, across age groups, within and across neighborhoods, and within and across communities. A general strategy is to start small, working with a core group that can demonstrate competence in problem solving and become comfortable with the relevant knowledge and skills. The core or nucleus group can then begin to reach out to others within its own reference group and across reference groups (see Chapter 13). We need documentation of such efforts and systematic trials of new techniques, to learn what it takes to get a spread of effect started and to germinate ever-widening areas of involvement in change.

A special frontier in this strategy is building linkages between local agencies and the surrounding community. Human service agencies have a symbiotic relationship with their communities and share common problems, if not always common objectives. Participatory problem-solving efforts across groups offer real potential for putting effective competency into the glib rhetoric of agency/community relations. In corrections, for example, the pressures for incarcerating more people for more time—despite the scarcity of monies for more prisons—are going to increase the need for community approaches to corrections. These efforts often put corrections agencies on a collision course with local communities. They point to the need for joint problem-solving efforts across correctional and other agencies, community groups and local businesses and industries. The core groups for initiating such efforts might well come from among corrections employees, citizens, and offenders or exoffenders.

Coping with Change

Change is a fact of life. Even if this were the best of all possible worlds—and we are far from an even tolerable world—change is forced on us by science, technology, shifts in populations, and assorted cataclysms. Change is something that happens to most people. Few people have any awareness of the forces (economic, political, ecological) determining the human condition. Few people are equipped by education or training to make rational attempts to cope with the need for change. Sadly, most people's response to rapid change is a sense that things are getting out of control and an increasing reliance on a few highly knowledgeable or trained experts and/or often unknowledgeable and untrained charismatic leaders. If people are ever to gain a sense of control over their lives (and to have actual control), they need opportunities to confront the need for change and to develop ways to meet change.

But opportunities are not enough: The crucial ingredient is knowledge, and the change problem is how to make people knowledgeable about changing forces determining the human condition and how to give them the skills needed to apply change-relevant knowledge to bring change about.

And finally, the effect of change must be observed. Are the results of one's actions what was intended? Does something that once worked no longer work? Is it time for a new integration of knowledge to meet new sets of circumstances?

What we need is a society in which more people spend their lives as students as well as workers, in which work provides the material for building knowledge that is applied to improve one's environment, not only for now, but with one eye on the future. The grass-roots management strategy outlined in this book offers a way to move in this direction, particularly if cross-group contagion becomes viable.

The Futures Problem

Hamil (1979: 115) has observed that:

> there are different views on the issues of who ought to control the new technologies. Almost all believe that individuals should become more involved in the planning process, if only to avoid the past mistakes of poorly guided government planners. The politicians, futurists, and others who try to generate greater community action often encounter marked apathy, and occasional deep pessimism, about personal and common futures. Also, as technologies grow in complexity, decisions on how to employ them fall more and more to specialists familiar with all the issues.

In the long run, though, the possibility of totalitarianism will disappear only if both intellectual expertise and popular sentiment contribute to decisions. The two-way flow of information needed to make this hope a reality would insure that the liberties guaranteed by democracy will remain intact in a technological world.

In one sense, all planning is related to the future. When people talk about "futures" or future studies, however, they are talking about planning more than two years down the road and planning on a scale so vast that it seems beyond the control of mere salaried employees and/or constitutes an exercise in futility. Not surprisingly, futurists are seen (and many see themselves) as an elitist group.

But as the future belongs to all, future planning—the opportunity to consider the decisions of today that will determine the future we will be living in tomorrow—should (and could) be democratized. As groups learn to understand and cope with the force fields within which their problem-solving efforts are located, this can include obtaining knowledge that is relevant to determinants of future force fields. We are talking about expanding frames of reference, learning to think about the immediate problem in a wider societal context and a broader time frame.

Confronting the possibilities of the future (particularly the idea of alternative futures) is an anxiety-provoking experience. "I find it easier," Brilliant (1979) writes, "to be a result of the past than a cause of the future." The peg for reducing anxiety in thinking about the problems of tomorrow is to be firmly grounded in coping with the problems of today. As people learn to use the knowledge generated in problem-solving efforts, they become able to understand and make use of new technologies rather than being alienated by them.

Corrections as a Frontier for Change Efforts

Corrections offers an extreme example of the problems being faced by institutions forming the structure of our society. All are suffering from the increased alienation of both client and staff groups, but leave solutions in the hands of fewer and fewer people.

Why cannot those who experience a problem address the problem? For example, correctional officers could be convoked to consider consequences of overcrowding and ways of ameliorating such consequences. CO groups could consider such topics as "arranging placement to minimize congestion," "lowering tension in the prison," "helping stressed inmates," "helping stressed staff," "rearranging resources to enhance programs," "filling idle time," "locating low-risk inmates," and "maintaining security in congested prisons."

This book has suggested a possible paradigm for grass-roots management. Other models could be explored. There are many modes of inducing problem solving, different time tables and ways of scheduling, and different leadership styles. The most urgent strategy is to explore the leadership potential of low-echelon staff. This can be done with (or without) prior modeling by consultants. Other variations include managers leading staff groups, middle manager groups, and mixed groups of staff, middle managers, and managers. A key concern must be spread of effect; the graduates of one change enterprise must offer a cadre that provides change agents for the next.

Many spread-of-effect variations are possible. Our own correction officers suggested ways in which other officers could assume managerial functions; they planned pilot projects for subsequent diffusion; they suggested spotting "talent" among officers (e.g., mental-health-related expertise) that could be shared; they envisaged groups—such as middle managers and correctional officers—that could work separately and later be combined.

The potential is limitless. Participation demonstrated at the top (through OD) and the bottom (through QWL) can extend to the middle. It can cross all sorts of boundaries.

In prisons, participation can include inmates.[2] Inmates can be surveyed and correctional officers can invite selected inmates to join problem-solving groups. The strategy is particularly apt in addressing the overcrowding problem, in which inmates have an obvious stake.

Prisons today are polarized: Inmates resent officers; officers fear inmates and resent managers. Reactions to prison tension (such as riot prevention measures) often feed tension. A prison in crisis often reacts by increasing crisis. The remedy lies in defusing crisis, in a "cool" approach that promotes problem solving in lieu of fear and despair. Such an approach assumes that people who live with a problem can (with help) rise to the challenges they face. Such a strategy makes the *problem* the enemy, rather than (as occurs now) making enemies of parties affected by the problem in each other's eyes. In this sense, participation can create community in previously polarized settings.

To face crises we need resources, and these include *human* resources. We have suggested in this book that there are such resources available in the grass roots of organizations, and that the exploration and use of grass-roots potential can improve the climate of human service agencies, and enhance their human service function.

We feel that corrections in particular has an opportunity to serve as a field laboratory for demonstrating how people can actively participate in efforts to improve their own condition. We have grass roots of our own in corrections (Grant, 1957; Grant, 1965; Toch, 1961), and at least the nostalgic hope that our colleagues may be wise enough to take advantage of a concept whose time, we suggest, has arrived.

As a closing thought, we are ready to propose and defend the proposition that the challenge of offender management and rehabilitation is basically the same problem as that of worker management, and that the response of grass-roots management holds the key (or provides one of the keys) to the challenge of crime. However, that proposition calls for another, very different, book.

NOTES

1. As it happens, we need not have worried. There were no manifest differences between alienated and nonalienated officers in our group.

2. We (among others) have used offenders to study crime-related problems. Some "graduates" of such programs today function as managers in corrections and other human service organizations (Toch, 1969; Grant, 1968; Grant, 1980).

REFERENCES

Alderfer, C. P. *Existence, Relatedness and Growth.* New York: Free Press, 1972.

Angell, J. E. "Toward an alternative to the classic police organizational arrangements: A democratic model." *Criminology,* 1971, 9, 185-206.

APA Monitor, October, 1981, 12 (1).

Argyris, C. *Personality and Organization.* New York: Harper & Row, 1957.

Bandura, A. *Principles of Behavior Modification.* New York: Holt, Rinehart & Winston, 1969.

Bardo, P. "The pain of teacher burnout: A case history." *Phi Delta Kappan,* December 1979, 252-254.

Bell, D. *The Coming of Post-Industrial Society.* New York: Basic Books, 1976.

Briggs, D. L. and J. M. Dowling. "The correctional officer as a consultant: An emerging role in penology." *American Journal of Correction,* 1964, 26, 28-31.

Brilliant, A. *I May Not Be Totally Perfect But Parts of Me Are Excellent.* Santa Barbara, CA: Woodbridge Press, 1979.

Broadbent, D. E. "Chronic effects from the physical nature of work," in B. Gardell (ed.) *Man and Working Life.* New York: John Wiley, 1978.

Caplan, R. D., S. Cobb, J.R.P. French, Jr., R. V. Harrison, and S. R. Pinneau, Jr. *Job Demands and Worker Health.* Washington, DC: National Institute for Occupational Safety and Health, 1975.

Carlson, H. C. "Organizational research and organizational change: GM's approach." *Personnel,* 1977, 54, 11-22.

——— "Measuring the quality of work life in General Motors." *Personnel,* 1978, 55, 21-26.

Cherniss, C., E. S. Egnatios, and S. Wacker. "Job stress and career development in new public professionals." *Professional Psychology,* 1976, 7, 429-436.

Cherniss, C. *Professional Burnout in Human Service Organizatios.* New York: Praeger, 1980.(a)

——— *Staff Burnout: Job Stress in the Human Services.* Beverly Hills, CA: Sage, 1980.(b)

Cloward, R. "Comment," in H. L. Wilmer and R. Kotinsky (eds.) *New Perspectives for Research in Juvenile Delinquency.* Washington, DC: U.S. Department of Health, Education and Welfare, Children's Bureau, 1955.

Coch, L., and J.R.P. French, Jr. "Overcoming resistance to change." *Human Relations,* 1948, 1, 512-532.

Colarelli, N. J., and S. M. Siegel. *Ward H: An Adventure in Innovation.* New York: Van Nostrand, 1966.

Comer, J. P. *School Power.* New York: Free Press, 1980.

Committee on Life-Course Perspectives on Middle and Old Age. "Life-course perspectives on middle and old age." *Social Science Research Council,* 1980, 34, 63-65.

Cooper, M. R., B. S. Morgan, P. M. Foley, and L. B. Kaplan. "Changing employee values: Deepening discontent?" *Harvard Business Review,* 1979, 57, 117-125.

Copley, F. B. *Frederick W. Taylor: Father of Scientific Management.* New York: Taylor Society, 1923.

Crockenberg, V., and W. W. Clark, Jr. "Teacher participation in school decision making: The San Jose teacher involvement project." *Phi Delta Kappan,* October 1979, 115-118.

Cronbach, L. J., and Associates. *Toward Reform of Program Evaluation.* San Francisco: Jossey-Bass, 1980.

Duckles, M. M., R. Duckles, and M. Maccoby. "The process of change at Bolivar." *Journal of Applied Behavioral Science,* 1977, 13, 387-399.

Duffee, D. "The correction officer subculture and organizational change." *Journal of Research in Crime and Delinquency,* 1974, 11, 155-172.

Ellsworth, R. B., and J. J. Ellsworth. "The psychiatric aide: Therapeutic agent or lost potential?" *Journal of Psychiatric Nursing and Mental Health Services,* 1970, 8, 7-13.

Emery, F., and M. Emery. "Participative design: Work and community life," (1974); reproduced in F. Emery and E. Thorsrud, *Democracy at Work: The Report of the Norwegian Industrial Democracy Program.* Leiden, Holland: Martinus Nijhoff, 1976.

Erickson, C. L. "Faking it: Principles of expediency as applied to probation." *Federal Probation,* 1977, 41, 36-39.

Fenton, N. *An Introduction to Group Counseling in Correctional Institutions.* New York: American Correctional Association, 1957.

Freire, P. *Pedagogy of the Oppressed.* New York: Continuum, 1981.

French, W. L., and C. H. Bell. *Organization Development: Behavioral Science Interventions for Organization Improvement* (2nd ed.). Englewood Cliffs, NJ: Prentice-Hall, 1978.

Freudenberger, J. J., with G. Richelson. *Burn-Out: The High Cost of High Achievement.* Garden City, NY: Doubleday, 1980.

Frizell, B. "Escoffier: God of the gastronomes." *Horizon,* 1961, 3, 120-128.

Fromm, E. *To Have or To Be?* New York: Harper & Row, 1976.

Frost, C. F., J. H. Wakeley, and R. A. Ruh. *The Scanlon Plan for Organization Development: Identity, Participation and Equity.* East Lansing: Michigan State University Press, 1974.

Goffman, E. *Asylums: Essays on the Social Situation of Mental Patients and Other Inmates.* Garden City, NY: Doubleday, 1961.

Grant, J. D. "The use of correctional institutions as self-study communities in social research." *British Journal of Delinquency,* 1957, 7, 301-307.

——— "Delinquency treatment in an institutional setting," in H. Quay (ed.) *Juvenile Delinquency.* New York: Van Nostrand, 1965.

——— "The offender as a correctional manpower resource," in F. Reissman and H. I. Popper (eds.) *Up From Poverty: New Career Ladders for Non-Professionals.* New York: Harper & Row, 1968.

——— "From 'living learning' to 'learning to live': An extension of social therapy," in H. Toch (ed.) *Therapeutic Communities in Corrections.* New York: Praeger, 1980.

——— and J. Grant. "Staff and client participation: A new approach to correctional research." *Nebraska Law Review,* 1966, 45, 702-716.

——— "Contagion as a principle in behavior change," in H. C. Richard (ed.) *Unique Problems in Behavior Readjustment.* Elmsford, NY: Pergamon, 1971.

Guest, R. H. "Quality of work life—Learning from Tarrytown." *Harvard Business Review,* 1979, 57, 76-87.

Hackman, J. R., and G. R. Oldham. *Work Redesign*. Reading, MA: Addison-Wesley, 1980.

Hamil, R. "The fate of democracy in a technological world. *The Futurist*, 1979, 13, 115.

Hammerstein, O., II. "Stout hearted men," in *New Moon*. Warner Bros., Inc., 1927.

Hammond, K. R., M. Wilkins, and F. J. Todd. "A research paradigm for the study of interpersonal learning." *Psychological Bulletin*, 1966, 65, 221-232.

Herbst, P. G. *Alternatives to Hierarchies*. Leiden, Holland: Martinus Nijhoff, 1976.

Herrick, N. "How dissatisfied is the American worker?" *Society*, 1981, 18, 26-33.

Herzberg, F. *Work and the Nature of Man*. Cleveland: World, 1966.

——— "Participation is not a motivator." *Industry Week*, 1978, 198, 39-44.

——— B. Mausner, and B. B. Snyderman. *The Motivation to Work*. New York: John Wiley, 1959.

Hulin, C. L. "Individual differences and job enrichment—The case against general treatments," in J. R. Maher (ed.) *New Perspectives in Job Enrichment*. New York: Van Nostrand Reinhold, 1971.

Jacobs, J. "What prison guards think: A profile of the Illinois force." *Crime and Delinquency*, 1978, 24, 185-196.

Johnsen, R. "Democratizing work and social life on ships: A report from the experiment on board M. S. Balao." *Working on QWL: Developments in Europe*. The Hague, Netherlands: Martinus Nijhoff, 1979.(a)

——— "Informal helping networks in prison: The shape of grass-roots correctional intervention." *Journal of Criminal Justice*, 1979, 7, 53-70.(b)

Jones, M. *The Therapeutic Community: A New Treatment Method in Psychiatry*. New York: Basic Books, 1953.

——— *Maturation of the Therapeutic Community*. New York: Human Sciences Press, 1976.

——— "Desirable features of a therapeutic community in a prison," in H. Toch (ed.) *Therapeutic Communities in Corrections*. New York: Praeger, 1980.

Josephson, E., and M. Josephson. *Man Alone: Alienation in Modern Society*. New York: Laurel Edition, 1975.

Kakar, S. *Frederick Taylor: A Study in Personality and Innovation*. Cambridge: MIT Press, 1970.

Karger, H. J. "Burnout as alienation." *Social Service Review*, 1981, 55, 270-283.

Karlinsky, S. "Job satisfaction among living unit and non-living unit staff in a Canadian penitentiary." Unpublished doctoral dissertation, York University, 1979.

Kauffman, K. "Prison officer attitudes and perceptions of attitudes: A case of pluralistic ignorance." *Journal of Research in Crime and Delinquency*, 1981, 18, 272-294.

Kelman, H. C. *A Time to Speak: On Human Values and Social Research*. San Francisco: Jossey-Bass, 1968.

Kopf, K. E. as quoted in "A view of central administration." *The Voice*, May 22, 1981.

Kornhauser, A. *Mental Health of the Industrial Worker*. New York: John Wiley, 1965.

Kreman, B. "Search for a better way of work: Lordstown, Ohio" in R. P. Fairfield (ed.) *Humanizing the Workplace*. Buffalo, NY: Prometeus, 1974.

Lawler, E. E., III. "Job design and employee motivation." *Personnel Psychology*, 1969, 22, 426-435.

Lefcourt, H. M. "The function of the illusions of control and freedom." *American Psychologist*, 1973, 28, 427-435.

Lewin, K. "Action research and minority problems" (1946), in K. Lewin, *Resolving Social Conflicts: Selected Papers in Group Dynamics*. New York: Harper & Row, 1948.

——— "Group decision and social change," in T. M. Newcomb and E. L. Hartley et al. (eds.) *Readings in Social Psychology*. New York: Holt & Company, 1947.

Lombardo, L. X. *Guards Imprisoned: Correctional Officers at Work*. New York: Elsevier, 1981.

Lytle, J. H. "An untimely (but significant) experiment in teacher motivation." *Phi Delta Kappan*, June 1980, 700-702.

Maccoby, M. "Changing work: The Bolivar project." *Working Papers for a New Society*, 1975, 3, 43-55.

Macy, B. A. "A progress report on the Bolivar quality of work life project." *Personnel Journal*, August 1979, 527-559.

Marrow, A. J., and J.R.P. French, Jr. "Changing a stereotype in industry." *Journal of Social Issues*, 1945, 6, 33-37.

Maslach, C. "Burned-out." *Human Behavior*, 1976, 5, 16-22.

Maslow, A. H. *Motivation and Personality*. New York: Harper, 1954.

May, E. "Prison guards in America: The inside story." *Corrections Magazine*, 1976, 2, 3ff.

Mayo, E. *The Human Problems of an Industrial Civilization*. Cambridge, MA: Harvard University Press, 1933.

McGregor, D. "Conditions of effective leadership in the industrial organization" (1944), in T. M. Newcomb, E. L. Hartley et al. (eds.) *Readings in Social Psychology*. New York: Holt & Company, 1947.

——— *The Human Side of Enterprise*. New York: McGraw-Hill, 1960.

Merton, R. K. *Social Theory and Social Structure* (rev. ed.). Glencoe, IL: Free Press, 1957.

Miller, M. J. "Interpersonal understanding: Laboratory and field investigations," in L. Rappoport and D. A. Summers (ed.) *Human Development and Social Interaction*. New York: Holt, Rinehart & Winston, 1973.

——— and U. Davies. "Communication and understanding between police and delinquent youth." *Program of Research on Human Judgment and Social Interaction*, Report No. 414, Institute of Behavioral Science, University of Colorado, 1972.

Mills, T. "Quality of work life: What's in a name?" *Civil Service Journal*, 1979, 19, 50-52.

Morrow, L. "The burnout of almost everyone." *Time*, September 21, 1981.

Morse, J. J. "A contingency look at job design." *California Management Review*, 1973, 16, 67-75.

State of New York, Council 82-AFSCME, Joint Committee on Quality of Work Life. *Proposed Budget Criteria*, 1981.

New York Department of Civil Service, Classification Standard, Correction Officer Grade 14. *Occupations Code 8700100*. Albany, NY: State Department of Civil Service, 1974.

New York Teacher. "Stress/burnout study sheds new light on the issues involved." December 20, 1981.

Oldham, G. R., J. R. Hackman, and J. L. Pearce. "Conditions under which employees respond positively to enriched work." *Journal of Applied Psychology*, 1976, 61, 395-403.

Ouchi, W. *Theory Z: How American Business Can Meet the Japanese Challenge*. Reading, MA: Addison-Wesley, 1981.

Packard, J. S., and D. J. Willower. "Pluralistic ignorance and public control ideology." *Journal of Educational Administration*, 1972, 10, 78-87.

Pines, A. M., and E. Aronson, with D. Kafra. *Burnout: From Tedium to Personal Growth*. New York: Free Press, 1981.

President's Commission on Law Enforcement and Administration of Justice. *The Challenge of Crime in a Free Society*. Washington, DC: Government Printing Office, 1967.

QWL Focus (the news journal of the Ontario Quality of Working Life Centre). 1981, 1, August issue.

Redl, F. "The phenomena of contagion and 'shock effects,' " in *When We Deal with Children: Selected Writings*. New York: Free Press, 1966.

Rodin, J. "Managing the stress of aging: The role of control and coping," in S. Levine and H. Ursin (eds.) *Coping and Health*. New York: Plenum, 1980.

――― and I. Janis. "The social power of health-care practitioners as agents of change." *Journal of Social Issues*, 1979, 35, 60-81.

――― and E. Langer. "Long-term effects of a control-relevant intervention with the institutionalized aged." *Journal of Personality and Social Psychology*, 1977, 35, 897-902.

Roethlisberger, F. J., and W. J. Dickson, *Management and the Worker*. Cambridge, MA: Harvard University Press, 1961.

Runcie, J. F. "By days I make cars." *Harvard Business Review*, 1980, 58, 106-115.

Rush. H.M.F. *Job Design for Motivation*. New York: The Conference Board, 1971.

Safire, W. "Burnout." *New York Times Magazine*, May 23, 1982, p. 10.

Sarason, S. Foreword to C. Cherniss. *Professional Burnout in Human Service Organizations*. New York: Praeger, 1980.

Schacht, R. *Alienation*. Garden City, NY: Doubleday, 1970.

Schulz, R., and B. Hanusa. "Experimental social gerontology: A social psychological perspective." *Journal of Social Issues*, 1980, 36, 30-46.

Seeman, M. "On the meaning of alienation." *American Sociological Review*, 1959, 24, 783-791.

Sheppard, H. L., and N. Q. Herrick. *Where Have All the Robots Gone?* New York: Free Press, 1972.

Sherman, L. W., C. H. Milton, and T. V. Kelly. *Team Policing: Seven Case Studies*. Washington, DC: Police Foundation, 1973.

Simpson, R. L., and I. H. Simpson. "The psychiatric attendant: Development of an occupational self-image in a low-status occupation." *American Sociological Review*, 1959, 24, 389-392.

Special Task Force to the Secretary of Health, Education, and Welfare. *Work in America*. Cambridge, MA: MIT Press, 1973.

Stotland, E. "The police feedback cycle," in V. J. Konecni and E. B. Ebbesen (eds.) *The Criminal Justice System: A Social-Psychological Analysis*. San Francisco: Freeman, 1982, 187-259.

Taylor, F. W. *Scientific Management*. New York: Harper & Brothers, 1947.(a)

――― "Testimony before the Special House Committee." *Scientific Management*. New York: Harper & Brothers, 1947.(b)

Teske, R., and H. Williamson. "Correctional officers' attitudes toward selected treatment programs." *Criminal Justice and Behavior*, 1979, 6, 64ff.

Thorsrud, E. "Policy-making as a learning process in working life," in B. Gardell and G. Johansson, *Working Life: A Social Science Contribution to Work Reform*. London: John Wiley, 1981.

Toch, H. "The perception of future events: case studies in social prediction." *Public Opinion Quarterly*, 1957, 22, 57-66.

—— *Legal and Criminal Psychology*. New York: Holt, Rinehart & Winston, 1961.

—— *Violent Men: An Inquiry Into the Psychology of Violence*. Chicago: Aldine, 1969.

—— *Peacekeeping: Police, Prisons and Violence*. Lexington, MA: D. C. Heath, 1976.

—— "Is a 'correctional officer,' by any other name, a 'screw?'" *Criminal Justice Review*, 1978, 3, 19-35.

—— "Alienation as a vehicle of change." *Journal of Community Psychology*, 1979, 7, 3-11.

—— "Liberating prison guards." *Proceedings of the 15th Interagency Workshop*. Huntsville, TX: Sam Houston State University, 1980.

—— J. D. Grant, and R. T. Galvin. *Agents of Change: A Study in Police Reform*. Cambridge, MA: Schenkman, 1975.

Tomkins, S. S. "The quest for primary motives: Biography and autobiography of an idea." *Journal of Personality and Social Psychology*, 1981, 41, 306-329.

Walder, A. G. "Participative management and worker control in China." *Sociology of Work and Occupations*, 1981, 8, 224-251.

Wanous, J. P. "Who wants job enrichment?" *S.A.M. Advanced Management Journal*, 1976, 41, 15-22.

Weingust, D. "Shared leadership—'The damn thing works.'" *Educational Leadership*, 1980, 37, 502-506.

Westley, W. A. *Violence and the Police: A Sociological Study of Law, Custom, and Morality*. Cambridge: MIT Press, 1970.

Wheeler, S. "Role conflict in correctional communities," in D. R. Cressey (ed.) *The Prison: Studies in Institutional Organization and Change*. New York: Holt, Rinehart & Winston, 1961.

White, S. E., and T. R. Mitchell. "Job enrichment versus social cues: A comparison and competitive test." *Journal of Applied Psychology*, 1979, 64, 1-9.

Wing, J. K. "Evaluating a program in the United Kingdom," in L. M. Roberts, S. L. Halleck and M. B. Loeb (eds.) *Community Psychiatry*. Garden City, NY: Doubleday, 1969.

ABOUT THE AUTHORS

HANS TOCH is Professor of Psychology in the School of Criminal Justice at the State University of New York, Albany. He received his B.A. from Brooklyn College and his Ph.D. in social psychology from Princeton University. Dr. Toch has authored and edited numerous books and journal articles on the psychology of crime and violence and on reform in the U.S. prison system, including *Therapeutic Communities in Corrections* (editor and contributor, 1980); *The Psychology of Crime and Criminal Justice* (editor and contributor, 1979); *Living in Prison: The Ecology of Survival* (1977); and *Men in Crisis: Human Breakdowns in Prison* (1975), for which he was awarded the Hadley Cantril Memorial Award.

J. DOUGLAS GRANT is President of the Social Action Research Center in San Rafael, California, and a faculty member of the Wright Institute, Berkeley. He received his MA in psychology and mathematics from Stanford University. Mr. Grant has conducted research and evaluation projects on criminal justice and youth programs for various government agencies, and is currently Co-Project Director of an umbrella evaluation for the schools initiative. He has contributed to numerous books and journals including *The Value of Youth: A Call for a National Youth Policy* (with A. Pearl and E. Wenk) and *Agents of Change: A Study in Police Reform* (with H. Toch and R. T. Galvin).